Groove

Historical Materialism Book Series

The Historical Materialism Book Series is a major publishing initiative of the radical left. The capitalist crisis of the twenty-first century has been met by a resurgence of interest in critical Marxist theory. At the same time, the publishing institutions committed to Marxism have contracted markedly since the high point of the 1970s. The Historical Materialism Book Series is dedicated to addressing this situation by making available important works of Marxist theory. The aim of the series is to publish important theoretical contributions as the basis for vigorous intellectual debate and exchange on the left.

The peer-reviewed series publishes original monographs, translated texts, and reprints of classics across the bounds of academic disciplinary agendas and across the divisions of the left. The series is particularly concerned to encourage the internationalization of Marxist debate and aims to translate significant studies from beyond the English-speaking world.

For a full list of titles in the Historical Materialism Book Series available in paperback from Haymarket Books, visit:
www.haymarketbooks.org/category/hm-series

Groove

An Aesthetic of Measured Time

By
Mark Abel

Haymarket Books
Chicago, IL

First published in 2015 by Brill Academic Publishers, The Netherlands
© 2015 Koninklijke Brill NV, Leiden, The Netherlands

Published in paperback in 2015 by
Haymarket Books
P.O. Box 180165
Chicago, IL 60618
773-583-7884
www.haymarketbooks.org

ISBN: 978-1-60846-484-5

Trade distribution:
In the US, Consortium Book Sales, www.cbsd.com
In Canada, Publishers Group Canada, www.pgcbooks.ca
In the UK, Turnaround Publisher Services, www.turnaround-uk.com
In all other countries, Publishers Group Worldwide, www.pgw.com

Cover design by Ragina Johnson.

This book was published with the generous support of
Lannan Foundation and the Wallace Global Fund.

Printed in Canada by union labor.

10 9 8 7 6 5 4 3 2 1

Library of Congress Cataloging-in-Publication data is available.

Graffiti on a wall in Turin. Photo by the author.

Contents

Introduction: The Meaning of Musical Time   1
   Music and Time   2
   The Meaning of Form   4
   Music as Symbolism   7
   The Structure of the Book   12

1 What is 'groove'?   18
   Four Elements of Groove   24
      1 *Metronomic Time*   24
      2 *Syncopation*   31
      3 *'Deep metricality' or Multi-levelled Meter*   42
      4 *Back-beat*   49

2 Is Groove African?   61
   The Making of Popular Music   72
   Rhythm in African Music   77
   Historicising Musical Meter   84

3 Bergsonism and Unmeasurable Time   92
   Bergson's Metaphysics of Time   94
   Deleuze and the Multiplicity of Time   97
   Zuckerkandl's Audible Time   104

4 Schutz's 'Vivid Present' and the Social Time of Music   116
   Schutz's Phenomenology   119
   Music as Phenomenon   125
   Growing Older Together   130
   Making Music   133
   Overcoming the Dichotomy of Inner and Outer   143

5 Adorno and Reified Time   147
   The Time of Jazz   149
   Time in Music   153
   'Serious' Music and Time   157
   Modernism and the Trend towards Stasis   162
   Music and the Empirical World   166
   Subjectivity and Collectivity   176

Presentness 180
Adorno's Contribution 184

6 Meter, Groove and the Times of Capitalism 187
   Abstract Labour and Abstract Time 195
   Exchange and Abstract Time 206
   Monopoly Capitalism and the Discipline of Abstract Time 213
   World Time 218

7 History, Modernism, and the Time of Music 222
   Time and Narrative 223
   The Structure of History 229
   The Historical Consciousness of Modernity 236
   Groove as a Musical Modernism 243
   Temporal Quality, Quantity and Measure 245
   The Politics of an Aesthetic of Measured Time 251

References 257
Index 270

INTRODUCTION

The Meaning of Musical Time

Groove music is the music of our age. Scan the radio channels and, unless you hit upon one of the few classical music stations, it is groove music that you will hear. The sounds emanating from the earphones of the millions of iPods and other audio devices that are so much a part of contemporary life are even more overwhelmingly dominated by groove music. And although some of the music that accompanies film and video draws on classical sources or pastiches of classical styles, groove music is nonetheless also the most likely kind of music to emerge from our television and computer speakers.

Musical groove began as a Western phenomenon, but, like many other aspects of Western culture in the era of globalisation, has now spread to other parts of the world. Not only is music featuring Western artists commonly available for sale and broadcast across the non-Western and developing world, but many indigenous non-Western musics have been deeply influenced and transformed by the groove concept. Groove music is becoming as ubiquitous across the world as it already is in the West; so dominant, in fact, that its presence goes largely unnoticed, its characteristics unconsciously accepted as simply the way music is.

So what is groove music? We shall thoroughly examine the features of groove, what makes it work and how it differs from other kinds of music, in a subsequent chapter. For now, let us provisionally and loosely describe it as syncopated music with a prominent, regular beat. Groove, then, is a way of organising the temporal aspect of music: it is a particular approach to musical rhythm and meter.

Groove emerges in Western popular music around the turn of the twentieth century and represents a distinct departure in the organisation of musical time. It constitutes something like a paradigm shift in musical temporality and, for better or worse, has had in just over a century a far-reaching impact on our musical culture and what we understand music to be. Why did such a transformation take place and how should it be understood?

In setting out to answer these questions, this book adopts a historical materialist perspective on art. That is, it is committed to the view that cultural phenomena, although governed by their own rules and procedures, do not belong to an autonomous realm, but are ultimately to be explained in relation to the material foundations of the societies that produce them. Significant new developments in artistic practice are not simply invented, or delivered by inspiration, but are driven, albeit in complex and often highly mediated ways, by developments in the way society is organised at a fundamental level. Simply stating this principle, however, does not automatically provide answers to two crucial questions for a study of musical temporality. What kind of relationship exists between musical time and the time outside music, social time? And what kind of methodology is appropriate for a historical materialist analysis of music? That is, where in the music should we look for traces of materiality, of concrete social existence? We will need to address these preliminary questions before moving on to the question of groove itself.

Music and Time

When we consider musical time, we find that, among the various musics produced during the course of human history across the world, there have been a wide variety of ways of organising musical temporality. The Western system of the last few hundred years involving the metrical organisation of beats and note durations is only one of these, and is far from universal. If we are committed to the position that these procedures, just as with any artistic practice, form or style, are not purely internal to the artform itself, but are connected to, as reflections or expressions of, other, non-artistic, human practices and experiences, how are we to explain these differences in musical temporality?

We might argue that all music, at least to some extent, represents an attempt to capture the reality of time, paralleling in the aesthetic sphere attempts to grasp the reality of time by scientists such as Newton and Einstein or philosophers like Aristotle or Bergson. This raises the possibility that some musics succeed better than others in this goal, and that it may ultimately be possible to create a music that adequately captures the reality of time. After all, it has been argued that while space is best grasped visually, temporality is auditory, it comes to us in sounds and rhythms.[1] But the fact that there are so many divergent ways of organising musical time suggests that music does not seek to pin down the reality of time in any objective sense.

More persuasive, perhaps, is the idea that just as the variety of styles and methods in the history of the visual arts represent 'ways of seeing', in John Berger's resonant phrase, musical styles are 'ways of hearing'.[2] From this perspective, figurative paintings should not be understood as attempts to capture definitively the objective reality of their objects, even if that is the intention of

---

[1] Scaff 2005, p. 8.
[2] Berger 1972.

their creator(s), but, rather, are expressions of the relationship between subject (artist) and object (what is being represented), a relationship which necessarily changes with historical and social circumstances. This position takes us beyond the issue of *how well* a painting captures its object (without making that issue irrelevant) to focus on *how* the painting captures its object. On this basis, it makes less sense to ask whether Picasso depicts the human body better than Velasquez than to examine why they do it so differently.

Applying this to music, we might say that the way in which a musical style, or, following Meyer, 'style-system', organises time is an expression of the way that its creators understand time generally, or put another way, it expresses the time consciousness of those who make and use it.[3] Paradoxically, 'time consciousness' may, for much of people's lives, be rather *unconscious*, or at least generally inexplicit and unquestioned, making music one of the activities in which it is most clearly expressed. So the study of musical time becomes a mechanism which can illuminate the implicit conceptions of time which predominate in a society.

Returning to the analogy with visual art, there are of course differences between the object of a figurative painting and time as the object of a piece of music. The former is a real object in the material world – the human body or a bowl of fruit – which the painter seeks to represent. But it is not so easy to be as unequivocal about the reality of time; even if we want to say that time exists, it does not do so in the same way as a human body or a bowl of fruit. In any case, music, in contrast to figurative painting, is generally regarded as a non-representational artform which does not seek to depict objects in the world and is ill-suited to doing so.[4] For these reasons we may want to qualify the comparison. First, we can recognise that if music does represent a way of hearing time, rather than an attempt definitively to capture its objective reality, then we can safely bracket the whole question of the objective nature of time when examining musical time. This does not necessarily lead us to a position which denies the connection between musical time and non-musical time: we can still retain the notion that musical time is a reflection of time consciousness, itself a way of grasping in thought the lived experience of time, on the part of those making and listening to the music in question. Time here is understood phenomenally, recast as the temporality of lived experience,

---

3   Meyer uses this term to denote something analogous to a language, reserving 'style' for describing what is common to the work of a particular composer or school of composers. Meyer 1956, p. 64.
4   Not universally, however: see Kivy 1984.

rooted in the specificities of socio-historical existence, rather than anything more universal or transcendent.

Secondly, compared to the object of a figurative painting, musical temporality has more to do with form than content, or, at least, as Joan Stambaugh points out, is form as well as content. The demarcation between form and content may be relatively straightforward in the case of figurative painting, but is notoriously difficult to determine in music. It is clear that a simplistic notion which regards content as themes (subjects) and motifs, and form as the structure into which they are organised, will not suffice. Stambaugh reminds us that musical temporality, though obviously formal in the way that it organises the succession of material into an overall structure, is also, through rhythm and meter, an integral part of the content as well.[5]

The Meaning of Form

What does seem to be the case, however, is that for any given style-system of music, the central temporal procedures are formal in the sense that they are given, accepted and largely unquestioned. Here, musicologist Susan McClary's concept of 'convention' proves useful. McClary describes a convention as 'a procedure that has ossified into a formula that needs no further explanation'. Procedures such as the ternary structure of a symphonic minuet or trio, or the fade-out of a pop song, she argues, should not be regarded as 'purely musical'. Rather than being simply technical in a way that transcends signification, they are in fact intensely meaningful, perhaps all the more powerfully so because of the unobtrusive way in which they operate.[6] McClary takes Western tonality to be a convention in this sense, an integrated set of procedures for the organisation of pitch which for three centuries in Europe was taken for granted. Like ideologies, artistic conventions such as this present themselves as natural and normative; in the case of tonality, as rooted in the physical relationships between pitches as frequency ratios. Yet, claims McClary, they are in fact historically produced phenomena, are imbued with meaning, and do a great deal of cultural work, albeit behind the scenes.[7]

McClary points out the similarity between her concept of convention and others' attempts to expose the meaning buried in apparently neutral forms. Such examples include, in the field of science, Thomas Kuhn's 'paradigms',

---

5   Stambaugh 1964, p. 273.
6   McClary 2000, pp. 2–6.
7   McClary 2000, p. 118.

while her definition of convention as the ossification of practices bears clear similarities to Adorno's description of form as sedimented content, which will be examined in Chapter 4. The way in which McClary's conventions operate at a level which is below consciousness, as given rather than chosen features, also recalls Fredric Jameson's 'political unconscious', his attempt to flesh out the mechanisms by which meaning – ultimately, for Jameson, political meaning – finds its way into cultural texts through the codification imposed by aesthetic form.[8] Jameson's is just one way among others of pursuing an approach to art suggested by the Marxist tradition which emphasises the historical over authorial intention as the starting point of cultural hermeneutics. On this reading of art, the most fruitful place to begin any investigation of meaning is not likely to be a specific work or even the entire oeuvre of an individual artist, but some broader periodisation of style-systems. The 'conventions' or 'form' of any given period are understood as having been historically established, and retaining a degree of stability and durability due to their suitability for giving expression to the shared values and assumptions of a society, or at least to those of its ruling elements. These sets of artistic procedures confront individual artists as givens, as artistic raw material, or as simply the way that an artform works. They may be bolstered by official systems of validation such as academies, but can be equally durable where such systems do not exist, as in popular culture. The work of individual artists can only be understood in relation to this bedrock of bequeathed conventions which provides the context of their work. The history of an artform is not, on this understanding, fundamentally, the history of the artworks or the artists that comprise it. Rather it is the history of artistic form itself, and its relationship to the range of social practices contemporaneous with it. Though it often appears that established conventions that have been unquestioned for hundreds of years periodically come under attack and are overthrown by specific artists, such as a Schoenberg or a Picasso, these events can only be fully explained by addressing the ways in which changed socio-historical circumstances encourage the development of new conventions and make old ones obsolete. As a result, these kinds of hermeneutical investigations of the arts, whether Marxist, or, like MacClary's, from the discipline of New Musicology, tend to be drawn to the points in history when old conventions are overthrown and artforms are refounded on a revolutionary new basis.

Hence, periodisation becomes a key technique in the study of art. Perhaps the most influential of such periodisations in the hermeneutical study of culture is Fredric Jameson's. Drawing on the Marxist debates over modernism

---

[8] Jameson 1983.

between Lukács, Adorno, Brecht and Benjamin, Jameson has developed a historical schema of cultural and artistic forms. Whereas those earlier debates centred on the artistic value of modernism vis-à-vis realism in terms of their ability to capture the truth of the world, Jameson, with the cushion of historical distance, has sought to explain modernism's rise in a materialist manner as the result of significant changes in the nature of capitalism in the years surrounding the turn of the twentieth century. For him, realism is the mode of artistic representation thrown up by capitalism in its early or classical phase, while modernist art registers the transformed cultural priorities of the advent of fully-fledged monopoly capitalism, the period when capitalist relations and the market had come to dominate almost the entirety of the lives of those in the advanced countries of Western Europe and North America. Jameson famously completes his schema with the addition of a third period, corresponding to capitalism's global saturation, in which postmodernism is identified as 'the cultural logic of late capitalism'.[9]

Whether or not one accepts Jameson's concept of late capitalism and a distinct cultural logic associated with it, and a number of Marxists do not, the analysis of modernism as a cultural response to monopoly capitalism remains central to a materialist historicisation of art.[10] The problem of modernism arises as an issue for this study because of the fact that groove, although apparently pulling in the opposite direction as a temporal aesthetic from the musical modernisms of the turn of the twentieth century, emerges contemporaneously with them. It seems plausible on chronological grounds to understand groove as driven by the same transformations in capitalism that produce the modernist artistic movements. But how, then, should it be characterised, given that it appears to share few, if any, of modernism's preoccupations? At the very least, groove seems to complicate any historical schema built on neat, clean transitions.

A very different kind of periodisation is adopted by Jacques Attali in his study of music's historical development. Attali rejects a hermeneutic method, arguing that 'the musician is not a mirror of the productive relations of his time. Gesualdo and Bach do not reflect a single ideological system any more than John Cage or the Tangerine Dream'.[11] Musical styles do not in reality succeed one another in a neat linear series; there is always a simultaneity of distinct codes and an overlapping of periods and forms. For Attali, therefore, it is not aesthetics or meaning but power that must be the key term in any

---

9   Jameson 1991.
10 For example see Anderson 1998; Davis 2005.
11 Attali 1985, p. 18.

periodisation of musical history. Thus he proposes a succession of *orders* or stages of the political economy of music, each constituting a different strategic use of music by power. It is certainly the case that no history of music could be complete without an examination of its political economy, and Attali's idiosyncratic methodology produces some interesting insights. But a full account must also integrate the various ways throughout history that music has organised sound (or noise, as Attali puts it), showing how political economy on the one hand, and musical form, style or code on the other, are connected, albeit in complex and contradictory ways. When Attali argues that the attempt to match a succession of musical codes with a history of economic and political relations is impossible because 'time traverses music and music gives meaning to time', he is making the mistake of assuming that time lies beyond the ambit of social relations.[12] My starting point is the contrary position: that the meaning of time, and possibly even time itself, is socially and historically constructed, and, therefore, a study of changes in the organisation of time in music is one way of tracing its history.

Music as Symbolism

If we are interested in aesthetic meaning, periodisation may be a useful starting point, but it still leaves us with the question of how to read the meanings of particular artistic forms. One possibility is to assume that music is in some way symbolic of aspects of the society which produces it. McClary's discussion of the establishment of tonality as a convention focuses on 'analogs' as the primary way by which meaning can be teased out of apparently neutral or 'purely musical' material. It is worth considering the validity of this, since neither McClary or others who deploy a similar approach take any time to defend it. Analogy is, of course, the practice of making a comparison between very different sorts of things by pointing to similarities between them. In this case, for McClary, it is a question of drawing parallels between the harmonic language of eighteenth-century music and the principal themes of post-Enlightenment European thought. She argues that tonality enables musical events to appear to generate themselves according to laws of cause and effect, analogous to the emphasis on rationality and the new spirit of scientific enquiry of the period;

---

12   Attali 1985, p. 19. Even where Attali follows Marx in identifying time as a measure of value in capitalism, he restricts its application to analysis of the political economy of music, without considering whether time-as-value can be traced, or heard, in the music itself (see Attali 1985, pp. 124–5).

and that tonal procedures impart a goal-orientedness to music, which is the musical analogue to the emerging ideals of progress, 'purposeful advancement', and 'the possibility of self-generation'. Adapting Meyer's emotion-based analysis of the tendency within tonal music for expected harmonic resolution to be delayed, she argues that musical strategies that postpone arrivals serve to confirm the belief that rational effort will achieve its goals.[13] She also suggests that tonality is well suited to the ideology of individualism which established its dominance in this period, although the analogy here appears to be less about tonality than the emergence of musical ensembles structured to feature an individual virtuoso supported by an ensemble backing. She concludes that tonality won out in the eighteenth century over competing procedures as 'cultural priorities came to focus almost obsessively on progress, rationality, intelligibility, quests after goals, and the illusion of self-contained autonomy'.[14]

This hermeneutic method is a form of *Ideologiekritik*, whose goal is to expose the ideology which is held to be at work within the very language of cultural form. Tonality is a particularly obvious target for this kind of critique, as it appears to function according to its own internally-derived and naturally-based laws: for example, that the dominant chord 'naturally' seeks to resolve to the tonic presents itself as a kind of necessity over which the composer does not have full control. In this respect, we might identify another analogy, one not drawn by McClary, between the ideology of tonality as a self-contained system working according to its own laws and that of the capitalist market as a 'hidden hand'. If Marx was right that the reified economy under capitalism was the source of alienation, it may be appropriate to apply the same critique to tonal music.

Christopher Small's critique of the Western concert-music tradition proceeds along similar lines, though he is more likely to use the term 'metaphor' than analogue. He writes: 'tonal-harmonic music is a metaphor for the rationalistic and individualistic temper of western man'; and 'the sound relations of a musical performance stand in metaphorical form for ideal human relationships as imagined by the participants'.[15] Small's use of the term metaphor is rather unspecific. His hermeneutical method is actually a mixture of different kinds of parallels drawn between broad characteristics of the music and the society which produces it. Elsewhere he uses the word 'model', but perhaps the best term to capture the methodology Small deploys is 'pattern', as in the following passage:

---

13   Meyer 1956, pp. 26–30; McClary 2000, pp. 67–8.
14   McClary 2000, p. 68.
15   Small 1977, p. 102; Small 1997, p. 129.

> When we take part in a musical performance, any musical performance, when we music, we engage in a process of exploring the nature of the pattern which connects, we are affirming the validity of its nature as we perceive it to be, and we are celebrating our relation to it. Through the relationships that are established in the course of the performance we are empowered not only to *learn about* the pattern and our relation to it but actually to *experience* it in all its complexities, in a way that words never allow us to do, for as long as the performance lasts.[16]

So music is understood to be 'patterned after' relationships between humans and between humans and the natural world. Hence, Small's critique of the Western concert tradition focuses on the ways that it reflects social domination – the domination of some people by others, and the domination of nature by humans through the application of abstract scientific logic, what Adorno referred to as 'instrumental rationality'. He also, however, adds a further, utopian dimension by suggesting that music not only symbolises aspects of society as they currently exist, but is also capable of pointing to how society should or could be. Music is:

> not only a metaphor, but also a way of transcending [society's] otherwise unspoken and unexamined assumptions. Art can reveal to us new modes of perception and feeling which jolt us out of our habitual ways; it can make us aware of possibilities of alternative societies whose existence is not yet.[17]

The utopian is an important aspect of art's meaning, but its introduction here produces a hermeneutical problem. If music is held to be the way it is because of its structural similarities with society as it exists, how then can it also be symbolic of aspects of society which do not (yet) exist? Analyses that proceed on this basis are open to the accusation of having cherry-picked their musical examples to bolster a preconceived political perspective. This problem merely highlights a more general one: can a theory of music as *symbolic* of society, one which proceeds by identifying structural similarities between musical form and aspects of society, produce secure attributions of meaning? Is analogue or metaphor, or any other form of symbolisation (others prefer to look for 'structural homologies'), adequate as a hermeneutical method?[18] The connections

---

16   Small 1997, pp. 141–2.
17   Small 1977, p. 2.
18   Shepherd 1982, p. 155.

drawn by McClary and Small between the intramusical and the extramusical are suggestive and illuminating, but without clarity about what kind of connections they are and what entitles them to be drawn, they remain somewhat conjectural. As Shepherd notes, 'without a firmly established and philosophically conceived cultural theory in which to locate socio-musical homologies, it is difficult to refute the possible criticism that such homologies are contrived'.[19]

This problem is not easy to solve. Tagg has attempted to develop a semiotic approach in order to pin down musical meaning in a much more concrete and definite way.[20] But, because he regards music as a form of communication, as a message being transmitted from musician to listener, Tagg assumes that musical meaning is transparent to sender and receiver alike at the surface of musical content, neglecting the possibility that ideology is buried within musical form. In focusing on the perceived connotations of music for film and TV, this kind of positivism runs the risk of telling us nothing more than how Hollywood studios and advertisers use musical clichés to manipulate our responses.

McClary's and Small's approaches have the advantage in recognising the ideology at work in the structure of music. However, because both tend to satisfy themselves by establishing links between certain musical characteristics and the dominant values and ideas of society, both fall short of being fully materialist. Small believes that by looking at music we can 'learn something of the inner unspoken nature of western *culture* as a whole'.[21] Aside from some comments about the alienation of industrial society and the social groups who benefit from it, the analysis does not go deeper than the level of the culture and ideas of society. Pressing further is not without its dangers. John Shepherd, for example, recasts tonality's postponed resolutions as 'delayed gratification' in order to link classical music not only to the asceticism of the Protestant work ethic, and hence to capitalism, but to specific classes in contemporary society – those prepared to endure several years of poverty at university or in professional training in order to reap the reward of affluence later. The music of the 'dispossessed', by contrast, displays an immediacy which corresponds to their lack of a stake in, or control over, the direction of society.[22] This is an example of an insufficiently mediated analysis, in which the links between types of music and social class are rigidly drawn, and which obscures the fact that Western popular music is also tonal and often uses the same devices of

---

19   Shepherd 1982, p. 149.
20   Tagg 1999; Tagg and Clarida 2003.
21   Small 1997, p. 2 (emphasis added).
22   Shepherd 1982, pp. 160–5.

delayed resolution as art music. In a similar vein are analyses by 'orthodox' Marxists such as Marothy, for whom tracing the degree of individualism or collectivity manifested by musical forms justifies the division of music into bourgeois and proletarian forms.[23] The question of the relationship between 'high' and 'low' culture and class is not irrelevant, and I intend to return to it later, but Marothy's formulation suggests that cultures are hermetically sealed from one another in a way that has never been the case.

How can a study of musical time help to clarify the relationships between musics and the societies from which they come while avoiding the pitfalls identified above? In the first place, musical time should be understood as highly conventional, in McClary's sense of the term. Devices such as meter, pulse, and the divisive conception of note durations established themselves as the standard components of temporal organisation in Western music contemporaneously with the emergence of tonality that McClary analyses. Like tonality, this form of temporal organisation is taken as natural and neutral, as a 'discovery' rather than a culturally specific construction, which disguises the ideological work that it does. It is my contention that 'groove', as both continuation and departure from the temporal procedures of Western music in the 'common practice era', has similarly established itself during the twentieth century as 'convention' for the vast majority of music heard daily in the West, and increasingly across the world. The uncovering of the unconscious meaning of this musical temporality through an exploration of its connection with contemporary temporality more generally, can tell us something about both groove music and the nature of the society that produces it.

This raises the question of what exactly is the primary object of this investigation, the temporality of music or that of the society that produces it? The answer is both: a study of the relationship between musical time and social time should prove capable of shedding light in both directions. For that reason, rather than conceiving music as a form of symbolic representation of society, Jameson's term 'figuration' may be more pertinent and useful, especially where time is concerned. For Jameson, figuration

> impl[ies] an operation, impossible or not, rather than some mere turning on or off of a function, some mere designation of a property or possibility. To pose the problem in terms of figuration is to ask questions distinct from the traditional ones about truth; as well as from literary ones about style or metaphor.[24]

---

23   Marothy 1974.
24   Jameson 2010, p. 479.

The suggestion here is the dialectical one that the temporalities of artistic forms do not simply passively reflect social time, whose reality is in any case disputable, but through the process of making it visible or explicit, contribute to its construction in some way. It is also a formulation which seems to allow for that aspect of art addressed by Small, namely its ability to escape the bounds of simply reflecting what is, and point towards what might be.

The Structure of the Book

The book begins with a musical analysis of groove in order to justify the claim that groove is an aesthetic of measured time. The definition of groove which I elaborate shows how several musical practices come together to produce an emphasis on strict chronometric time. In a sense, not only does groove depend on a concept of measured time, but groove music itself becomes a measure of time. As Clemence points out, 'any repetitive phenomenon whatever, the recurrences of which can be counted, is a measure of time'.[25] The time-measuring aspect of most contemporary music is evident every time one hears the tick-ticking spilling from other people's iPod earphones. I have chosen to use the term groove, despite the fact that some others writers use this term to emphasise *deviations* from strictly measured time in musical performance, human looseness rather than precision.[26] I have done so because I believe my use of the word is close to its usage by practising musicians, and also because the rhythmic discrepancies that others focus upon are, in a very real sense, dependent for their aesthetic impact upon a degree of measured temporal accuracy which is, therefore, prior to them.

Chapter 1 is also the only place where significant numbers of notated musical examples occur and are included to illustrate the various elements that I bring together in my definition of groove. Because of the nature of my argument and especially because of the refutation in Chapter 2 of the view that groove has African origins and is therefore only really found in 'black music', I have deliberately avoided selecting examples from those artists with whom the term is most associated. There is no Stevie Wonder, James Brown, Earth, Wind and Fire, Chic or Tower of Power, not because these artists do not make groove music, far from it, but because I want to secure the 'conventionality' of groove in twentieth-century music. That goal depends on being able to

---

25 Clemence 1968, p. 406.
26 For example, Charles Keil's theory of 'participatory discrepancies' which will be addressed in the next chapter.

demonstrate the ubiquity of groove across popular music and beyond, and illustrate its presence in even the 'less artistically credible' pop. Hence I have tried to choose examples from 'mainstream' rock and pop artists, without attempting to be in any way exhaustive or fully representative.[27] The fact that many of the examples cluster around a particular time period should not be taken as indicative of anything more significant than my own age. (Readers without the inclination to follow the musicological arguments may be advised to skip Chapter 1, and possibly Chapter 2 as well, in order to concentrate on the philosophical, aesthetic and political discussion presented in the subsequent chapters.)

Having established that groove is a musical convention based on measured time, the task is then to address its significance. This is where a study of the meaning of musical time may have an advantage over studies of other aspects of music. The fact that, unlike tonality, time is both intramusical and extramusical has important implications for hermeneutical method. In contrast to the claims of thinkers such as Langer and Schutz that musical time is a special or 'virtual' time, a Marxist position must insist that the time of music is, at some level, the same time as the time of the world. As Adorno argues, musical time is not simply 'real, external time', otherwise it could not have varied so widely between musics at different points in history, but it 'always reflects real, external time'.[28] 'Time as such' does exist in music, albeit transformed aesthetically.[29] The outcome of this is that some of the problems of drawing connections between the intramusical and the extramusical can be bypassed. If it is the case that there is no gulf in substance between the temporality of music and the temporality of empirical existence, it may not be necessary to rely upon a symbolic theory of music's relationship to society in order to expose musical meaning. Some of the weaknesses inherent in the methodology of positing analogues, metaphors or other structural similarities between music and aspects of the world can perhaps be avoided. Instead, at least at a general level of analysis, we can operate on the assumption that the temporality of music *is* the temporality of society in aestheticised form, and is not merely symbolic of it.

How deeply materialist would such an analysis of temporality be? Is the temporality of music a reflection of the *time consciousness* of a society or of time itself? If the analysis goes no further than investigating the former, it is open to the kind of criticism I made of McClary and Small earlier. But in

---

27 The exception is the reggae, selected for its particularly clear use of layered off-beats.
28 Adorno quoted in Leppert 2002, p. 144.
29 Adorno 1997, p. 182.

addressing the latter, we are confronted again with the issue of the reality of time which I argued could be bracketed for the purposes of this analysis. As a way of working through this problem, I begin by discussing musical time in relation to *ideas* of time, specifically measured time, or the measurability of time. This involves discussion of a number of non-Marxist thinkers on the question of time, which is necessary either because of the influence they have had on Marxist appraisals of, in particular, modernist art; or because they are capable of throwing light on the problem of temporality despite the weaknesses of their overall perspective. The central figure in the first category is Henri Bergson, whose notion of time as intrinsically continuous and unmeasurable, addressed in Chapter 3, lies behind many modernist assumptions and many critiques of metrical music. Chapter 4 examines Alfred Schutz's phenomenology of musical time, an approach which has relevance given its consistency with the bracketing of time's reality that I have already argued for. Schutz, though in no way a materialist, is sufficiently concerned with the social aspects of temporality to recognise the importance of the collective nature of the practice of music-making to musical temporality. Adorno is the towering figure in Marxist musical aesthetics and Chapter 5 addresses his argument that the temporality of groove exhibits, in a sense, too much materiality, that it is simply the incorporation, without aesthetic modification, of the rigid temporality of reified, industrial society.

In Chapter 6, I attempt to account for modern time consciousness in a materialist way, by deepening the analysis to include the temporality of the capitalist economic system itself. Here, temporality is understood not as time consciousness, nor even as time consciousness which is shaped or generated by concrete, lived experience in a social context, but as something real produced by the material processes at the heart of capitalism. The result is a kind of flattening of the distinction between time consciousness and time itself which, I hope, does not represent a collapse into idealism or rationalism, but is justified by the specific nature of capitalism and helps to provide a materialist explanation for its dominant musical forms.

On the face of it, this kind of materialist analysis appears to have no place for judgements of musical value. The formulation of an explanation as to why a particular music takes the form that it does, one which seeks to trace the ways in which music is shaped by the fundamental characteristics of the society that produces it, would seem to be a value-neutral project, akin, perhaps, to an anthropological investigation. This is the position taken by the initial, musicological, part of the book, consistent with the view that groove is something like a 'cultural logic' which has imposed itself upon all but a small fringe of musical practice since the early twentieth century. There may be good groove music and bad groove music, but the initial analysis I undertake does not attempt to make any distinction, and the musical examples chosen for Chapter 1 should not be assumed to have value implications.

However, the questions raised by this analysis are, at another level, highly value laden, indeed political. The debates between Marxists referred to earlier focused on the aesthetic merits of modernist artistic procedures, not simply the reasons for their emergence, and were highly politically charged. Jameson simultaneously offers an explanation for postmodernism and registers his dismay – political and aesthetic – at its effects. Adorno's extremely perceptive writing on music reminds us that the best analysis is also critique. Against the positivism prevalent in some cultural theory, I take the view that there can be no neutral theory and that taking a position on one's object of study does not compromise understanding, but rather aids in getting to the truth of it. In this respect, the approach adopted in this book differs markedly from the kind of analysis pursued by 'postmodern Marxists' such as Adam Krims and Henry Klumpenhouwer, for whom the task of Marxist musical scholarship in the era of 'late capitalism' is to be analytical rather than critical, not to make judgments but simply to trace the functioning of capital accumulation 'in the very sound of the musical tracks'.[30] Given the total commodification of cultural products, they argue, and the fact that art cannot transcend its socio-historical circumstances, there can be no moment of resistance or opposition within artforms that requires to be exposed through a Gramscian or cultural studies-type reading, and all attempts to locate the elements of beauty or truth in art are futile and distracting.[31] Marxism, for these authors, should have nothing to do with the concept of aesthetics, and to the extent that aesthetic concerns feature in Marx's writings, they are a hangover from bourgeois idealism which compromise his materialist thought.[32]

Clearly there is a political corollary to the view that culture under capitalism can never express anything but the logic of the system: it is the defeatist one that all resistance is futile.[33] There may be something to be said for being suspicious of the search for resistive meanings in cultural works, but it remains central to any genuine Marxism that capitalism is fundamentally contradictory

---

30   Krims 2003, p. 142. There is also a fundamental misunderstanding of Marx's theory of commodity fetishism at work in Krims's and Klumpenhouwer's project of 'reading' cultural commodities. In a strange reversal of Marx's view that commodity production serves to obscure the reality of social relations under the blank interchangeability of exchange values, they argue that it is only in commodities that social relations can express themselves.
31   Klumpenhouwer 2001, p. 401.
32   Klumpenhouwer 2001, pp. 399–400.
33   '[I]t is pointless to struggle towards an exit in such a closed system as capitalism' (Klumpenhouwer 2001, p. 398).

and that those contradictions are expressed and fought out in the 'superstructural' spheres of politics, ideology and culture. The necessary existence of a class within capitalism whose interests are antagonistic to capital's – the proletariat – provides the material basis for political, ideological and cultural expressions which are at odds with the dominant ones, notwithstanding the system's undoubted ability to turn many of the latter to its own advantage through commodification.

It is certainly true that the grooves of popular music circulate fully within a system of commodity exchange, controlled by an industry moved solely by the logic of capital accumulation. Marx argued that cultural production was commodified (and 'productive' from the point of view of capitalism), 'in so far as [it] is subsumed under capital and only takes place so that capital may valorise itself'.[34] I have taken the view, consistent, I believe, with Marx's use in this sentence of 'in so far as' and 'only', that artistic production under capitalism can exceed this purely 'productive' component, and that indeed, capitalist cultural production is parasitic upon those instances of 'unproductive', or free, artistic labour which produce innovation and cultural significance. It may no longer be possible to be a Milton, expressing one's nature freely in literature 'in the way that a silkworm produces silk', or to be 'a singer who sings like a bird', as Marx puts it, but without at least an *element* of such free labour, those musicians who do not (yet) earn a living from their art, or who struggle to express themselves despite their dependence on the culture industry, the record companies would soon have no use value to commodify.[35] Free and alienated labour exist in extreme tension in cultural production under capitalism and it is the task of Marxist analysis to unravel this complex relationship. Indeed, were there not some aesthetic kernel at the heart of artistic activity, albeit one always under threat of annihilation by commodification, some promise of the possibility of the cultivation of human senses for their own sake rather than mere utility, there could be no more justification for a Marxist study of cultural products than one of cars or computers.[36]

Consequently, once the initial definition of groove has been completed, value becomes a continuous thread in what follows. In many ways, the argument I have attempted to make can be understood as a defence of groove, on aesthetic, historical, and ultimately political grounds, against a variety of types

---

34   Marx 1994, p. 137.
35   Ibid. As Hobsbawm puts it, 'Tin Pan Alley no more *invents* its tunes and fashions in a sort of commercial laboratory than the canning industry invented food: it discovers what is most profitably processed and then processes it' (Newton 1959, p. 19).
36   See Eagleton 1990, ch. 8.

of critique of it. The final chapter attempts to grapple with the problem that we have already encountered in relation to Small's work, that of how art can be intimately connected to the society which produces it without simply endorsing or acting as apologist for it; how, if fundamental elements of the social structure can be shown to be present within its very form, it can avoid ideologically reinforcing those elements; how music which is, in the deepest sense, *of* a society can at the same time contribute to a critique of that society, point beyond it, or expose something of the truth of it.

In order to unravel these issues, Chapter 7 discusses history, narrative and modernist time, concluding that the aesthetic structuring of measured time effected by groove, although derived from the abstract time of capitalism, represents a modernist, non-narrative, collective response to the experience of life dominated by abstract time, one capable of figuring a liberated temporality beyond the reified temporal structures of contemporary capitalism. Groove's political charge lies in its ability to turn measured time against itself. Groove is the dialectical negation of abstract time.

CHAPTER 1

What is 'groove'?

How should we define the term 'groove'? The word has been in common vernacular usage among musicians involved in popular music for a number of decades but has only recently found its way in to the theoretical realm, where it remains vague, underdefined and subject to a variety of interpretations.

Ask a musician what groove means and the reply would probably be that it relates to the rhythmic feel of a piece of music, how the individual parts or layers of the music, particularly the instruments of the rhythm section, interlock and interact with each other to create a unified rhythmic effect – the groove. A musician would be aware of the concept of 'groove-based music', music whose rhythmic component is its primary meaningful element, more important than, say, its melody or harmony. She would probably associate this in particular with the 'black music' of the 1970s, funk and its related styles, if only because of the prominent use of the term in that era by musicians themselves, an instance of which is George Clinton's celebrated slogan, 'One Nation Under a Groove'. The word has often been used by musicians for naming record labels,[1] bands,[2] albums,[3] and songs.[4]

The word groove, of course, also has a connection with the technology of music recording, that part of the vinyl disk which 'holds the music', a meaning which, despite its superseding by digital technology, persists in the term, 'rare grooves' used by record shops who specialise in particular kinds of dance music recorded in the old format.[5]

Though the word has a long history in the field of practical music-making, its occurrences in books on popular music theory are rare. It is not found in text-books or glossaries like Roy Shuker's *Understanding Popular Music* or *Key Concepts in Popular Music*, or the *Oxford Companion to Popular Music*. The second edition of *The New Grove Dictionary of Jazz* defines groove as 'a persistently

---

1 As in 'Groove', a 1950s subsidiary of RCA-Victor, and the more recent 'Nu Groove Records'.
2 As in Groove Armada, Groove Theory, Infectious Grooves.
3 As in Bob Dylan's *Down In The Groove*, King Curtis's *The Groove*, plus thousands of compilation albums.
4 As in Madonna's 'Into the Groove', Limp Bizkit's 'Getcha Groove On', Earth, Wind and Fire's 'Let's Groove', Milt Jackson's 'Bag's Groove'.
5 Mark Katz exploits this double meaning of the word – that it refers to both the music and its recording medium – in his history of hip-hop DJ-ing, *Groove Music*. Katz 2012.

repeated pattern' and traces the use of the term back to the wartime swing era.[6] 'Groove' also gets a mention in the entry on 'Form' (written by Richard Middleton) in Horner and Swiss, *Key Terms in Popular Music and Culture* which says the following:

> the concept of 'groove' – a term now theorized by analysts but long familiar in musicians' own usage – marks an understanding of rhythmic patterning that underlines its role in producing the characteristic rhythmic 'feel' of a piece, a feel created by a repeated framework within which variation can then take place.[7]

Susan McClary's use of the word in *Conventional Wisdom* is much more impressionistic, one which is held to pertain as much to a psychological state as to how the music is organised. She also makes the common association between groove and physicality. Discussing a gospel recording by the Swan Silvertones, she writes:

> When the backup singers enter, they lay down a slow groove that rocks the hymn physically. The groove registers even more powerfully in the chorus when clapping enters to mark the backbeats. As St. Teresa wrote of her ecstatic states, 'the body has some part, even a considerable part, in it'; and even if we can't see the group moving with the pulse they create, we can hear their physical investment in the performance. To appreciate their performance properly – that is, to become part of the community here offered – we would have to surrender ourselves likewise to the groove, with all its carefully placed cross-rhythms.[8]

Both Middleton and McClary relate groove to what they regard as the African element in Afro-American music, and in particular the cultural practice identified by Henry Louis Gates as 'signifyin(g)', or the 'changing same', a way of structuring cultural forms radically at odds with the European narrative model. I will return to this argument in the next chapter.

The psychological strand of McClary's description, the notion of 'losing oneself' in the groove, with its implication of a trancelike state, is also mentioned by Ingrid Monson's musician interviewees, one of whom described grooving as

---

6 Kernfeld 2009.
7 Horner and Swiss 1999, p. 143.
8 McClary 2000, p. 25.

'a euphoria that comes from playing good time *with* somebody'.[9] Allen Farmelo conceives groove as having 'unifying consequences'; it represents a shared and alternative reality based on a trace-like state of consciousness.[10] This conception has a 1960s countercultural inflection but places an important emphasis on the essentially collective aspect of groove.

An unexpected place for the word 'groove' to pop up is in the section on rhythm in Roger Scruton's *The Aesthetics of Music*, where it appears in the context of jazz:

> Rhythms are quickly wearisome, unless refreshed by a countervailing foreground which groups the tones against the meter. The ever-so-slight rubato of a solo instrument playing in front of the beat is familiar to jazz-lovers. To play jazz properly it is not enough to move with the beat: you must also enter the 'groove' of it, which means riding alongside it with those playful gestures that ruffle the rhythmic surface and fill it with light. The distinction between beat and groove is a special case of the general distinction between foreground and background in rhythm.[11]

This points us in the direction of another set of meanings implied by the term, slightly at odds with Middleton's emphasis on repetition. That is that groove concerns the *irregularities* in rhythm, those elements which disrupt its strictness, repetitiveness and uniformity. It is this emphasis which underpins the only serious attempt by music theorists to grapple with the concept of groove, that of ethnomusicologist Charles Keil, who has gone so far as to propose a branch of study called 'groovology' based on the notion of 'participatory discrepancies' or PDS.

For Keil, groove is a *process* rather than a thing, a verb rather than a noun, and it is intimately related to other terms used by musicians such as 'beat', 'vital drive', 'swing', 'pulse', or 'push'.[12] Crucially, the effect that is groove, or rather grooving, is a product not of the tightness of integration of the elements that interact to make it up, but of their divergence. As Keil says, 'everything has to be a bit out of time, a little out of pitch to groove'. Groove, therefore, is the fundamentally imperfect result of a collaborative process, whose value lies precisely in both its collaborative, collective, negotiated nature and its inherent imperfections:

---

9   Don Byron quoted in Monson 1996, p. 68.
10 Farmelo 1997.
11 Scruton 1999, p. 37.
12 Keil and Feld 1994, p. 96.

What's at stake in the premise that PDs [participatory discrepancies] are where the juice, the groove, the funk, and the delights of music, and of life, are, is a real basic worldview that says that the universe is open, imperfect, and subject to redefinition by every emergent self.[13]

Though groove is essentially processual, Keil's collaborator Steven Feld argues that it does produce an objective result, but suggests a relationship between the activity and its outcome which is more like that between 'form' and 'content' than 'composing' and 'composition':

> In the vernacular a 'groove' refers to an intuitive sense of style as process, a perception of a cycle in motion, a form or organizing pattern being revealed, a recurrent clustering of elements through time. Such consistent, coherent formal features become one with their content but are uniquely recognizable by the way they shape content to articulate specifically in that form. Groove and style are distilled essences, crystallizations of collaborative expectancies in time.[14]

The concept of participatory discrepancies and Keil's advocating of a science of groovology has led to research on the part of other scholars, usually ethnomusicologists, to find and measure the discrepancies. Some of the results were published in a special issue of the journal *Ethnomusicology* in 1995. J.A. Prögler's paper, 'Searching for Swing: Participatory Discrepancies in the Jazz Rhythm Section', is an account of a number of quite basic experiments involving jazz bassists and drummers playing 12-bar blues changes in a swing feel. Prögler declares he is looking for the 'productive tensions' that are central to a good swing feel, and hence to the jazz groove. His research, therefore, consists of the rather arid exercise of measuring the extent to which the players are out of time with each other and presenting the results in a series of tables and diagrams. However, he himself is forced to admit that this is all somewhat contrary to how musicians themselves regard the construction of groove. Quoting Berliner, he says:

> to many musicians a critical element of striking a groove is the synchronization between the drummer and the bass player, and he found that many musicians discuss this in terms of 'precision', 'unison', and being 'tight'.[15]

---

13   Keil and Feld 1994, p. 171.
14   Keil and Feld 1994, p. 109.
15   Prögler 1995, p. 31.

Charles Keil found similar attitudes amongst musicians who had 'conceptions of swing based on unity and maintaining tempos' rather than discrepancies. Monson also emphasises synchronisation when she suggests that at the heart of the aesthetic ideal of the jazz groove is 'how well the walking bass line *locks* or is *in the pocket* with the ride cymbal rhythm'.[16] Certainly, most musicians would tend to endorse Chernoff's suggestion that the grooves get better the more tightly people play with each other.[17] On the other hand, many would agree that the musical appeal of groove is undermined by the total precision of timing which music computer software imposes.

In an article written in 2005, Keil acknowledged the failure of the PD project to make a real theoretical breakthrough, speculating that if groove really is about process then it may not be possible to pin it down in a minute analysis of the 'text'. As he puts it, reiterating his radical opposition to any kind of syntactical understanding of music:

> I might go back to the musical structures as 'texts' myself at this point if I hadn't already convinced myself that as structures they are empty of feeling and meaningless. No symbolism. No semiotics. No fullotics. All the emotion and meaning is in our heads, not in the music. All the emotion and meaning is in the relationships of the musicking moment. All the emotion and meaning is in the 'motion and feeling', in the grooves and sounds. . . . in the moment. . . . in our heads.[18]

If this were true, then the study of music as text is redundant. All that remains is the study of people engaged in 'musicking', to use Christopher Small's neologism, either on the 'production' or 'reception' side of the process.[19]

Also adopting what might be described as an anti-objectivist approach is David Brackett. In his *Interpreting Popular Music* he combines a number of the ideas we have already encountered. First, groove is a feature of the West African musical tradition; second, it is the result of a relaxed and flexible attitude to the underlying metronomic pulse or 'time-line'. Third, lest those elements of a definition should suggest 'too positivistic a formula', Brackett adds:

---

16   Monson 1996, p. 56 (emphasis added).
17   Keil 1995, p. 6.
18   Keil, 'Groovology and the Magic of Other People's Music'.
19   Small 1997.

> Discerning why some bands 'groove' more than others is a complex affair.... a groove exists because musicians know how to create one and audiences know how to respond to one. Something can only be recognised as a groove by a listener who has internalised the rhythmic syntax of a given musical idiom.[20]

Clearly, before any discussion of groove can begin, it has to be recognised as such by performers or listeners. But to deny that further analysis can take place, and to suggest, as Brackett does, that distinguishing between a ' "good" groove and a "bad" one' is primarily a subjective matter is to risk treating an important element of musical experience as something that emerges almost magically from performance.

Adopting a rather cautious perspective which sits on the fence both on the issue of the extent to which groove is 'experiential [and] phenomenological' rather than 'syntactical', and whether it is dependent upon 'equal subdivisions of each beat' or 'temporal discrepancies' from the pulse, is Garry Tamlyn's encyclopaedia entry on the subject.[21] Here we encounter the notion that 'getting into the groove' describes the experience of a 'sense of comfort resulting from the congruity of stylistic (and mostly rhythmic) elements and the interpretative or semiotic rules that are generally associated with a musical style'. This formulation suggests that groove is nothing more than the satisfaction derived from the competence to appreciate the rhythmic aesthetic of any given style. On this definition, groove can be experienced through the performance of any music whatsoever: since all music has rhythm, all music can produce groove. The lack of specificity in this approach so dilutes the concept of groove that it is of little help in explaining why the term only arises in connection with the non-art musics of the twentieth century.

However important the insights into groove's processual nature might be, I shall argue that it is possible to define, identify, and study groove as an objective element of music. Groove's processual aspect arises because groove is associated primarily with traditions in which music is either improvised or partly improvised in performance, or generated through improvisational processes prior to performance such as 'jamming'.[22] Keil and Feld find it in the participatory components of what is marketed as 'world music' from around the

---

20   Brackett 2000, pp. 143–4.
21   Tamlyn 2003, p. 610.
22   Derek Bailey associates the term with Western improvisation, and claims that, like 'swing', 'rock' and 'ride', it is of sexual derivation (Bailey 1992, p. 4).

globe as well as in Western popular music: the 'lift-up-over sounding' music of the Kaluli of Papua New Guinea (Feld), and Polish-derived polka bands of the USA (Keil). The implication is that it does not exist in the Western classical musical tradition not because of anything in that music itself, but because of the division of labour and roles between composer and performers, and between performers and listeners embodied in that tradition.

I will argue that groove is a musical phenomenon that is unique to twentieth-century Western popular music. Although the connection between collective improvisation and groove is undeniable, groove is not excluded from situations in which there is no improvisation or in which there is a single performer. It is possible to locate groove in the musical 'text' and identify it as a particular way, or a set of multiple ways, of organising musical events temporally; as, in other words, a way of organising musical time which is peculiar to twentieth-century popular music.[23] As such, my concept is intended to be more precise than some of the vaguer uses of the term encountered above. But I will also apply it more broadly than others by attempting to show that it is a feature not only of 'African-American music', or those genres that are commonly described, or describe themselves as, 'groove-based', but to the overwhelming majority of twentieth-century 'popular' music.

But in order to begin to do that, it is necessary to abandon all the impressionistic and non-musical senses of the meaning of the word groove, and to define it as precisely and unambiguously as possible. I propose that groove consists of a combination, or constellation, of four elements, all of which must be present to at least some degree.

Four Elements of Groove

1   *Metronomic Time*
The presence of groove in music depends first on a strict attitude to the pulse. Most Western music, arguably most music anywhere in the world, is organised

---

23   'Text' here does not mean score, but neither does it exclude score. Tamlyn speaks for many who emphasise the processual nature of music when he argues that 'groove emanates from musical performance..., not from a musical score'. But this is rather less significant than he intends given that it is also true of all aspects of music: sound, melody, timbre, form etc. Notation should be regarded not as another form that music can take, but as a set of instructions for a performance, or, in the case of musics which are not notated before their performance, as a useful way of capturing some of their aspects visually to facilitate other performances or for analytical purposes. I will, therefore, be using notation in the course of this analysis of groove (Tamlyn 2003, p. 610).

around a regularly occurring beat, an isochronous pulse. Groove music falls within the set of musics which share this characteristic: indeed it requires a particularly close adherence to a regular pulse; one might say it is highly metronomic. Such a characteristic does not mark out the groove music of the twentieth century as unique, but neither is it so universal as to make the observation meaningless. There have been historically, and there remain, musics which are not so organised. From the evidence of what survives of it, much of the religious and ritualistic vocal music of the pre-modern era in Europe and the near-East operates without the existence of a regular pulse. For the chants of the Christian and Jewish traditions, such as Gregorian plainchant, the sung word is the crucial element, and the music follows the rhythm of the text. In fact, it seems justifiable to argue that music which results exclusively from the transformation of the spoken word into song, especially if it is performed by a single voice, tends to lack rhythmic regularity since the rhythm of speech is not organised around a pulse. The Islamic 'call to prayer' falls in the same general category, often with the addition of melismatic flourishes which are also in free rhythm.[24]

The origins in European composed music of musical pulse in the loosest sense lie in the emergence of the polyphonic music of the thirteenth to the sixteenth centuries. This music is described as 'mensural', deploying notation which presented note lengths in proportion to each other, clearly differing in this respect from the free rhythm of plainchant.[25] Some of the surviving manuscripts of the music of the troubadours and trouvères of the same period are notated in this way, but it seems that the degree of measurement implied by mensural notation was probably relatively vague.[26] It is possible for music to be metrical without the presence of a measured pulse, in the way that poetry is metrical. The rhythmic modes of the thirteenth century comprised such a system in which standard groupings of note length proportions served as equivalents of poetic feet. The primary aim was to reproduce the accent patterns of poetry or speech; the note length proportions can be regarded as a means to that end and mean that this early mensural music was not organised around a regular pulse in the way that later music came to be.[27]

---

24 Neubauer and Doubleday, 'Islamic religious music', *Grove Music Online. Oxford Music Online*.
25 Pryer in Latham 2002, 'Mensural music', *The Oxford Companion to Music, Oxford Music Online*. See also Kennedy 1984 and the entries 'Mensural Music' and 'Mensural Notation'.
26 Stevens et al. 'Troubadours, trouvères', *Grove Music Online. Oxford Music Online*.
27 Latham 2002, 'Metre', *The Oxford Companion to Music, Oxford Music Online*.

It is of course in the instrumental music designed for accompanying dancing that we find the highest degree of rhythmic regularity, particularly music played by ensembles which included the drum. The late medieval period saw the spread across Western Europe of the practice of a single musician playing pipe and tabor simultaneously, and Arbeau's examples of tabor and tambourine rhythms for various dances show simple patterns based on a regular pulse, mostly in triple time.[28] Such rhythms in the European folk music tradition remain fairly rudimentary, necessarily so if performed by the pipe and tabor 'one man band', an arrangement which conceivably allows for a degree of temporal flexibility. It is not until the development of larger instrumental ensembles in the late Renaissance period that the use of an isochronous pulse became an essential and standard way of organising musical rhythm.

However, if we make the direct comparison between twentieth-century groove music and the nineteenth-century orchestral and chamber music repertoire which dominates in the concert halls and 'classical' recording catalogues, I believe it is valid to argue that the former displays a closer adherence to an isochronous pulse than the latter. It surely is the case that part of the meaning of the term 'groove' is the sense of the music's being locked into a temporal straightjacket. Monson refers variously to 'playing time' and 'keeping time' as central to groove, while Iyer defines the term 'groove-based music' as 'meaning that it features a steady, virtually isochronous pulse that is established collectively by an interlocking composite of rhythmic entities'.[29] He goes on to argue that 'European classical music ... would not fall into the realm of groove-based music because of the former's reliance on tempo variation for expressive purposes'.[30]

Groove music's strict adherence to the pulse is an unwritten rule, a musical practice which has become genuinely conventional in the sense of being unconsciously accepted and unquestioned among its practitioners and audience. Nineteenth-century Romantic music's adherence to the beat is very different: it is flexible, contingent and subject to conscious performance decisions. It is regarded as a means to the end of ensuring that the musical phrases speak meaningfully.

One way of pursuing the contrast is to note that there exist a range of circumstances in nineteenth-century art music in which divergence from the regular pulse is not only permissible but is encouraged. A number of these are obvious as they are indicated by the composer in the score: slowings down

---

28   Arbeau 1966, pp. 67–9.
29   Monson 1996, pp. 52, 56.
30   Iyer 2002, pp. 397, 399.

(*rallentandos, ritardandos, allargandos* etc.) and, less common, speedings up (*accelerandos, strettos* etc.). Of course, slowing down is a practice found in various popular musics, especially as a way of bringing a piece to a close, but such endings are much rarer than in classical music and are usually rather uncomfortable and unsatisfactory, opted for as a last resort in solving the 'problem of the ending' in groove music. Perceptible slowings virtually never occur in the middle of pieces of any genre of groove music, while acceleration is very rare. Musical training of popular musicians puts great emphasis on avoiding involuntary acceleration, which is regarded as destructive to a good sense of groove, and where it is employed as a deliberate musical technique in particular cases, such as in Dexy's Midnight Runners's 'Come On, Eileen', it is a kind of novelty effect of strictly limited usefulness.[31]

Two other performance instructions found in the classical tradition which override the presence of a regular beat are the pause (or *fermata*), an indication that the beat should be allowed to stop and rest for an indeterminate period before resuming – effectively the temporary cessation of musical time – and tempo changes, the deliberate switch to a new pulse rate which is often accompanied by a change in meter (time signature). A comparison of the first with its apparent equivalent in groove music – the 'stop' or 'stop bar' – is illuminating. The difference is that in the 'stop', although all instruments are silent, musical time, in the form of the pulse, is held to continue unaltered during the silence and the length of the stop is precisely measured. This ability to apparently make time audible through silence is a powerful and unique feature of groove. As for the second, occurrences of tempo and time signature changes are not unknown in groove music but are relatively rare and are arguably confined to those genres with 'classical' pretensions, such as prog rock and certain kinds of contemporary jazz.

However it is perhaps in the *unwritten* aspects of performance style that the difference in attitude to the beat of each musical tradition is most clearly seen. Most nineteenth-century classical music cannot be performed successfully without employing the technique known as *rubato* (or, more fully, *tempo rubato*, literally, robbed time). Both Hudson and Latham draw a distinction between historically earlier and later uses of the technique.[32] In the eighteenth century the fluctuations in tempo were permitted in the lead or melody part, often a violin or voice, while the accompanying instruments continued to maintain the pulse. Mozart is quoted as saying that when *rubato* is used by

---

31   Dexy's Midnight Runners 1982.
32   Hudson, 'Rubato'; Latham, 'Rubato'.

pianists, 'the left hand should go on playing in strict time'.[33] The form of *rubato* that developed in the nineteenth century involved the use of tempo fluctuations in *all* parts for expressive effect. This amounts to the hastening and retardation of the musical pulse itself. One of Liszt's students characterised his teacher's use of the technique as 'a sudden light suspension of the rhythm'. This kind of *rubato* is most easily practised by a solo performer, and it is a central feature of the rich solo piano repertoire of the nineteenth century, but it is also regarded as a necessary element of the successful performance of ensemble, even orchestral, works. A study of temporal fluctuations in performances of Viennese waltzes found that it was customary to lengthen the middle beat of each bar sometimes by as much as 50 percent.[34]

One theory of the more modern *rubato* requires that the speedings up should be balanced by the slowings down, that the time is really be borrowed rather than robbed and should ultimately be paid back in full, so that overall the music returns to the point in time where it would have been if *rubato* had not been used. However, since, unlike in the earlier form of *rubato*, there is no instrument keeping regular time, that condition is never really put to the test and performers are in practice free to be as flexible with the beat at any moment as they wish. *Rubato* became in the late nineteenth century a license for performers to use their musicianship and interpretive skills to delay or hasten the arrival of a beat in the interests of the successful performance of a phrase, of 'making the phrase speak'. Though the opportunities for this are more limited in ensemble music than in solo pieces, it nevertheless takes place, especially in chamber music: a successful string trio, for example, will be one whose players are sensitive enough to adjust to one another's minute variations in tempo as they employ this technique, a subject which will be discussed further in Chapter 5.

The kinds of conscious, generalised deviations from the pulse represented by *rubato* are anathema to groove music practice. Iyer argues that 'groove-based music... is much less forgiving in the realm of tempo variation and *rubati* than a string trio might be'.[35] If it is appropriate to talk about the use of *rubato* in, for example, jazz, it is only as a return to its earlier form in which performers responsible for the lead line manipulate the timing of phrases so that it diverges temporarily from the underlying pulse. A singer may start a phrase late, then push ahead through it to catch up. A jazz soloist may 'sit

---

33   Mozart 1777.
34   Research by Ingmar Bengsston cited in Alén 1995.
35   Iyer 2002, p. 399.

behind the beat'. What remains in strictly pulsed time and unaffected by these fluctuations is the accompaniment provided by the rest of the band. In other words, unlike the Romantic *rubato* described above, the overall pulse of the music is *not* permitted to fluctuate perceptibly; what is being manipulated is simply the relationship of a single part to the rest of the musical texture. This type of temporal manipulation might therefore be better described as a form of syncopation.

As for the less conscious forms of temporal fluctuation found in the art music tradition, these too exist in groove music, as they inevitably must given that musical performance is a human, rather than a mechanical, activity. These are what Keil et al., are addressing with the notion of participatory discrepancies, albeit without sufficient emphasis on the strict time that underlies them. What has been said about good string quartet playing is also true of rhythm sections, in that the establishment of a successful groove has at least as much to do with the collective temporal interaction between players as each individual's metronome sense and ability to play in time.[36] However, whatever temporal discrepancies may be detected in a performance by the kind of investigations undertaken by Prögler, and whatever the significance of the discoveries of music psychologists as to the factors which affect the perception of musical timing, the intention of groove performance is, 'to *give rise to the perception of a steady pulse*'.[37] Regular micro-fluctuations in timing, such as a consistently late snare drum beat, for example, are permitted within the context of temporal stability at a macro-level, and, as Iyer argues, are endowed with extra expressiveness because of their isochronous context.[38] Occasional deviations from strict timing may be deployed by a sensitive rhythm section paradoxically in order to maintain the sense of temporal regularity at points in the music, such as the transition from one section to another, where other factors might give the impression of disrupting it. Overall, the impression of strictly isochronous pulse must prevail.

Quite distinct from the issue of *rubato* are passages of music without a regular beat at all. These became marginalised in the Western tradition with the rise of measured music and the development of meter. The practice has survived in jazz in the *colla voce* accompaniment of a singer. Here, the singer is permitted to deliver the phrases of the song in 'free time', i.e., without regular pulse, while the accompanist, usually an individual pianist, follows her lead.

---

36 The issue of this kind of collective interaction is discussed in Chapter 7.
37 Iyer 2002, p. 398.
38 Ibid.

This practice is particularly associated with the 'verse' section of jazz standards which, if performed at all, is used as an introduction to the better-known 'chorus' which forms the main body of the piece. It should not be confused with the jazz ballad in general, which, despite being at a slow tempo, depends on a strict pulse. That the *colla voce* technique is virtually never used for a whole song, and is confined to that portion of the piece which is thought of preceding its true beginning, confirms its marginalisation in twentieth century music in favour of the groove principle.

Does this mean that groove musicians have a more acute sense of metronome time than their classical counterparts, that, as Iyer suggests, a 'heightened, seemingly microscopic sensitivity to musical timing' is exclusive to groove musicians? As we shall see, it has been argued that 'metronome sense' is an attribute which derives from African musical origins, finding its way into Western popular music as a result of the influence of African-American musicians.[39] Leaving aside for the moment the question of its alleged African origins, which will be challenged in the next chapter, does it makes sense to attribute groove music's commitment to a strictly isochronous pulse to an enhanced 'metronome sense'? Philip Tagg, keen to oppose the racialised nature of the argument for a unique 'metronome sense' in African and Afro-American music, cites evidence showing that the ability to play in time has long been a valued skill amongst Western composers, conductors and instrumentalists.[40] This leads Tagg to doubt the distinctiveness of groove music's relationship to the pulse, whereas, in fact, it merely challenges the theory that 'metronome sense' is the basis of the distinction. The flexible attitude to the pulse of non-groove music is not the result of its practitioners' undeveloped time sense. In fact, what I have argued about *rubato* and the other subtle fluctuations in the pulse employed in classical music could be used to support the contrary argument. Rather, the different attitudes to temporal regularity adopted by different musics are evidence of fundamental aesthetic differences between them.

Nevertheless, as a result of the importance of metronomic time to groove music, the ability for temporal accuracy – 'tightness' – is cultivated and prized as perhaps the primary skill. Tagg's eighteenth-century evidence notwithstanding, what came to be a priority in nineteenth-century performance practice was intensity of expression, and the belief that isochronicity was detrimental to such expressivity. In the groove ensemble, timing and synchronisation errors are the flaws which require eradication above all others. They are also likely to be exposed due to the nature of the ensemble itself. Compare the constitution of the orchestra to the kinds of instrumentation common in twentieth-century

---

39 Ibid.
40 Tagg 1996.

popular music. The bulk of the orchestra is composed of stringed instruments, the acoustic properties of whose sound (the absence of a sharp attack, at least when bowed) do not put timing accuracy to a severe test. (The real tests of a string section's timing accuracy are *pizzicato* passages, in which some of the best orchestras do not fare so well). Horns and winds tend either to be submerged in the strings-dominated texture or to be playing solo passages, and, in addition, the acoustics of the concert hall tend to mask timing errors.

Conversely, most groove music ensembles are dominated by guitars, drums and the piano, percussive and plucking instruments which make sounds with sharp attack characteristics which expose the slightest timing discrepancy. Orchestral musicians are never asked to synchronise their playing with the drums or percussion, the hierarchy of the orchestra ensures it is always the other way round; while the percussive stabs and rhythmic interjections of horn sections in many styles of popular music demand a more aggressive tonguing technique than is generally demanded by the classical tradition, often (and completely alien to the classical tradition) applied to the ends of notes as well as their beginnings.

Even the way the ensembles are led confirms these differences. The reason why the role of conductor does not exist in groove music is not that the ensembles are rarely as big as the symphony orchestra; jazz big bands are a comparable size but generally only require timing direction for the beginnings and ends of pieces. It is because beating time with the hands is too inaccurate a method for the kind of temporal strictness required in groove music. The conductor's downbeat is sufficiently accurate to coordinate a *tutti* orchestral chord given the acoustic leeway discussed above, and her beat is capable of indicating broad fluctuations of tempo such as *rallentandos*. But a conductor's beat cannot ensure that the four notes of a chord in the French horns are tongued simultaneously or that the tympani are in time with the double basses. Its function has much more to do with interpretive feeling than with timing. Groove musicians' emphasis on timing means they prefer a count-in to a waved downbeat for starting a piece because it ensures greater accuracy for the first note and gives an indication of the ongoing tempo. Conducting and counting-in will be addressed in the context of Schutz's phenomenology in Chapter 5.

2   *Syncopation*

However, an attentiveness to the isochronous pulse is not sufficient to generate groove. A second factor is the more or less continuous presence of syncopation. The term syncopation may be more or less narrowly defined. The Grove Dictionary limits its meaning to 'the regular shifting of each beat in a measured pattern by the same amount ahead of or behind its normal position in that pattern', e.g. a series of crotchets displaced by a quaver or a series of off-beat quavers separated by quaver rests.[41] The specificity of this definition is intended to distinguish syncopation from the related phenomena of cross-rhythm, cross-accent, and polyrhythm. However, other writers are content to use syncopation more generically as 'the displacement of the normal musical accent from a strong beat to a weak one', leaving more open the question of precisely how this is achieved.[42] I intend to follow this latter usage but to add that we might also describe syncopation as the deliberate misalignment of emphasised notes in a musical part with the underlying pulse of the music.

This immediately raises a question. The pulse of the music, the isochronous beat discussed above, does not exist independently of the music, but is produced by the music. In other words, it only exists at all because some of the notes or events of the music are making it happen, are spelling it out. A significant number of events occurring off the beat must threaten the very existence of the beat. Syncopation, therefore, requires both events which establish the pulse and events which contradict it. These may occur in the same part (i.e., the same instrument), or, more important for twentieth-century groove music, between different parts or different instruments within a band.

The precondition for understanding how syncopation works and the differences between different types of syncopation is an understanding of meter. The question of meter will be dealt with more fully later, but for the moment let us accept its basic definition as 'a synonym for time signature'.[43] That is, meter refers to the relationship to a main pulse of a second, slower pulse, produced by grouping the main pulse into regular multiples. The name given to these groupings in Britain is 'bar' and in other countries 'measure', and its size, or the number of pulses it contains, is the main information indicated by the time signature. A bar of four beats (the most common in Western music and even more dominant in groove music) is understood to impart certain characteristics to each of its four beats: beat 'one' is the strongest and is known as the downbeat – it is the successive beats 'one' that generate the slower pulse mentioned above, in this case running at one-quarter the speed of the main pulse; beat 'three' is the next strongest, falling half way between successive beats 'one'; beats 'two' and 'four' are weaker and are known as the off-beats, while beat 'four' has the addition characteristic of being the up-beat, that is, the beat that prepares for the subsequent downbeat. (There is a subsidiary sense in which beats two and three are also upbeat and downbeat respectively).

---

41   'Syncopation', *Grove Music Online, Oxford Music Online*.
42   Scholes and Nagley 2002, 'Syncopation', *The Oxford Companion to Music, Oxford Music Online*.
43   London, 'Metre', *Grove Music Online, Oxford Music Online*.

The pattern of relative strengths in the whole cycle might be represented thus:

ONE – two – THREE – four   or   1 – 2 – 3 – 4

Syncopation in the narrow sense defined by Grove occurs in Western art music, but often taking a low profile as the rhythm of the accompaniment, as it does, for example, in the second subject of the first movement of Schubert's *Unfinished Symphony*:[44]

In its more general meaning, syncopation's use in the classical tradition is much rarer. This means that, especially in melodic lines, when a note occurs between beats, there is generally a note on the next beat as well. Thus rhythmic units such as the following, common in groove music, are rare in the classical 'common practice period':

The final note of such rhythms, in the Western 'classical' tradition, are felt to require 'stabilisation' by the presence of a note on the subsequent beat:

This applies to all their equivalents at half the above durations, etc.

Syncopated rhythms do appear in classical music, often inserted as deliberate references to folk music, one of the earliest used being the 'Scotch snap':

This is a syncopation because the longer note of the pair falls between beats. But it is a relatively weak one because it syncopates against the second beat of the bar, itself a weak beat. Nevertheless, it is this syncopation, in the following form:

---

44   Schubert 1986, pp. 44–5.

which is an essential ingredient in the cakewalk and became one of the important rhythmic elements of ragtime as groove music emerged at the turn of the twentieth century.

Also to be found in classical music was another form of syncopation, made celebrated use of by Beethoven in his *Leonore Overture No. 3*.[45] It is the figure:

This syncopation is both stronger and weaker than the previous one: stronger because the syncopation is against the beat three of the bar, a strong beat; weaker because it uses a relatively long duration interval between syncopated note and beat, a crotchet rather than the semiquaver of the cakewalk figure.

In general, the effect of syncopation is greater the shorter the duration between syncopated note and beat syncopated against. Experiments in the field of the perception of musical timing suggest that beats (understood as points in time which have no duration) are perceived categorically rather than absolutely. Snyder conceives each beat as having a perceptual 'capture zone' around it, enabling events which fall within it to be perceived on the beat even if they are actually slightly early or slightly late.[46] He speculates that the sizes of such zones may be culturally determined, but what is certainly true is that they are stylistically specific, there being, logically, two key factors determining them. The first is the degree of adherence to a metronomic pulse: styles which deploy heavy *rubato* require an enlarged beat category, allowing more events to be perceived as falling on them, and conversely reducing the possibilities for syncopation. The second factor is the size of the prevailing subdivision of the beat. The terms 'density referent' and 'quantize value' will be discussed later, but it is clear that subdividing each beat into many small units necessarily limits their conceptual range, thereby increasing the possibility of syncopation. If the 'capture zone' is curtailed by either or both of these factors, musical events very close to beats can be perceived as syncopations. These are the conditions

---

45   Beethoven 1986. George Bernard Shaw was among those who claimed that the syncopation in popular music was nothing new: 'the rowdiest jazz sounds like The Maiden's Prayer after Beethoven's third Leonore overture ...' (cited in Van der Merwe 1989, p. 276 fn. 12).
46   Snyder 2000, p. 167.

for highly syncopated music, both in terms of frequency (possibility) and degree (strength).

All these examples – the Scotch snap, the cakewalk rhythm, and the *Leonore* figure – should be thought of as precursors to the syncopation proper of groove music. This fully-fledged syncopation of the twentieth century divides into two types – *anticipation* and *polyrhythm*. In a sense, all syncopation can be thought of as anticipation – the playing early of a note which would otherwise fall on a beat. However, mature anticipation involves the systematic use of this form of syncopation against the strongest available beat, preferably beat one. A clear example of it is the anticipation of the final note of a cadential phrase, such as the last phrase of a song. It is useful to think of such anticipations as embellishments of simpler musical lines and to compare such phrases to their imaginary, unsyncopated forms. For example:

With the application of anticipation to the final notes of the phrases, becomes:

A kind of half-way stage is possible where vocals are involved, in which the final syllable of the lyric is anticipated, but the pitch of the note is not:

Bob Marley, 'No Woman, No Cry'.[47]

The amount of syncopation-by-anticipation within a phrase can be thought of as having been added to an unsyncopated phrase by degrees. It can be viewed as extending note-by-note from an initial starting point. Here is a famous line presented 'straight', i.e., without syncopation:

---

47   Marley 1974.

The following shows the syllable on the final strong beat – 'for-' – anticipated:

Now the anticipations can be extended forward to include the following syllable – 'nia-':

Performing a similar operation on strong beat of the previous bar, anticipating the syllable 'Ho-', requires that the previous two syllables also be anticipated in order to create 'room'. Here the following 'tel' has also been anticipated:

Finally, as it is sung on the recording, with the 'come' syllable also anticipated:

Eagles, 'Hotel California'.[48]

As can be seen, the permutations and combinations are various, and a performer has the possibility of choosing from them at will. Applying anticipation to almost every note adds groove to what would have been a rather uninteresting line:

---

48   Eagles 1976.

Becomes:

Norah Jones, 'Don't Know Why'.[49]

Anticipation is not merely confined to vocal or other lead lines but can be found in similar abundance in rhythm section parts. Rock guitar parts are frequently built around such combinations of on-beat elements and anticipations:

Rainbow, 'Since You've Been Gone'.[50]

The other form of syncopation found in twentieth-century groove music is *polyrhythm*. Polyrhythm in essence consists of the effect of a repeated rhythmic figure with a periodicity at odds with that of the underlying meter. Alternatively, we might think of this as the temporary establishment of a second meter, conflicting with the first – a state of temporary polymetricality. The prime example of this form of syncopation found in the Western classical tradition is the *hemiola*, which is the insertion into triple meter of a phrase or figure in triple meter at half the tempo of the first:

---

49 Jones 2002.
50 Rainbow 1979.

A celebrated example of *hemiola* is Leonard Bernstein's use of it in the song 'America' in *West Side Story* in which the two meters, written 6/8 and 3/4 in this case, alternate bar by bar rather than being played simultaneously. The *hemiola* also forms of the basis of the jazz waltz rhythm, but because it combines two triple meters its disruptive effect is relatively limited as synchronisation of the respective downbeats is reached after just one unit of the slower meter. By contrast the superimposition of triple meters against duple or quadruple ones is more radical and it is this form of polyrhythm that is found more commonly in groove music, not least because of the preponderance of duple/quadruple meters in this music. Such polyrhythm is generated by the placement of accents on every third of the duple or quadruple subdivisions of the beat, creating the sense of a compound (triple) meter against the main meter. In its simplest form, it produces what has become known as the rumba rhythm:

As will be seen, this bears some similarity to Beethoven's *Leonore* rhythm, cited earlier, but represents a higher degree of syncopation due to the fact that its syncopated note (the second note) is much closer to the beat it is syncopated against (the third beat) than Beethoven's.[51]

The rumba rhythm also comprises one half of the *clave*, the rhythmic pattern which underpins twentieth-century Latin American rhythms:

But, the rumba rhythm is by no means the preserve of Latin American music. It is a universal component of Western popular music, found in virtually every style from country to hiphop. Here it is in a classic 1980s rock tune used as a film soundtrack, where it occurs at twice the speed relative to the beat as written above, and in the second half of the bar. The polyrhythm is emphasised by its contrast to the very square rhythm in the other instruments:

---

51   *contra* Bernard Shaw!

WHAT IS 'GROOVE'? 39

Survivor, 'Eye of the Tiger', or 'Theme from Rocky IV'.[52]

The principle of setting groups of three against groups of four can be adapted or extended to produce other syncopated rhythms. It is common to displace the rumba rhythm so that its final note coincides with a strong beat, usually the first beat of the bar, in what might be called the 'reverse rumba' rhythm:

or

The following is an example of a bass line built around the reverse rumba rhythm concluding on beat 3 of the bar, also a strong beat. The bracketed notes are all three semiquavers apart while the underlying meter groups the semiquavers in fours:

Bill Withers, 'Lovely Day'.[53]

---

52   Survivor 1982.
53   Withers 1977.

The rumba rhythm establishes a polyrhythm which is fairly short in duration. An extended version of the principle is often found in various kinds of groove music in which the triplet groupings are maintained for twice as long. This results in a bar of 16 semiquavers being divided into groups of 3 + 3 + 3 + 3 + 2 + 2:

The longer the groupings of three are maintained the more they suggest a permanent alternative meter, coexisting with the main meter as expressed by the time signature, which would make the music genuinely polymetric. But Danielsen is right to argue that even this extended rumba pattern represents only a *tendency* to polymetricality: in Western music, unlike in traditional West African music, alternative meters are never allowed to persist long enough to challenge the dominance of the main meter. In any case, the above rhythm need not be viewed as an extended rumba at all – it may be understood as a standard rumba each of whose notes have been divided into halves.

This extended rumba rhythm is a standard feature of rock in particular. The following example from is from Queen, identical to the above except for the final anticipations:

Queen, 'Don't Stop Me Now'.[54]

while the accents in the guitar break from The Beatles's 'Here Comes the Sun' mark out the same rhythm, although this time across two bars rather than one:

George Harrison, 'Here Comes the Sun'.[55]

---

54   Queen 1978.
55   The Beatles 1969.

Both these forms of syncopation – anticipation and polyrhythm – are found in ragtime, the first genuine groove music to emerge in the United States.

Scott Joplin, 'The Entertainer', 1902.[56]

In bar 1, triplet groupings set up a polyrhythm against the regular quavers of the left hand part (not shown), with the lower note of the figure (E) spelling out the rumba rhythm. In addition, there are two anticipations (marked 'A'), one against the downbeat of bar 2 and the other in bar 3. Later in the piece the rumba rhythm is very clearly stated:

One of Joplin's other very famous pieces, the 'Maple Leaf Rag', provides a particularly clear example of a combination of reverse rumba and rumba rhythms:

Scott Joplin, 'Maple Leaf Rag', 1897.[57]

A very similar rhythmic figure was used by George Gershwin for his 'I Got Rhythm' of 1930:

George Gershwin, 'I Got Rhythm'.[58]

---

56 Joplin 1998, opening bars.
57 Joplin 1998, pp. 19–22.
58 Gershwin 1934, pp. 32–5.

Late twentieth-century popular music continued to deploy combinations of the two types of syncopation identified here: anticipation and polyrhythm. This classic rock example opens with the 'I Got Rhythm' polyrhythmic figure and ends with four anticipated chords:

Van Halen, 'Jump', 1984, opening bars.[59]

3   'Deep metricality' or Multi-levelled Meter

As already mentioned, central to the temporal aspect of Western music is meter, that is, a certain regularity in the groupings of pulses, or, as I described it earlier, a second pulse running at half, a third, or a quarter of the rate of the main beat, depending on whether there are two, three, or four beats in each bar. Perhaps even more than the question of isochronous pulse, the presence of meter in Western music can be traced historically. Arnold Whittall says:

> The rhythmic character of music from the Baroque, Classical, and Romantic periods is often very different from that of much earlier or more recent music. Obviously, regular accentuation and phrase-structure did not suddenly appear with Monteverdi and Bach and vanish with Schoenberg and Stockhausen, but the rhythmic characteristics which prevailed in music between Monteverdi and Schoenberg cannot always be found in music from other periods, or of other cultures.[60]

When Whittall speaks of regular accentuation and phrase structure he is speaking of meter. The groove concept of popular music inherits the metricality of previous musics, but intensifies it and makes it a more central organising principle.

Somewhat like syncopation, the term meter can be defined in different ways. As we have seen, the basic theory regards meter as represented by the time signature; that is, it amounts to no more than how many beats there are in each bar and whether the result is duple, triple, quadruple or compound time. On this definition, any periodicity longer than the bar is not considered in terms of meter, but as a matter of form. However, the theory of musical temporality has been developed by various writers with the aim of integrating the

---

59   Van Halen 1984, pp. 1–4.
60   Whittall 2002, 'Rhythm', *The Oxford Companion to Music*, Oxford Music Online.

temporality of events at the micro level with the large-scale, structural organisation of music.[61] Sometimes these systems of analysis take the form of situating meter as a distinct level somewhere in the middle of a range of structural levels which posit micro-timings as the lowest level and form as the highest.[62] But the notion that music involves a hierarchy of temporal levels opens up the possibility that meter is itself a hierarchically-organised, multi-levelled, recursive structure.

Such a conception of meter appears to be particularly appropriate to twentieth-century groove music, which, partly because of the level of repetition involved, often displays a symmetrical structure in which bars are grouped into twos, fours, eights and so on. This is often interpreted, even by those sympathetic to popular music, as a defect which contributes to this music's mundaneness. Peter Van der Merwe says the following of the songs of Tin Pan Alley and Broadway, many of which provided the raw material for jazz:

> What is characteristic of the thirty-two-bar song is not so much the rhythmic repetition itself as its combination with a squareness of layout that produces a deadly predictability hardly equalled in music. In the feebler examples, once one has heard the first eight bars one seems to know already how the remaining twenty-four will go. Perhaps the truth is that this is simply a decadent form, designed to be turned out by the least inspired hack and understood by the meanest musical intelligence.[63]

Logically, there is no reason to consider four-bar phrases any more predictable than four-beat bars. The regular phrase structures of groove music should be considered an aspect of their metrical structure, or perhaps as the influence of the meter upon the form. The crucial contribution that a hierarchical meter imparts to music is an increase in its ability to measure time. As Eric Clarke explains:

> The strictly hierarchic [metrical] organization reduces the need to track the number of... units [beats] that have elapsed as long as the listener can retain an awareness of the hierarchic depth to which units are embedded. In short, hierarchic organization employing units with constant or simply related durations resolves the need for an additive counting process.[64]

---

61 See for instance, Lerdhal and Jackendoff 1983; Cooper and Meyer 1960.
62 See Clarke 1987, p. 233.
63 Van Der Merwe 1989, p. 271.
64 Clarke 1987, p. 231.

The most fruitful way of conceiving meter in groove music, and possibly more generally too, is as a series of levels running from sub-beats through beats, bars, and phrases to larger-scale sections.

If we start with the basic pulse of a piece of music, the pulse that runs at the speed that we might tap our foot and which would provide the basis of a count-in, and is sometimes referred to as the *tactus*, we can than think of the metrical levels as extending recursively in both directions from this basic beat. In one direction are the lower, or divisive, levels, the subdivisions of the beat into smaller units. The standard possibilities here are duple, triple and quadruple subdivisions, corresponding in notational terms to quavers, quavers in compound time, and semiquavers respectively (assuming the beat is crotchets). Moving in the opposite directions are the higher, or multiple, levels of the meter which often comprise of groups of two, four, eight bars and so on, combining to form hyper-bars, phrases, sections and choruses as appropriate.[65]

I propose adopting the following nomenclature for referring to metrical levels: the level of the tactus shall be referred to as M and will usually correspond to the time-signature; higher levels (i.e., hyper-bars, phrases, sections etc.) will be notated as M^1, M^2, M^3 etc.; and lower levels (i.e., subdivisions of the beat) as m_1, m_2, m_3 etc. Music with a deep metrical structure can be described by identifying the type of meter – duple, triple, quadruple, or other which pertains to each level. Thus the metrical structure of the standard tunes such as 'Sweet Georgia Brown' decried by Van Der Merwe for its regularity could be represented thus:[66]

Unit	Metrical level	Description (value)
Chorus	M^3	Duple (two 16-bar sections)
Section	M^2	Quadruple (four 4-bar phrases)
Phrase[67]	M^1	Quadruple (four bars)
Bar	M	Quadruple (4/4 meter)
Beat	m_1	Duple (quaver subdivision)

Bernie, Pinkard and Casey, 'Sweet Georgia Brown', 1925

---

65   'Hypermeasure' is a term coined by Edward T. Cone for a metrical unit larger than a bar, usually four bars long, in which each bar 'behave[s] as a single beat' within a larger metrical structure. However, for Cone this phenomenon represents 'the tyranny of the four-measure phrase' and is avoided, or at least disguised, by the greatest composers (Cone 1968, p. 79).
66   As recorded by Django Reinhardt: Reinhardt 2001.
67   'Phrase' seems more appropriate than hyper-bar for this tune as it is melody-led.

Though we think of the most common meter as quadruple (having the time signature 4/4, or 'common time'), it might be more consistent to regard the basis of meter as duple. Paul Fraisse's explanation of pulse generation as ultimately deriving from the symmetricality of the human body is consistent with Victor Zuckerkandl's formulation of the metric wave as essentially an oscillatory movement – to-and-fro or away-and-back.[68] If we follow this, then our paradigm of musical meter would be duple at every metrical level, consisting of two-beat bars (common time would be 2/4 rather than 4/4), combining in pairs at each higher level. While in the other direction, beats would divide initially in halves, then quarters, and so on. This is in fact an accurate picture of some of the most groove-oriented of twentieth century music such as the one-chord funk grooves of James Brown and George Clinton discussed by Anne Danielsen.[69]

One implication of this is a downgrading of the triplet to the status of special or unusual case. This requires qualification. In groove music, genuine triple time is indeed rare. Some music does appear to be in triple time, for example, jazz waltzes and pop songs like 'Golden Brown' by The Stranglers.[70] However, the fast pace of the pulse in these instances means that the triplets are really at the level of the beat (m_1) rather than the bar (M), which remains duple or quadruple. The triple subdivision is quite common in groove music from the classic 12/8 blues onwards but is usually combined with duple/quadruple organisation at higher metrical levels. One exception, of course, is the twelve-bar blues which is structured in three four-bar phrases. Using the nomenclature proposed above, a twelve-bar blues with a slow 12/8 feel could be described in the following way:

Unit	Metrical level	Description (value)
Chorus	M^2	Triple (three 4-bar phrases)
Phrase	M^1	Quadruple (four bars)
Bar	M	Quadruple (four beats)
Beat	m_1	Triple (triplet subdivision)

Twelve-bar blues with a 12/8 feel

---

68   Clarke 1999, p. 474; Zuckerkandl 1973, pp. 166–8.
69   Danielsen 2006.
70   The Stranglers 1981, which also includes 4/4 bars.

We could extend the schema upwards to further levels provided they exhibited regularity. For example, if a performance of our blues involved the lead instruments or voices taking two choruses each, the level M^3, which we might describe as the hyper-chorus level, would be duple. In fact, such regularity at that metrical level would be rare: at the higher levels irregularity is much less disruptive to the sense of meter established at lower levels. Though level M is usually stable in most genres, Prog Rock and related styles being an exception, irregularity is fairly common even at M^1 and M^2. Even the Broadway songs Van der Merwe regards as hopelessly square are not universally 32 bars long, for example Gershwin's 'A Foggy Day' of 1937 has an extra two bars in its final phrase, while Jerome Kern's 'All the Things You Are' of 1939 has a barely noticeable extra four.

Towards the lower levels of the meter, groove music is marked by its tendency for regularity. Indeed, this is another feature that can broadly be said to distinguish groove music from the classical tradition. One can over-generalise here, but it generally holds that while the art music of the nineteenth century does not stick to a single subdivision of the beat for anything but the shortest periods, the reverse is true of popular music. Since bar and phrase lengths are often similar between genres of popular music, one of the key defining features of any groove is the length of its shortest subdivision (or note duration) which tends to remain constant throughout. Some writers have referred to this as the 'density referent', a term which derives from ethnomusicology, but another description might be 'quantize value', from digital sequencing practice. Grooves can be distinguished from each other by their quantize value: funk usually uses 1/16s (semiquavers) while in much mainstream rock 1/8s (quavers) are the smallest unit. Many classic blues have a triplet, or 12/8 feel, while the jazz swing feel is based mostly on swung duplets, that is, pairs of notes in a flexible long-short configuration.

The existence of 'swung quavers' – duplets of unequal length – alerts us to the possibility of a similar phenomenon occurring at higher metrical levels. The obvious example is 5/4 meter, which is best regarded not as a quintuple meter but as an uneven duple meter whose beat lengths are in the ratio 3:2. This is like the effect achieved by propping the metronome at an angle or someone walking with a limp. On this basis, Dave Brubeck's 'Take Five' has the following metric structure:[71]

---

71 As recorded by the Dave Brubeck Quartet: Brubeck 1959.

Unit	Metrical level	Description (value)
Chorus	M^3	Triple (AAB)
Phrase	M^2	Duple
Hyper-bar	M^1	Quadruple
Bar	M	Uneven duple (3:2)
Beat	m_1	Triple (beat 1)
		Duple (beat 2)
Sub-beat	m_2	'Swung' (uneven) duple

Paul Desmond, 'Take Five', 1959

The fact that such tables as the above are possible is an indication of the strong sense of meter of much groove music. Meter depends on regularity – 'irregular meter' is virtually an oxymoron – and though irregularity is not completely absent, groove is best generated when the metrical value which applies for each metrical level (or, strictly speaking, for the interface between each adjacent pair of levels) remains constant throughout the piece. Such regularity is accentuated by repetition, which, rather than being treated with caution as it came to be in Western art music, is employed as a central structural principle of groove music.

Of key importance here is the *riff*, a suitably pithy phrase whose role is to contribute, through multiple repetition, to the metrical structure, usually at the level of hyper-bar. That the riff is not found in the classical tradition is testament to the relative weakness of meter in such music – after Mozart metrical regularity is confined increasingly to the level of the bar, and in the twentieth century not even there. The musical phrase is more likely to be valued for its intrinsic properties and its developmental potential rather than its ability to generate larger level structures. Middleton describes this small-scale type of repetition as *musematic* and contrasts it with the larger scale *discursive* repetition associated with the narrative-type aesthetic of Western art music.[72] The question of narrativity will be discussed later, but it seems more useful initially to focus on the scarcity of exact repetition on any scale in the classical tradition. Even the 'recapitulation' of large sections of music which plays such a crucial role in symphonic form is repetition-with-a-difference. It is also repetition-at-a-distance, the difference being due to the effect of the intervening material.

---

72 Middleton 1990, p. 269.

In conclusion, groove depends on the regularity guaranteed by a strong sense of meter. Though that regularity need not extend to the higher levels, it is usually necessary for meter to be stable at the level of sub-beat, beat, bar and hyper-bar. The feature which encapsulates groove's minimum metrical requirements is the *vamp*. Like the riff, the vamp operates through repetition at the level of hyper-bar and specifies all the metrical relationships necessary to establish the groove. Unlike a riff, a vamp would normally involve the entire rhythm section; it is essentially rhythmic but also contains an element of harmonic movement, albeit circular, and thus is a groove *in nuce*.

Nevertheless, despite the importance of these repetitive elements to groove music, the analysis of groove presented here, in contrast to some others, is not one that regards it as dependent on the repetition of material, such as occurs in a vamp.[73] The establishment of deep metricality will usually require a degree of rhythmic repetition but does not necessitate the exact repetition of pitches in the form of riffs, chord sequences, etc. It is this that makes possible adaptable grooves capable of flexibly articulating relatively lengthy harmonic progressions such as those found in some jazz standards.

The significant difference between groove and other metered music is not the repetition of material but the extension of meter from a distinct level within the temporal hierarchy of the music to the dominating principle at all levels. In the tonal music of the 'common practice' period, meter would function as 'a cognitive framework around which events are organized' at lower levels of the structure, but would give way to other types of temporal organisation – melodic periodicity and the tonal framework – at the higher levels.[74] In groove, all elements of the music are marshalled to make a contribution to the measuring function performed by multi-levelled meter.[75] This conception also allows us to reject the analysis of syncopation as musical cues which contradict meter but not enough to undermine it.[76] Rather we can understand syncopation as manifestations of lower levels of the metrical structure from the perspective of a higher one.

---

73   See for instance, Hughes 2003, pp. 14–15.
74   Clarke 1987, p. 233.
75   Lerdahl and Jackendoff argue that there is an upper limit to the effect of meter within the structural levels of music (Lerdhal and Jackendoff 1983, p. 21). Two points are relevant: (1) they consider only Western art music (Mozart's fortieth Symphony is their example); (2) the large scale structures which they regard as non-metrical are in any case beyond the temporal scope of most pieces of groove music.
76   Lerdahl and Jackendoff 1981, p. 485.

4 Back-beat

It is one of the more perplexing characteristics of the grooves of twentieth century popular music that they hinge upon *back-beat*, that is, an emphasis on the off-beats of the bar (beats two and four) and often the off-beats of other metrical levels as well. This emphasis may be highly obvious, marked with a thunderous snare beat drenched with studio reverb, or generated in a subtle manner by the rhythmic contours of the musical phrases, but it is always present and provides the skeleton on which the flesh of the groove hangs.

Gunther Schuller believes this phenomenon has its roots in what he calls the 'democratisation' of rhythm, about which he says:

> By the 'democratization' of rhythmic values, I mean very simply that in jazz so-called weak beats (or weak parts of rhythmic units) are *not* underplayed as in 'classical' music. Instead, they are brought up to the level of strong beats, and very often even emphasized *beyond* the strong beat.

He continues:

> Another manifestation of the same principle is the so-called drum backbeat on the second and fourth beat of a bar, especially popular in modern jazz drumming and rock and roll music. Similarly the average jazz musician will count 1-2-3-4 but snap his fingers on 2 and 4, thus putting greater emphasis on these ordinarily weak beats than on 1 and 3. (What a far cry from the 1-2-3-4, 1-2-3-4 of military marches!).[77]

Theodore Gracyk, writing specifically about rock music, echoes Schuller's democratisation argument and cites Langdon Winner:

> The most fundamental defining characteristic of rock and roll, of course, has always been a 4/4 time signature in which the second and fourth beats are heavily accented. In rock rhythms and dances the ineluctable 'one-TWO-three-FOUR' is the force which sustains the motion.

For Gracyk, the rock aesthetic represents a 'reject[ion of the] standard Western assumption that the first beat of the measure is the strongest'.[78]

There is some inconsistency here. On the one hand, 'democratisation' implies an *equalisation* of the strength and importance of the four beats of the bar. On the other, both authors argue that in rock and other 'modern' music

---

77   Schuller 1968, pp. 8–10.
78   Gracyk 1996, pp. 134–5.

beats two and four become *stronger* than beats one and three. Clearly, the question of back-beat is intimately tied up with that of meter discussed above.

Earlier, in the section on syncopation, the standard explanation of 4/4 meter as a series of relative beat strengths in the relationship *Strongest–Weak–Strong–Weak* was presented. The fact that back-beat, therefore, involves an emphasis on the weak beats of the bar appears contradictory. How can beats which the meter defines as weak, or which must be weak in order to generate the meter, also be strong? Does back-beat simply represent the reversal of the *strong-weak* schema such that strong becomes weak and weak becomes strong? If that were the case, we would expect that the meter would continue to be perceived as *strong-weak-strong-weak*, simply having been displaced by one beat. What began as off-beats would be perceived as on- or down-beats and the effect would be lost.

For beats 'two' and 'four' to become the emphasised beats without becoming the strong beats would seem to require a radical revision of our understanding of meter. A key insight here is provided by Victor Zuckerkandl who argues that the conventional view of meter is erroneous. Meter is not produced from a pattern of strong and weak accents but is much better understood as oscillation, as a 1 – 2 – 1 – 2 etc., where '2' is not weak but 'away-from-one'. At the heart of meter is a cyclical motion or wave comprising a motion of 'to-fro' or 'away-back', and the standard understanding of causality in meter must be reversed: 'it is not a differentiation of accents which produces meter, it is meter which produces a differentiation of accents'.[79] For Zuckerkandl, meter is a *dynamic field* which imparts its force to tones (notes) according to where they fall within it. He describes rhythm as '*motion in the dynamic field of meter*'.[80]

Conceiving of meter in this way puts the emphasis on the *character*, rather than the strength, of each beat within the metric cycle and allows for the possibility that the off- or back-beats can be strong in a way which does not threaten to usurp or displace beat one. The status of beat 'one' depends not on its relative strength but on its character as an 'on' or 'away' beat and on its role in marking the start of the cycle. Conversely, beats 'two' and 'four' have quite a different character, that of a 'return' or preparation for the next on- or away-beat.

But the question remains as to why the strictly metronomic, syncopated and highly metrical music that is groove should need to emphasise the back-beats? The answer has something to do with meter and measurement. The idea that in some way music *measures* time clearly predates modern popular

---

79   Zuckerkandl 1973, p. 169.
80   Zuckerkandl 1973, pp. 172–4.

music: that sense finds expression in the musical terms *meter* and *measure* themselves. But groove music takes this characteristic to a new level.

If we combine Zuckerkandl's conception of the metric wave with the notion of metrical levels discussed in the last section, we begin to see meter as a tiered structure of beats whose character as on- or off-beats depends on which level of the metrical structure is being considered. If we limit ourselves, following Zuckerkandl, to duple relationships, and show only the 'on' and 'off' beats at each level, a single 4/4 bar could be represented thus:

Metrical level	**1**	2	3	4	**2**	2	3	4	**3**	2	3	4	**4**	2	3	4	**1**
Bar (M)	On								Off								On
Half bar (m_1)	On				Off				On				Off				On
Beat (m_2)	On		Off		On		Off		On		Off		On		Off		On
Half beat (m_3)	On	Off	On	Off	On	Off	On	Off	On	Off	On	Off	On	Off	On	Off	On

The diagram makes it clear that each off-beat at a particular metrical level becomes an on-beat at the next lowest level, thereby bringing into play new off-beats at half-way intervals which were merely latent at the higher levels. (Naturally, given what was argued in the last section, this pattern could theoretically be extended to the upper (multiple) metric levels, creating the notion of off-bars and off-hyper-bars etc.)

The above diagram's similarity to a ruler is striking – not a modern metric (decimal) ruler, to be sure, but one showing half, quarters, eighths and sixteenths of an inch.[81]

---

[81] These diagrams look similar to those in Lerdahl and Jackendoff 1983; and Clarke 1987. However both those retain the beat-*strength* understanding of meter rather than Zuckerkandl's superior beat-*character* formulation. For Lerdahl and Jackendoff, the levels are arranged in relation to each other on the basis that 'if a beat is felt to be strong at a particular level, it is also a beat at the next larger level' (Lerdahl and Jackendoff 1983, p. 19). Our theorization substitutes 'on' for 'strong', but is better explained by proceeding in the other direction: each new lower level is formed by inserting off-beats – and thereby additional temporal specificity – between the beats of the level above.

This similarity is not a coincidence since the method by which it operates is similar to the measurement of length, too, in that it requires a procedure of refinement, of increasing accuracy, in the measuring process. When using a ruler to measure length, if the point to be measured falls exactly on one of the strongest lines of the ruler, then the measurement is a round number of units. If not, then we must look to where it falls in relation to the next strongest lines. Again, if its length does not coincide with one of these, the next longest set of lines come into play, and so on, until a subdivision is found which coincides with the point to be measured.

The same is true of any note or musical event occurring in the groove. In order for its temporal position to be correctly understood by the listener, it must be identified as at least an off-beat at some level of the metrical structure, which involves bringing into play as many metric levels as is necessary to do so. Returning to the diagram of a bar above, a note coinciding with beat 4 of the bar, for example, necessitates consideration of the half-bar level (m_1), while one falling on the tenth, say, of the smallest subdivisions shown (semiquavers) can only be positioned by invoking the lowest level shown on the diagram (m_3).

It now begins to become clear why off-beats have such a crucial role. Since there are no on-beats without intervening off-beats (no successive 'aways' without 'backs' in between), a note is measured, that is, its temporal position is identified, once we have (cognitively) reached the level at which it is an off-beat. There is no need to define it as an on-beat by proceeding further to the subsequent level. Understanding it as an off-beat is sufficient to position it temporally, or in musical terms, rhythmically.

It follows that marking out off-beats is far more productive rhythmically than marking out on-beats as it is the most economical way of bringing into play an extra metrical level and thus providing more temporal information. Consider a series of notes spaced at the interval of a half-bar (minims). If we synchronise the first of them with beat one of the bar, making them on-beats, we present this much metrical information:

The amount of metrical information imparted here corresponds to the metric level of the bar, the top level of our diagram, level M.

However, if our minim-spaced beats are displaced by one beat, placing them on off-beats, it results in the following:

WHAT IS 'GROOVE'?

Provided we have something occasionally marking out where beat one of a bar is so that we do not mistake our off-beats for on-beats, the same periodicity as before has articulated the metric level one below our starting point, level m_1. The same principle applies to the next level down. The following pulse, despite being double the frequency of the last one, does not take us any further down the scale of metrical levels than we have already reached:

But displaced by half the temporal interval between the notes – that is, syncopated by half a beat – and we arrive at the next metric level (m_2) and our groove now has a quantize value (or density referent) of quavers:

A pulse with the same frequency as before, placed on the off-beats relative to its own spacing, immediately invokes the next metric level of the groove, making it correspondingly more fruitful in rhythmic terms. Considered in terms of meter, this is precisely the effect of syncopation, according to the very first definition of it we encountered earlier: to invoke the lowest possible metrical level with the resources available.[82]

Not only does increasing the metric depth of the groove generate more rhythmic interest, it also helps ensure metronomic accuracy and temporal stability. In terms of the isochronous beat, an intervening off-beat is crucial in ensuring the accurate placement of the next on-beat. Schuller referred above to the way jazz musicians emphasise the two and four when they count time. In fact, the count-in commonly used in jazz looks something like this:

---

82   As in the example from Schubert's *Unfinished Symphony* in which a series of syncopated crotches articulate the quaver level of the meter.

In order to provide metric clarity and stability, two metrical levels are specified in the count, rather than the simple 'one-two-three-four' or even just 'three-four' common with other kinds of music.

When a finger snap is added, it invokes in bar one the metrical level to be counted out in bar two, helping to secure the accurate measurement of the half-bar space between 'one' and 'two':

Returning to the history of music, back-beat has its roots in the accompaniments of nineteenth-century popular song. As folk tunes increasingly came to be accompanied by chordal harmony, their backings often took on an oom-pah rhythm, itself derived from the European, especially German, dance bands. This style, involving the playing of the bass note on the on-beat followed by the chord on the off-beat(s) is very common in both music hall and vaudeville song arrangements, but it had already been used by composers such as Chopin as a way of organising left-hand piano accompaniments, especially those in triple time such as waltzes and mazurkas. It is essentially the same style, though firmly in duple time, that characterises the left hand of ragtime and its later adaptation by 'stride' pianists.[83] The fact that the bass notes and the chords are in different registers permits them to be heard as though they are distinct lines of the musical texture: the bass notes as a series of on-beats, the chords as a series of off-beats. Once separated in this way, the chords function as back-beats at the main metrical level of the groove.

In later genres of popular music involving ensembles with drum kit, much more flexibility is permitted in the rhythms of bass and the chords, with the role of marking the main back-beat falling to the snare drum. Iyer, while correctly identifying back-beat as a central element of groove, makes the mistake of identifying it exclusively with the snare of the drum kit. This leads him to argue that its origins lie in 1950s rock-and-roll rather than half a century earlier.[84] Nevertheless, in post-war popular music, it is generally the snare drum that articulates the main back-beat. When there is relatively little syncopation in the rhythm section parts, as is often the case in many rock styles, it is the presence of a snare back-beat that is crucial to the groove. See, for example,

---

83   Robinson, 'Stride', *Grove Music Online*, *Oxford Music Online*.
84   Iyer 2002, p. 405.

WHAT IS 'GROOVE'?

The Police's 'Every Breath You Take', whose rhythm parts are completely unsyncopated and where syncopation in the vocal only really begins at bar 5:

The Police, 'Every Breath You Take'.[85]

There is nothing about this guitar figure that definitively identifies it as part of the rock or pop genre. Harmonically it is firmly within the Western post-Renaissance tradition and one can quite easily imagine it in a completely different context played legato as a left-hand piano or even a string accompaniment.[86] It is the back-beat snare alone that contributes the groove element, serving to accentuate the main metrical level and producing a sense that the guitar and bass parts are locked into strict time.

The role played by the snare in rock and related genres might be regarded as an instrumental replacement for clapping. The back-beat handclap is the crucial ingredient that turns *a capella* singing into groove music, a technique put

---

85   The Police 1983.
86   The only possible harmonic give-away as to its pop/rock provenance is that it uses root position chords throughout.

to effective use in black American gospel music. The back-beat at the main metrical level forms a kind of skeleton of the groove, the minimum of metric information required to make sense of a melody in groove music. The Police vocal above, especially the more syncopated passage from bar 5 onwards, becomes rhythmically unintelligible if performed without the back-beat.

The off-beats at the main metrical level are the prime instances of back-beat. But in much groove music it is possible to detect a back-beat at several metrical levels simultaneously. This is very clearly the case in reggae, whose archetypal groove structure comprises the superimposition of the backbeats at three metrical levels:

Here, the 'main' back-beats, those of level M, are played by guitar, while the drums are responsible for the off-beats of the adjacent metric levels on either side: the bass drum those of M^1, the hi-hat those of m_1. Note that provided the conventions of reggae are understood, that those involved know that the guitar 'chops' do not mark on-beats, there is no need for anything to happen on beat one of the bar. (Often beat one is avoided by the bass also). In fact, in one sense, there are no on-beats being played at all. The fact that the chord is changing every bar helps to orient us, but otherwise nearly everything we need to know about the metrical structure is supplied by off-beats rather than on-beats.

Emphasising the necessity for knowledge of the conventions of the genre in this way seems to take us too close to Brackett's and Keil's 'subjective' position and away from the possibility of an objective analysis of groove. It raises the question of correct and incorrect understandings of the groove: the possibility that 'strong' off-beats might be mistaken for on-beats by listeners lacking the appropriate cultural reference points. It is theoretically possible, for example, for a listener to 'hear' the groove of Burning Spear's 'Marcus Garvey' in this way:

rather than 'correctly' in this way:

Burning Spear, 'Marcus Garvey'.[87]

But it is not likely, partly because of the problem of making sense of the first 'C' in the bass if it is heard as falling on beat 'four', but more crucially because it is more difficult to reconcile the bass drum falling on beat 'two' than on beat 'three'. Some artists play with this possibility of rhythmic misunderstanding by deliberately misleading listeners with an ambiguous element of the groove whose correct interpretation only becomes clear once the rest of the band has entered. One striking case of this occurs in Rose Royce's 'Car Wash' which opens with a handclap rhythm which suggests the following interpretation:

Other parts are then introduced gradually, but it is not until the entry of the full ensemble at bar 23 that it becomes clear that our rhythmic perception is being toyed with. The rhythm is actually built around back-beats and the correct perception of it is:

Rose Royce, 'Car Wash'.[88]

That such games are possible emphasises that groove is not merely a subjective matter.

The back-beats discussed so far have been continuous features of the instrumental parts in which they appear. The picture is a little more complex in that

---

87   Burning Spear 1975.
88   Royce 1976.

Americanisation of Brazilian samba, the *bossa nova*, as shown by the following transcription of Stan Getz's recording of Jobim's 'Desafinado':[89]

At the level of the tactus or M, which in Latin American music is usually written in minims, is the bassline. This appears to be a straight, unsyncopated rhythm to which the term back-beat would not apply. After all, an off-beat only becomes a back-beat if its preceding and succeeding on-beats are not played. However, because of the oscillating nature of the bass's root-fifth pattern, which recalls Zuckerkandl's 'away-back' metric wave, a back-beat is suggested by the fifth, in this example by the dotted crotchet 'C's. A continuous back-beat at level m_1 is found in the pedal hi-hat, playing regularly on the second and fourth crotchets of each bar (cross-heads, stems down), doubled by the accents on the shaker. It is the guitar that displays the additional complexity here by playing a rhythmic figure which alternates between the back-beat at level m_1 in the first half of each bar and back-beats at level m_2 in the second half. One way of conceiving these two off-beat quavers is as an anticipated version of the crotchets 'four'-'one'. Finally, against this web of off-beats sits a rumba-based cross-rhythm of the 'I Got Rhythm' type played on the rim of the snare (cross-heads, stems up), setting up a temporary polyrhythm which further accentuates some of the back-beats.

It should be clear, then, from these examples, that the phenomenon of back-beat is not a perverse addition to the groove concept, but emerges logically from the combination of syncopation and deep metricality. In fact, it could be argued, following the reasoning used above, that syncopation itself is a prod-

---

89   Getz 1962.

uct of a drive to articulate the full extent of the metricality of the music, to ensure it has maximum measuring power.

These, then, are the four elements which combine to generate groove. It is not the case that groove music is quantitatively more metronomic, more syncopated or more deeply metrical than other kinds of music. As we have seen, all these characteristics can be individually present in other musics. Rather, it is a matter of a qualitative effect that emerges when all four of these characteristics come together in specific constellations.

Of the non-groove musics which have some of the characteristics of groove but fall short of having all four, a comparison with those that have exerted some influence on the development of twentieth century popular music is relevant here. European folk music for dancing had a metronomic pulse and was regular at a number of metrical levels, but was not generally syncopated or polyrhythmic (or was only occasionally and mildly so) and, crucially, did not have a back-beat. (We should not be misled by the fact that most so-called folk music today is performed according to contemporary conventions and has thus been transformed into groove music).[90]

Traditional West African music is likewise strictly metronomic, and also highly polyrhythmic. However, I will argue in the next chapter that its lack of a unitary meter prevents it from being groove music. This, too, applies to much twentieth-century minimalist music, whose overlaid patterns, although sharing a common isochronous pulse, typically repeat according to different periodicities, producing start points which continually shift in relation to each other, thereby precluding the establishment of a common meter.

As for the 'common practice period' of the Western art-music tradition, it does not consistently display any of the four elements of groove. Though, broadly speaking, much Baroque and Classical music adheres to a regular pulse (Baroque operatic recitatives and Classical concerto cadenzas being obvious exceptions), and the music of the Classical period displays a degree of what I have called 'deep metricality', both these characteristics are increasingly eroded in nineteenth-century Romanticism.[91] As I have argued, syncopation is rare in this tradition and where present takes a weak form, while back-beat does not feature at all. Even those syncopated figures which are found, for example in the nineteenth-century nationalist schools of composition of Central and Eastern Europe, are often incorporated as deliberate references to folk or peasant dance music.

---

90 Hence the reason for my description of it in the past tense.
91 The classical period is to be understood here in its narrow definition as the period which includes Haydn and Mozart.

Nineteenth-century Western art music had at its disposal another temporal device: tonality. The transition between, and juxtaposition of, key centres functions, in the large-scale symphonic works of the Western tradition, to articulate a long-duration, quasi-historical form of time which is more or less independent of rhythm and meter at the level of themes and motifs. This kind of macro-time is not a feature of the groove musics of the twentieth century, even though Western popular styles continue to employ the principles of Western tonality. For one thing, popular songs and instrumental pieces are almost never on a scale which would make such procedures viable.[92] But in addition, though small-scale harmonic progression is entirely compatible with groove, including modulation to distant keys as in the bridge sections of many Broadway songs which became jazz standards, there is a tendency in groove music to marginalise the harmonic element. At its most extreme, as in much of the work of James Brown and George Clinton considered by Danielsen, the grooves are articulated within the context of a single chord, that is, without any harmonic movement at all.[93] Thus, the temporality expressed by groove is of a type that depends entirely on the four elements identified above, not on tonal structure.

By the turn of the twentieth century, as the groove concept was crystallising in ragtime and other popular musics, Western art music, under the influence of artistic modernism, was increasingly eschewing any sense of audible temporal regularity. Either, as in the expressionism of the Second Viennese School, the use of *rubato* combined with rhythmic complexity obliterates any sense of pulse for the listener (even though it still exists in the score in order to co-ordinate the performance); or, in music which retains a strong sense of pulse, such as in many of Bartók's and Stravinsky's works, any metrical regularity beyond the level of the beat is avoided with the use of irregular and changing time-signatures and accents. The apparent bifurcation of twentieth-century Western music into two strands – modernist and popular – defined by their attitude to measured time, is one of the central issues this book seeks to address.

---

92   When Hobsbawm describes jazz as 'little music' this is probably what he means (Newton 1959, p. 146).
93   Danielsen 2006.

CHAPTER 2

Is Groove African?

The suggestion that Western popular music derives at least some of its characteristics from African musical practices and traditions has penetrated deeply into writing and thinking about popular music. By far the most frequently cited of those characteristics, though not the only one, concerns rhythm: the notion that what gives much American popular music its particular emphasis on rhythm, its sense of 'beat', its syncopation, in short, its 'groove', has its origins in West African music, in particular, in the drumming which is a central element of the music of that part of the world.

The argument is made in many forms. In its widely diffused, commonsense version it amounts to the view that early Western popular music was a fusion between African rhythm and European harmony. Most theoretical and academic writing rejects such a simplistic notion, but the idea that the rhythms of ragtime, early jazz and rhythm and blues, which exercised such a formative influence over subsequent popular music genres, were essentially African rhythms appears repeatedly in the literature on popular music.

Such ideas form a spectrum from 'strong' versions of the theory which posit a highly racialised, quasi-genetic and very direct connection between the practices of African and black American musicians, to 'weaker', more culturalist versions of it which emphasise mediation and syncretisation in the processes by which stylistic traits are held to have been transmitted from one tradition to another. But one element is always present: the notion that Africa is the source while America and the West is the destination in this transmission process. Implicit in this theory is the concept of inheritance, the sense of musical traditions having been passed down the generations from some ancestral source, a sense captured in the term 'roots music'.

There are two aspects of these arguments that demand investigation. The first concerns the mechanisms by which the supposed continuity between musical traditions from distinct parts of the world and different historical periods was achieved. Obviously, the idea of the African component of Western popular music rests on the forced migration of millions of Africans to the New World during the period of slavery. Often, cultural continuity is simply assumed from this fact, and little attempt to made to explain the means by which it occurs. After all, it seems evident that very few elements of the culture of West Africa in the seventeenth and eighteenth centuries, taken in its general sense as 'way of life', survived amongst twentieth-century African-Americans. Even where it may be possible to identify an element of musical continuity, it is unlikely to have survived in a pure form, unchanged by the radically altered material circumstances under which it exists. To suggest otherwise, is to endorse an idealism which accords cultural and ideological phenomena an unwarranted autonomy.

One of the first ethnomusicologists to tackle the question of the relationship between African and American musics, Richard A. Waterman, initially describes the African elements that he detects in American music as 'influences' and 'survivals' that have resulted from the syncretism between African and European musical cultures which already had much in common, or at least, few traits that were in direct conflict with each other. Unlike other musical traditions in the world, 'almost nothing in European folk music … is incompatible with African musical style, and much of the European material fits readily into the generalized African musical mold'.[1] Here, at least, is the beginnings of a theory which aims to explain the conditions which allowed certain African musical practices to become part of a new, syncretised musical culture. The emphasis seems to be on fusion and hybridisation.

Waterman identifies a number of African features in American music, all of which are rhythm-related, and uses the term 'hot rhythm' to describe them. Associating 'hot rhythm' with 'Negro music' allows Waterman to posit a direct link between African music and jazz.

> Those who have had opportunity to listen to Negro music in Africa or the New World have been almost unanimous in agreeing that its most striking aspect is its rhythm.... Everywhere, Negro music differs from the music of impinging non-Negro groups in being 'hotter'.[2]

Already, we have lost the sense of syncretism and fusion of traditions. Despite the assertion that this tradition is not racially inherited, 'hot rhythm' on this description clearly is a racial characteristic which appears in 'Negro music' *everywhere* it is to be found. The fact that Waterman makes no mention of the famous white exponents of jazz from his period, for example bandleaders like Benny Goodman, reinforces this interpretation.

One element of this rhythmic inheritance identified by Waterman is 'metronome sense', a facility required by African music which has manifested itself in jazz, and:

---

1 Waterman 1951, p. 209.
2 Waterman 1948, p. 24.

entails habits of conceiving any music as structured along a theoretical framework of beats regularly spaced in time and of co-operating in terms of overt or covert motor behaviour with the pulses of this metric pattern whether or not the beats are expressed in actual melodic or percussive tones....

This clearly has some affinity with what we are describing as groove. Waterman goes on:

Because it amounts to an unverbalized point of view concerning all music, this traditional value which differentiates African from 'pure' European music systems of appreciation is a typical example of the variety of subliminal culture pattern most immune to the pressures of an acculturative situation.[3]

The emphasised beat and syncopations of jazz are not a product of American cultural conditions, nor even are they the result of the interpenetration of African and European traditions, despite Waterman's initial emphasis on the *similarities* of those traditions for understanding African influences and survivals. Now the argument is that the 'hot' element of African music has survived in the new context of America because of its *distinctiveness* from the European tradition and its consequent *resistance* to incorporation. It is not a hybrid but rather a pure trait from outside that has not only survived against all odds, but has also resurfaced after a period of dormancy:

The concept of 'hot' went underground, as far as most of the population of the United States was concerned, until it reappeared in jazz music. The demonstration that the tradition of 'hot' rhythms, born in Africa, has survived the tremendous social, economic, and religious changes that have fallen to the lot of the carriers of that tradition, is no less important in indicating the almost incredible toughness of basic musical culture-patterns than it is in attesting the genuine musical value of the concept. For the 'hot' rhythm of Negro music, now so influential in the music of the New World, has proved its strength by the sheer fact of its survival.[4]

If Waterman might be said to fall into this essentialist position unwittingly, this cannot be said of those writers who espouse a consciously black nationalist

---

3   Waterman 1951, p. 211.
4   Waterman 1948, p. 37.

position. Olly Wilson, writing in 1974, proposes on the basis of the 'obvious empirical evidence' that the zone of West African musical influence should centre on the Atlantic and include West Africa, northern South America and the Caribbean, and North America. His aim is to defend what he admits is the most problematic part of that thesis by showing the extent of the West African influence on the music of North America, or more particularly, 'Afro-American music'.[5] Wilson makes the familiar suggestion that West African and Afro-American musics share a propensity for 'multi-meter practice' involving the 'clashing of rhythms'. But there is a warning: if such polyrhythmic practices are isolated and regarded as the prime principle of black music, as some writers have done, it is possible to confuse Afro-American music with a good deal of music written, presumably by whites, in the twenties and thirties.[6] We encounter here the problem of definition inherent in the concepts 'black music', 'Afro-American music' and its more modern counterpart, 'African-American music', which plague many of the discussions of this issue, and which have been addressed and challenged so pugnaciously by Philip Tagg.[7]

Wilson asserts, without citing any evidence, that during slavery, blacks who were used as musicians 'approached the instruments with a certain stylistic bias' – 'a percussive polyrhythmic manner of playing which was part of their West African tradition'. Later he makes the equally unsupported statement that 'the distinct manner of playing an instrument as if it were an extension of the voice has been a unique Afro-American feature throughout the history of black American music'. He continues: 'It is well known that the performance technique a black jazz musician uses is not the same as that of his white symphonic counterpart'.[8] The purpose of the racial epithets in this sentence is a mystery since it would be true without them, with them reversed, or with two completely different ones substituted, and consequently proves nothing.

Wilson sums up his entire position like this:

> My basic premise [is] that African-American music is a unique branch of West-African music in that . . . there is a basic store of African ways of creating music buried deep in the collective psyche of black Americans which historical and sociological forces make necessary for them to tap in order to retain some semblance of a unique identity.[9]

---

5   Wilson 1974, p. 6.
6   Wilson 1974, p. 9.
7   Tagg 1989.
8   Wilson 1974, p. 15.
9   Wilson 1974, p. 19.

Here, the 'collective psyche of black Americans' is offered as the mechanism whereby a series of cultural practices and attitudes have been preserved from their African origins. If this is a reference to Carl Jung's theory of a collective unconscious, it raises more questions than it settles. First, for Jung, the collective unconsciousness was not racially determined but common to all humanity. Second, Jung's identification of the 'archetypes' which constitute the collective unconscious as 'primitive' make its use particularly problematic in the context of race, a fact which Franz Fanon exploited in his critique of Jung in *Black Skin, White Masks*.[10] Wilson seems unaware of this and his use of the concept suggests that he endorses a genetic, idealistic, indeed a racialist, theory of culture. For him there are primordial musical archetypes in a collective unconscious to which only those with a certain heredity have access.

Wilson's writing predates a later theorisation of the unity of black culture across diverse geographical and socio-historical conditions, that of Henry Louis Gates, Jr. Gates's theory, which hinges on the concept of 'Signifyin(g)' as unique to black cultural forms, has had an influence on much writing on music. Samuel A. Floyd, Jr. traces the distinctive characteristics of 'Afro-American music' to the 'Ring Shout', a circle dance and chanting tradition practised during slavery which is held to be of 'ancient African provenance'.[11] Floyd cites Stuckey for an exhaustive list of musical practices which derive from this archaic musical form. They include:

> calls, cries and hollers; call-and-response devices; additive rhythms and polyrhythms; heterophony, pendular thirds, blue notes, bent notes and elisions; hums, moans, grunts, vocables, and other rhythmic-oral declamations, interjections, and punctuations; off-beat melodic phrasings and parallel intervals and chords; constant repetition of rhythmic and melodic figures and phrases (from which riffs and vamps would be derived); timbral distortions of various kinds; musical individuality within collectivity; game-rivalry; hand-clapping, foot-patting, and approximations thereof...

---

10 Jung 1968; Vannoy Adams 1996. Fanon does not object to the concept of a collective unconscious, but against Jung's genetic explanation, asserts that it is cultural: 'purely the sum of prejudices, myths, collective attitudes of a given group'. He turns the tables on Jung's Eurocentrism by arguing that at the heart of the European collective unconscious is 'an archetype: an expression of the bad instincts, of the darkness inherent in every ego, of the uncivilized savage, the Negro who slumbers in every white man' (Fanon 1967, pp. 187–8).

11 Floyd 1991, p. 266.

They also include 'the metronomic foundational pulse that underlies all Afro-American music'. Without pausing to question whether any of these practices might also be part of any other musical tradition, Floyd feels able to assert,

> Consequently, since all of the defining elements of black music are present in the ring, Stuckey's formulation [of regarding the ring as foundational to all subsequent Afro-American music-making] can be seen as a frame in which all black-music analysis and interpretation can take place...[12]

Any attempt to apply the categories of European aesthetics or musical criticism, caricatured by Floyd as consisting of concepts like 'transcendent, abstract beauty' and 'proper harmonic progressions' which emphasise form over content, is doomed to failure.[13] Thus 'swing', the rhythmic feel associated with jazz, resists 'Eurocentric' musicological analysis, being instead 'a natural and perfectly explicable product or by-product of the tropings of black music', and a prime example of 'Signifyin(g)'. 'Signifyin(g)' turns out to be something of a catch-all category in Floyd's hands, used to collect under a single cultural heading not only the organisation of 'sound-events on the time-line, against the flow of its pulse' to create 'swing'; but also 'self-criticising and self-validating comments during performance'; the 'dialogical, conversational character of black music'; and the way that an improvised solo 'does not repeat the melody that preceded it', but somehow comments upon it.[14]

On the basis of a single cultural form which appears to have survived from West Africa to slave communities in the Americas, a wide range of practices, many of which can be shown to also be a feature of a number of other musical cultures, are essentialised as 'black cultural tropes'. No explanation is offered as to how such practices survived between successive generations in changing historical conditions.[15] 'Signifyin(g)' is simply a marker of blackness.

---

12   Floyd 1991, pp. 267–8.
13   Floyd 1991, p. 274.
14   Floyd 1991, pp. 273, 275, 277, 280.
15   Iyer, in his study of the psychology of groove, also draws upon the Ring Shout as part of his claim that groove is an African-American musical innovation. Having dated the origins of backbeat as late as the 1950s, however, he has no way of justifying the following statement: 'The backbeat is best understood as a contemporary, popular remnant of what is probably some very ancient human musical behavior, filtered through a sophisticated, stylized African ritual and through centuries of African-American musical development'. (Iyer 2002, p. 406).

James A. Snead's examination of the question of repetition highlights the relationship of the concept of 'Signifyin(g)' to postmodernist thinking. The dominant modes of thought of European modernity emphasised history and progress, and in the hands of Hegel explicitly excluded Africans from world history. Snead's strategy is not to resist such exclusion but to embrace it, arguing that 'black culture' is free from the modernist roots of its European counterpart, especially in relation to conceptions of time. European culture under the influence of historicism, he asserts, has lost its pre-modern cyclical conceptions of time, and now treats even repetition as progress, as 'differentiation within repetition'.[16] Thus, even recurrent holidays and festivals are not free from this thinking: influenced by paradigms of growth and accumulation, Christmas celebrations and Olympic Games must be seen to get bigger and better with each recurrence.[17] European culture is goal oriented:

> In European culture, the 'goal' is always clear: that which always is being worked towards. The culture is never 'immediate' but 'mediated' and separated from the present tense by its own future-orientation. Moreover, European culture does not allow 'a succession of accidents and surprises' but instead maintains the illusions of progression and control at all costs.[18]

By contrast, black culture has no goal, accepts 'accidents' as central to its procedures, and celebrates 'the pure beauty and value of repetition' for its own sake. This results in a music which is constructed on a wholly different foundation from that of the European tradition. The peculiarity of black music, according to Snead, is 'that it draws attention to its own repetitions', whereas in European music, 'the repetition has been suppressed in favor of the fulfilment of the goal of harmonic resolution'.[19] He continues,

> Despite the clear presence of consistent beat or rhythm in the common classical forms of the ostinato or the figured bass or any other continuo instrument, rhythm was scarcely a goal in itself and repetition seldom pleasurable or beautiful by itself.[20]

---

16 Snead 1984, p. 65.
17 Snead 1984, p. 66.
18 Snead 1984, p. 67.
19 Snead 1984, p. 69.
20 Snead 1984, p. 72.

All this is of a piece with the concept of 'Signifyin(g)' as defined by Henry Louis Gates as:

> a rhetorical practice unengaged in information-giving. Signifying turns on the play and chain of signifiers, and not on some supposedly transcendent signified.[21]

In other words, black cultural strategies are revealed to have been postmodern all along, more concerned about their own artistic procedures than the expression of any particular content, happy to explore the 'play' of signifiers rather than any possible signifieds.

Snead may have a point when he draws distinctions between the music of the European art tradition and other musics. His discussion of the specific musical temporality that arises with modernity contains some valid insights. The main problem is the slippage in his theory from historical-geographic categories to ethnic ones, the reduction of the concept of 'African' as applied to specific socio-historical circumstances to the concept of 'blackness'. It is one thing to draw a distinction between modes of thought in the Europe of early modernity and those in pre-modern Africa. It is theoretically illegitimate to apply the same distinction between groups of people living in the same society in late modernity on the basis of their heredity – or more precisely, on the basis of what is taken to signify heredity, their skin colour.

This problem of racial essentialism is one that consistently bedevils Gates's literary theory of 'Signifyin(g)'. As Myers comments:

> Gates recognizes [that] as a 'principle of language use', ... signifying is 'not in any way the exclusive property of black people ...'. To his credit, then, Gates perceives that it would be an error to ascribe the unique characteristics of Afro-American literature to race. But he is not sure what else to ascribe them to. His reasoning runs in circles. Black writers form a tradition. How do you know? They all use the 'trope' of signifying. What makes this trope distinctively black? All black writers use it.[22]

Myers suggests that Gates is at least partly aware of the problem of his theory. The same cannot be said of those, like Floyd and Snead, who draw upon it to discuss music. It is possible that they feel more justified in applying it to music because the concept of 'black music' has won wide acceptance beyond black

---

21   Gates 1984, p. 287.
22   Myers 1990, p. 63.

American critics to a degree that 'black literature' has not. Much of the analysis of Wilson, Floyd and Snead finds its way into David Brackett's analysis of James Brown's 'Superbad'. Brackett, like some of his European counterparts, is uneasy about the racialising tendency of these writers, but clearly feels justified in taking this approach in the case of the musician James Brown because of the way that others have viewed him as 'symbolising the figure of blackness... par excellence'. He quotes:

> JB was proof that black people were different. Rhythmically and tonally blacks had to be from somewhere else... – it was in that voice.... If there is any black man who symbolizes the differences between black and white cultural and aesthetic values, Soul Brother No. 1 [James Brown] is that man.[23]

Brackett's claim that this need not be an essentialist view, but rather a discursive one, is somewhat undermined by his subsequent use of many of Wilson's and Floyd's arguments and his own persistent use of the term 'black music'. We end up with the same problem identified by Myers in relation to Gates. One cannot have it both ways: either 'black music' refers to music made by blacks, in which case it is unlikely to share uniform characteristics; or, if it is merely a set of musical practices and modes of expression open for use by anyone, it must lose the epithet 'black'. There is surely an inconsistency in claiming for 'black music', as Brackett does, the chord sequence of Gershwin's 'I Got Rhythm' but not the song from which it comes.[24] (The same issue arises with any of the many Broadway show tunes written by white, often Jewish, composers which were adopted as source material for black jazz musicians to improvise – or 'Signify' – upon).

The same kind of schizophrenia is apparent in some of the writing of Simon Frith. Like Brackett he is aware of the racist ideology which underpinned attitudes towards the music of black Americans, particularly in the era of classic imperialism in the late nineteenth and early twentieth centuries. However, what is presented is a warning against 'over-essentialising' rather than a rejection of the categories entirely. Having thoroughly exposed descriptions of jazz rhythms as 'primitive', 'uncultured', 'natural', 'intuitive', 'animal', 'libidinal', 'sensual', 'untamed', 'dangerous', etc., as inherently racist, whether those using them were intending positive or negative value judgements in doing so, Frith nevertheless is reluctant to dismiss the concept of 'blackness' from his thinking

---

23   Brackett 2000, p. 108.
24   Brackett 2000, p. 118.

entirely.[25] He cites what sounds like a highly unscientific 1944 study of black and white St. Louis children singing playground rhymes which claimed that the black children 'syncopated the rhythm and ... accompan[ied] the handclapping with a "jazz" and "swing" rhythm of the body'. Frith comments:

> The point here is not that young black children were naturally more physical than white children ... but that they were more rhythmically *articulate*, better able to bring together verbal and bodily expressive devices ... under the name of 'rhythm'.[26]

Frith appears to believe that the claim that children with a certain skin colour are naturally more 'rhythmically articulate' avoids the racial essentialising inherent in the claim that they are naturally more 'physical'.

Moreover, again after a warning that 'sweeping comparisons of "African" and "European" musics are decidedly unhistorical', Frith launches into a discussion of African music which simply assumes that it shares features with 'African-American music'.[27] Thus, a discussion on the mode of listening required by traditional African music is illustrated by a quotation about Motown musician James Jamerson's bass playing without any explanation of the connection.[28] It might be possible to make a case for the relevance of West African musical practices to the music of 1960s Detroit, but Frith does not attempt to make it. We are left with the tacit implication that the connection is to do with the 'blackness' of James Jamerson or of the Motown record label or both, contravening all of Frith's own anti-essentialist arguments.

A similar procedure occurs in Danielsen's book on the funk grooves of James Brown and Parliament in which an acknowledgement of the problems of the concept of 'blackness' in cultural theory acts as a caveat or disclaimer prior to the deployment of that very concept.[29] Danielsen clearly shares the view she cites that funk is 'blackness in its purest form', and moves directly to a discussion of its African sensibility on the tacit assumption that 'blackness' = African.

Christopher Small, though more sophisticated in his approach, also ends up falling into the same trap. Small seeks to avoid attributing definite musical characteristics to musical traditions, preferring to focus on the cultural values that underpin them. He asks why black people in the Americas have been so

---

25   Frith 1998, pp. 127–9.
26   Frith 1998, p. 136.
27   Frith 1998, p. 134.
28   Frith 1998, pp. 139–40.
29   Danielsen 2006.

creative and why their music has become so dominant throughout the world, despite its challenge to 'official culture'.[30] This is a reasonable question, but Small fails to explain why the starting point for his answer must be a discussion of the traditional musical practices of West Africa. So the claim, 'It is the musicking of the blacks which has been at the root of all the most potent developments in western musicking today' is assumed to be answerable on the basis of values and attitudes to music-making which derive from black Americans' African ancestry.[31] Underlying Small's position is a Third Worldist political perspective which shares much common ground with the black nationalism of Wilson, Floyd and Snead. The folk musics of Europe and America, he argues, cannot mount a challenge to the ossified and oppressive classical musical traditions of the West, not 'even those of the urban working class ... for they are ... so absorbed in its values that they can point to no alternatives'.[32] The problem here is not that Small takes a political approach to aesthetic questions, but a distorted political perspective which fails to notice that most blacks in the West are part of the urban working class, and which erroneously sees all struggle through the prism of colonial oppression in which race is the determining factor.

Small, Frith and Danielson are not wrong to identify the relationship between certain aspects of African music and Western popular music. A comparison between these two traditions is fruitful and will form the second part of this chapter. My criticisms of the above approaches are, first, that they are all, to a greater or lesser extent, ahistorical; and, worse, they all deploy, often either unconsciously or dishonestly, a racially essentialist connection between African music and those genres of Western popular music which can be called 'Afro-' or 'African-American'.

The musical element of continuity mostly identified in this connection is rhythm, and the genres of popular music assumed to be most 'African' are those about which the term 'groove' is mostly applied. Writers are often misled by claims made by musicians themselves about the Africanness of their work. This tendency has a long tradition. But the fact that the following comes from a black musician, the early twentieth-century bandleader James Reese Europe, does not make the notion of a racial musical characteristic any more plausible:

---

30 Small 1987, p. 11.
31 Small 1987, p. 134.
32 Small 1987, p. 482.

We accent strongly...the notes which would originally be without accent. It is natural for us to do this; it is, indeed, a racial musical characteristic.[33]

Similarly, one suspects that the reason why funk is a particular focus for the 'African' argument is the association of the genre and many of its practitioners, James Brown included, with the black nationalist and Africanist ideas of the 1970s. Writers like Wilson and Floyd are clearly influenced by a black nationalist ideology; their assertion of the African roots of black Americans and of a continuing African heritage is part of a conscious political project. European writers are too quick to follow this lead, despite, as I have shown, often harbouring criticisms of it. Notwithstanding the claim that 'black' musical practices and attitudes are open for use by all musicians, too often James Brown and James Jamerson are deemed to be the unquestioned paradigms of a genre such as funk, while the Average White Band are just average, (mostly) white imitators of a black style.[34]

The Making of Popular Music

Against the idea of a pure African tradition or specific set of musical practices which survive, more or less unchanged, in the African-American music of the twentieth century, most historical studies emphasise the complex intermingling of the myriad musical traditions brought by the range of immigrants to America. It may be possible to identify the origins of certain features of various forms of popular music-making as they emerge during the nineteenth century, but the process of their amalgamation and transformation makes unravelling them completely a hopeless task.

Part of the reason for that is that even as far back as the period of slavery, music-making was never an entirely segregated affair. House slaves soon learned to play European instruments and were often used as musicians for society balls, a tradition which continued long after slavery was abolished. In the nineteenth century, being a musician was often thought of as 'nigger work': regimental marching bans were often all black, while 'in many places the profession of dance musicians was reserved by custom for Negroes, just as was, for

---

33   Kingman 1979, p. 302.
34   The Average White Band (or AWB) was a six-piece Scottish band (five white, one black) who had a million-selling hit in 1975 entitled 'Pick Up the Pieces' which reached no. 1 in the US charts. It is arguably one of the great funk instrumentals of the period.

example, the occupation of barber'.[35] These were black musicians playing European-derived styles of music, but the intermingling of traditions went much further than that. In the period of religious revivalism of the early nineteenth century, mass outdoor camps took place featuring circuit-riding preachers, mass conversions and collective hymn singing. Kingman describes the frontier, where much of this activity took place, as the most democratic region in America at the time, with camp meetings being places where blacks and white met uninhibitedly.[36] Chase argues, 'Since both Negroes and whites attended the same camp meetings and sang the same songs, there is no need, at this stage at least, to make any kind of racial distinction'.[37]

There are contemporary descriptions which suggest that as a result of these shared experiences, there was no significant difference between 'negro part-singing' and the folk singing of the New England reformers. Chase argues:

> That Negro singing in America developed as the result of the blending of several cultural traditions is certain; and it seems equally certain that one of these traditions was the folk style of early New England psalmody and hymnody, carried southward in the late eighteenth and early nineteenth centuries.[38]

Similarly, whether taking part in the Methodist or Baptist church services of this period, both white and black sang in the same highly ornamented, 'unmodern' way known as 'lining out'.[39] This involves a degree of polyphonic improvisation, or 'basing', which is often held as a uniquely black American trait associated with the blues and early jazz. Chase disagrees:

> The Negroes undoubtedly had their peculiar intonation, rhythm, and intervals; but the singing of tunes with improvised melodic embellishments, and the filling-in of 'gaps' or holds with interpolated notes, was a firmly established practice in Anglo-American folk music long before the development of Negro spirituals and the blues. The *manner* of jazz improvisation may be unique, but the principle has a long tradition in both the folk and the art music of Europe.[40]

---

35   Chase 1966, pp. 76–7; Van Der Merwe 1989, p. 63; Southern 1984, p. 284.
36   Kingman 1979, pp. 163–4.
37   Chase 1966, p. 209.
38   Chase 1966, p. 239.
39   Van Der Merwe 1989, p. 78.
40   Chase 1966, p. 452.

Further undermining the basis for distinct cultural traditions, there was increasing miscegenation between the growing free black population of the nineteenth century and poor whites. Berlin tells us:

> Under the pressure of common conditions, poor blacks and whites became one. They lived together, worked together, and inevitably slept together, hopelessly blurring the colour line.
>
> The intersection of Bourbon and Orleans Streets in New Orleans was 'distinguished for the equality which reigns between black and white – all is hail fellow well met, no matter what the complexion'.[41]

Van Der Merwe gives the following pertinent warning against the over-simplified schemas of distinct African-derived black musical traditions and European folk-based white ones:

> If we are to remember only one fact about the American music of the past, let that fact be its sheer *variety*. White music varied from the most rustic to the most urbane, and black music varied from the near-African – itself representing several contrasting strains – to every degree of approach to every kind of white music. And all of these types did not remain static and isolated: they jostled each other, intermingling and interacting from the seventeenth century to the present.[42]

Indeed, he suggests that one reason why such fusion was possible was because of pre-existing similarities between European folk musics and African music which were in turn due to a common Arab influence. This influence on the music of West Africa has long been acknowledged. A.M. Jones comments in his seminal study of African music:

> The Islamic tradition can at once be recognized by the very nasal and stringy quality of the voice that is invariably used. But added to the nasal vocalization there is the very frequent use of mordents to embellish the melody notes.[43]

Likewise, Van Der Merwe regards the 'strident, nasal manner of singing' characteristic of some European folk musics as evidence of Middle Eastern Islamic

---

41 Berlin 1992, pp. 260–2 cited in Van Der Merwe 1989, p. 57.
42 Van Der Merwe 1989, pp. 57–8.
43 Jones 1959, p. 207.

influence, which has survived longest in the folk music of Scotland and Ireland because of their isolation on the extreme edges of the continent. Similar conditions of poverty and inaccessibility applied to the zones where Scots-Irish migrants to the Americas found themselves, places such as Newfoundland and the Appalachians, and, as a result, the traditions survived. So the encounter in America between black and white folk musics was one between styles that shared certain features as a result of this common Islamic heritage, a fact which completely undermines the notion of pure, black African musical traits.[44] Indeed, Van Der Merwe believes that the 'ring shout' which is so central to Floyd's picture of African-American music may itself be of Afro-Arab origin.[45]

That influence can be detected in the highly ornamented, semi-improvised manner of hymn singing discussed above, but also in the blues. The rhapsodic, melismatic vocal practices associated with the blues and the 'field hollers' which preceded it are common in the musics of a large area of Asia, Europe and North Africa, including the western savannah, and clearly have Arabic roots. The *hora lunga* discovered by Bartók in Romania, attributed to Persia, and Irish 'caoin' or lament are examples from European folk music of this florid style which, when transmitted to America, became known as the 'old way of singing' or 'long meter songs'. The fact that this style may be found as readily in solo performances of old Scottish tunes such as 'Amazing Grace' as in the blues or soul demonstrates the difficulty of disentangling Celtic, African and Middle Eastern influences. This is not to deny that the blues has African features, but to argue that many of those features are not exclusively African, and, further, that the form itself is not African. As Van Der Merwe says, 'All the components of the blues mode are to be found somewhere in West Africa, but separately, awaiting assembly on American soil'.[46] But he also credits the 'catalytic influence' of British folk music on the way that process of assembly worked itself out.[47]

What of the other forms generally held to be part of an African-American musical tradition? The call-and-response worksong is found nearly all over the world wherever there is communal manual labour, but tended to disappear in America with the mechanisation of work, surviving only in prisons.[48] Van Der Merwe suggests that American worksongs retained an African character

---

44   Van Der Merwe 1989, pp. 13–14.
45   Van Der Merwe 1989, p. 77.
46   Van Der Merwe 1989, pp. 131–8.
47   Van Der Merwe 1989, p. 145.
48   Kingman 1979, p. 53.

probably because this kind of work was performed by the lowest class of people, slaves and the least assimilated blacks. However, just as with other forms, it would be a mistake to think of them as purely African, untouched by other influences.[49]

The issue of worksongs introduces to the discussion the question of class divisions amongst black Americans, a factor that is missing in the accounts of the likes of Wilson and Floyd. The blues, too, began as the music of the poorest blacks, the outcasts and itinerants.[50] It is not until the 1920s that an accepted urban form of the blues develops, adopting a standardised form to cater for a large audience, many of whom are white.[51] Kingman describes a general process whereby innovation from the bottom strata works its way through society as a whole:

> Each [important development in American popular music] began as an uninhibited and more or less coarse form of Negro music-making, cultivated in a milieu characterized as 'lowbrow'. Each in turn was resisted by the musical 'establishment', and opposed by that segment of the populace with more cultivated tastes (both white and black), while being cultivated by 'radicals' within that segment (largely of the middle and upper classes). Each, after commercially successful imitation by white musicians, eventually permeated and permanently changed our vernacular music.[52]

This is similar to the model proposed by Keil which takes the process further by suggesting that the successful assimilation and commercialisation of a style provokes in turn a renewed drive to innovate among those in the bottom layers of society, motivated by the search for a form of expression free from the sanitising influence of respectable society and/or big business.[53] Van Der Merwe makes the point that the cultural pull on a minority community operates in two directions: blacks have always had to decide whether to hang on to African heritage or whether to adopt white ways. This explains why 'during the twentieth century black American music has grown, not less (as one would expect) but *more* African' as black musicians have sought to assert their distinct

---

49   Van Der Merwe 1989, pp. 69–70.
50   See Oliver 1970; Kingman 1979, p. 53.
51   Kingman 1979, p. 201.
52   Kingman 1979, p. 211.
53   Keil 1966.

identity in the face of what many have regarded as the exploitation of their skills by white society.[54]

This way of understanding what is African in American music is, however, completely at odds with the model offered by Wilson, Floyd and Gates. What is being suggested here is an active, conscious process of identification rather than the unconscious transmission of cultural heritage by (quasi-)genetic means. As a process of selection and choice, it is obviously open to musicians of any and all backgrounds to engage in.

But it also needs to be remembered that what is taken to be authentically African is itself socially constructed and mediated. The minstrel and 'Coon Shows' of the late nineteenth century clearly involved black performers accommodating to white stereotypes of black people in what is regarded now as a highly degrading fashion. But the funk musicians of the 1970s may have been engaging in a process which is more similar than they (and we) would care to admit when they sought to assert their African heritage through the adoption of a narrow range of musical characteristics which had come to be regarded in America as quintessentially African: an emphasis on rhythm at the expense of harmony, certain 'non-singing' vocal techniques, and the inclusion of handdrums alongside the drumkit.

In other words, to say, as Van Der Merwe does, that 'American music has grown more African' is already to capitulate to the kind of essentialism that the rest of his study does an excellent job in undermining. The most we can say is that throughout the twentieth century, there have been impulses to seek to make music more African, to 'return to the roots', but that each attempt makes it still less possible to identify anything uniquely or purely African.[55]

Rhythm in African Music

The idea that African music is inherently more rhythmic than European music is a very pervasive one which runs through many of the classic studies of African music. A.M. Jones, for example, goes so far as to argue that 'Rhythm is to the African what harmony is to Europeans and it is in the complex interweaving of contrasting rhythmic patterns that he finds his greatest aesthetic

---

54   Kingman 1979, p. 53.
55   This is part of the process of identity formation described by Paul Gilroy. In adopting what he calls an 'anti-anti-essentialism', Gilroy appears to regard the term 'black music' as unproblematic (Gilroy 1993, pp. 36, 102).

satisfaction'.[56] Generalisations such as these are tendentious and deserve to be treated with suspicion, but Agawu surely pushes his objection too far when he asserts that ' "African rhythm", in short, is an invention, a construction, a fiction, a myth, ultimately a lie'.[57] As long as we reject any fixed, ahistorical or quasi-genetic conceptions, it is possible, as a result of concrete, empirical studies, to determine a set of governing rhythmic principles which underlie the traditional musical practices found in a range of language groups and geographical areas of Africa, which may be contrasted with those of musics from other parts of the world and other historical periods. A survey of such studies reveals a fair degree of agreement on the nature of those principles, as well as some understandable disagreement over the extent to which the tools of Western musicological analysis can be applied to them. I will present the key elements of those studies here before proceeding to address the question of this chapter: Is groove African?

Most scholars agree that a central feature of the traditional musics of West, Central and Southern Africa in particular is the clash of rhythms. Jones calls this a 'cardinal principle' and talks of 'polyrhythmic cross-accented combinations' and 'staggered polyrhythms', while Chernoff puts it like this: 'The fundamental characteristic of African music is the way in which the music works with time in the dynamic clash and interplay of cross-rhythms'.[58] We have already encountered Waterman's notion of 'metronome sense', and whatever deficiencies can be identified in Waterman's application of it to music in America, it is certainly the case that African music is generally organised around a regular, isochronous pulse. What engaged Waterman, and is also noticed by other writers, is the fact that the pulse or beat is often not actually being played, or as Arom puts it, 'it is not necessarily materialised'.[59] Chernoff argues that the combination of the clash of rhythms and the fact that the pulse is not always explicitly stated demands of the listener 'an ability and a need to *mediate the rhythms actively*... the "beat" of the music comes from the whole relationship of the rhythms rather than from any particular part'.[60] This echoes Waterman's description:

> The maintenance of a subjective meter, in terms of the metronome sense, requires effort and, more particularly, a series of efforts regularly spaced in time. The regular occurrences of these 'rhythmic awarenesses' involves

---

56 Jones 1959, p. 26.
57 Agawu 2003, p. 61.
58 Jones 1959, p. 203; Chernoff 1979, p. 95.
59 Arom 1991, p. 211.
60 Chernoff 1979, p. 95.

the expectancy, at the moment of any beat, that the next beat will occur precisely at some succeeding moment determined by the tempo. Subjectively, the beat does occur.[61]

Waterman argues that instances of notes falling between beats have the psychological effect of strengthening the subjective perception of the beat. This is certainly a description that might fit the experience of some Western groove musics. Waterman's use of the term 'metronome sense' implies that the pulse produced by the combination of instruments and the subjective effort of the listener is a strictly regular one, while Chernoff also asserts that African music demands a higher degree of rhythmic accuracy than is found in the Western tradition: 'compared to us, Africans acquire a rather exact sense of time'. Jones agrees: 'When we Europeans imagine we are beating in strict time, the African will merely smile at the "roughness" of our beating'.[62] This is a dubious claim, but what does seem to be true is that in African music it is rarely the case, if ever, that the pulse is treated flexibly. Arom states that Central African percussion ensembles, for example, display 'regular, stable movement, free of *accelerando, rallentando*, or *rubato*; the music is measured and contains strictly proportional durations'.[63]

The regular pulse provides the basis for the construction of larger periodicities. Jones cites what he terms the 'unit of time rule', which means that 'normally in African music all rhythms are compounded of notes whose value is a simple multiple of the basic unit of time, and that the whole complex structure rests on this simple mathematical basis'.[64] More specific in his analysis, Kubik identifies three levels of timing in the music of sub-Saharan Africa: what he calls the 'elementary pulsation' comprising an infinite series of the smallest pulses in any performance; the 'reference beat', sometimes referred to as the 'dancers' feet', and probably corresponding to Waterman's 'metronome', formed of regular compounds of the elementary pulse-units; and cycles of regular units of reference beats.[65] The 'elementary pulsation' or 'unit of time' is what others, including Arom, refer to as the density referent, a term which has been applied to Western popular music.[66] Both the tendency for the pulse to be strictly isochronous and for it to be a multiple of a consistently present smaller

---

61   Waterman 1951, p. 213.
62   Chernoff 1979, p. 97.
63   Arom 1991, p. 229.
64   Jones 1959, p. 24.
65   Kubik, 'Africa', *Grove Music Online, Oxford Music Online*.
66   See Danielsen 2006.

time unit appear to be rhythmic characteristics shared by traditional African music and Western groove music.

However, Kubik goes on to say:

> A central reference beat exists in many forms of African music. However, in contrast with European, Mediterranean, and some Arab musics, the beat in sub-Saharan African music, as in North American jazz, is usually conceptualized without pre-accentuation; there are no preconceived strong or weak parts of the meter.[67]

The reference to jazz is contestable here, but others agree that the beat does not signify emphasis. Jones argues that a beat clapped in accompaniment to a song:

> is not in the least us[ed] ... to indicate any accentual stress in the melody. The clap has no influence on the melody at all. The latter is perfectly free to pursue its own course, with its own accents arising from its form, so long as it fits the total number of claps required to make the song feel complete.... The claps carry no accent whatever in the African mind. They serve as a yard-stick, a kind of metronome which exists behind the music. Once the clap has started you can never, on any pretext whatever, stretch or diminish the clap-values. They remain constant and *they do not impart any rhythm to the melody itself.* The rhythm of the melody is derived partly from the rhythm of the words as they would normally be spoken, and partly from the rhythm naturally produced by imitative sequences and, as in the West, by the whole build of the tune.[68]

The majority of students of African music, though not all, agree that most African rhythm does not involve meter in the Western sense, despite the existence of a regular pulse. Arom reminds us that 'isochrony means only equality of duration and has nothing to do with accentuation', and adds:

> One of the essential features of most traditional African music is the absence of *regular* accents.... [There is an] absence of a temporal reference matrix based on the regular alternation of an accented sound with one or more unaccented sounds; the notions of measure and strong beat which are intrinsic to such a framework are dispensed with.[69]

---

67 Kubik, 'Africa', *Grove Music Online, Oxford Music Online*.
68 Jones 1959, pp. 20–1.
69 Arom 1991, pp. 182, 191, 229.

This means that although, in addition to the isochronous pulse, there is a regular periodic structure (isoperiodicity) generated by the repetition of cycles of identical or similar musical material, there is no intermediate level between the pulsation and the period corresponding to that of the bar in Western music and based on the occurrence of regular 'strong' beats.[70]

If this is the correct way to understand the functioning of the pulse, it has implications for the question of whether the instances of notes which are played off the beat – a frequent occurrence given that, as we have seen, the beat itself often goes unarticulated – should properly be described as syncopation. Arom argues that the term syncopation is meaningless for such music since the idea of syncopation is inseparable from the theory of accentuation: 'there can be no syncopation in a musical system which makes no use of the contrast between strong and weak beats'. The most that can be said about the prevalence of off-beats in African music, according to Arom, is that it is more *contrametric* than *commetric*.[71] We should note that even if we reject the orthodox accent-based conception of meter in favour of Zuckerkandl's theory of the metric wave, as I have proposed, it does not substantially alter the argument that syncopation depends upon meter and cannot properly exist without it.[72]

Jones discusses syncopation in relation to the time-lines of African music, or *topoi*, in Agawu's terminology. Time-line patterns are 'characterized by irregular, asymmetric structures presented within regular cycles ... [which] often represent the structural core of a musical piece, a condensed and extremely concentrated representation of the rhythmic possibilities open to the musicians and dancers'.[73] One of the most ubiquitous of these is the so-called 'standard pattern', for Jones, the 'African signature tune', which occurs in the music of West, Central and East sub-Saharan Africa. It is a repeating cycle consisting of claps or drum strokes on the first, third, fifth, eighth and tenth of a group of twelve pulse-units. In Western notation it is often rendered as a repeating bar of 12/8, thus:

'Standard pattern'

giving the strong impression that it is a syncopated figure. 'But', says Jones, 'this is a travesty of what the African actually claps'. He continues:

---

70   Arom 1991, p. 211.
71   Arom 1991, p. 208 (Kolinskys' terminology).
72   See Chapter 1, 'What Is Groove'?, pp. 50-1.
73   Kubik, 'Africa', *Grove Music Online, Oxford Music Online*.

He treats his clap-pattern as existing in its own right and not as an off-beat derivative.... No one who has heard a party of villagers clap this pattern could possibly think that there was the slightest suggestion of syncopation in it, that is, the suggestion that it is 'out of step' with some primary background existing in the performer's mind.[74]

This is emphasised by the fact that, as Kubik points out, time-lines are not heard primarily against the beat – four dotted crotchets beats of a 12/8 bar in the case of the above example – but rather against a silent, unvoiced pattern that fills the gaps between the strokes. Kubik shows how a 7-stroke manifest pattern is supplemented by a 5-stroke latent one (or vice versa) in another 12-pulse standard pattern, using a less culturally biased form of notation:[75]

7-stroke	x	.	x	.	x	x	.	x	.	x	.	x
5-stroke	.	x	.	x	.	.	x	.	x	.	x	.

The 5-stroke pattern above is clearly the source of the 'reverse clave' of Latin American music, albeit in a triplet rather than duplet form. In Cuban and Brazilian music, the clave plays a similar role to the African time-line, as a kind of *Ur*-rhythm at the core of the music. However, unlike African music, modern Latin genres such as salsa and samba are metrical, so the clave is heard as syncopated against the meter of the music.

Brandel, too, argues that African rhythms are misinterpreted as being syncopated if they are notated or even simply conceived as operating within a metrical context. Taking as an example the melody of a Mangbetu song, she deploys Western notation in two ways to bring out the difference in conception, first by notating the melody in a regular meter (3/4):[76]

---

74 Jones 1959, pp. 211, 223.
75 Kubik, 'Africa', *Grove Music Online, Oxford Music Online*.
76 Agawu 2003, p. 87.

She comments that the second version is truer to the African conception, and that 'The subsuming of an independent, asymmetric line under a "counter" line of regularity... would be a falsification of the rhythmic intent of the music'. Agawu objects that Brandel has overlooked the choreographic component', namely the regular pulse that would be an element of a performance of this music which finds expression in the dancers' feet.[77] But the argument is not that this music has no regular pulse, only that the pulse does not, in Jones's words, 'indicate any accentual stress in the melody', and 'do[es] not impart any rhythm to the melody itself'.[78] The accents in the melody are derived from the accents of the words being sung which have not been adjusted to fit the musical meter in the manner that we are accustomed to in modern Western song. Certainly, from a notation-reading perspective, the perverse positions of the accents in relation to the meter make the first example very difficult to grasp as a melody, while the second reveals its accentual structure.

The term 'polymetric' is often used in relation to African rhythm: Waterman states that African music uses two or more metrical frameworks simultaneously, while Kubik regards simultaneously performed cycles of different periodic lengths as an example of polymeter.[79] Chernoff argues that African music 'cannot be notated without assigning different meters to the different instruments of the ensemble', and his transcriptions, along with those by Jones are characterised by the use of different time signatures for different instruments and staggered bar-lines.[80] Logically, however, polymetricality must be an impossibility. Meter is a standard that requires universality to be meaningful: either there is a single meter which applies to all parts of the music, or the music is not metrical. For Arom, the term polymeter should be reserved for cases of 'the simultaneous unfolding of several parts in a single work at different tempos *so as not to be reducible to a single metrum*'. What he has in mind are rare instances in modernist works by composers like Charles Ives or Elliot Carter in which the tempo and meter of the material played by one section of the ensemble bears no relation to others being played simultaneously. Such pieces, if genuinely polymetric according to Arom's definition, require multiple conductors. Alternatively, if the various parts of the ensemble share elements of a common rhythmic organisation, the piece is at most polyrhythmic rather than polymetric.[81] African music, with its common pulse units and

---

77   Agawu 2003, 90.
78   Jones 1959, p. 21.
79   Waterman 1951, p. 213; Kubik, 'Africa', *Grove Music Online, Oxford Music Online*.
80   Chernoff 1979, p. 43.
81   Arom 1991, p. 205.

reference pulse, clearly falls into this latter category. It is, therefore, better described as non-metric rather than polymetric.

Historicising Musical Meter

In summary, the main authorities generally agree that, although African music is organised around a strictly isochronous pulse, that pulse is not necessarily explicitly articulated sonically, it is not grouped into a metrical scheme, nor does it constitute a level within a metrical hierarchy, and it does not impart any accentual element to the musical material. Arom points out that there is a historical precedent within the Western tradition for music which, like traditional African music, is pulsed but non-metrical. It is the 'measured' or 'mensural' music of the roughly three hundred-year period beginning with the *ars nova* of the fourteenth century. As we saw in Chapter 1, the term 'measured music' is not at all synonymous with the concept of meter. It simply means that the durations of the notes are in proportion to each other without implying bars (or 'measures'). The unit of measured music was the *batuta* (beat) or the *tactus* (touch), a term which is still used in modern musicology. At that moment in Western music's history, there is no conception of the grouping of the beat into twos, threes or fours that came later with the emergence of bars. The ancient way of marking the beat in performance was the 'bending finger' method, by which the director or choirmaster 'did not count, let us say, 1, 2, 3, 1, 2, 3 ... but rather 1, 1, 1, 1 ...'.[82] Alternatively, time was kept by clapping or tapping on a desk. (The conductor's baton apparently originates for the purpose of striking the lectern in this way, a practice which survived at least until the eighteenth century as testified by Rousseau's recorded complaint about the 'unavoidable evil' of the sound of beating time at the Paris Opera). Souris testifies that in early mensural music, 'the beat is a neutral pulsation with no metric accentuation....', while even music as late as the sixteenth century, according to Emmanuel, 'conceive[d] of rhythm as based on beats, but not on beats marshalled into measures'.[83]

Arom makes the case that there is a marked resemblance between African musical practice and that used in the West in the late Middle Ages and the Renaissance:

> The arrangement of durations in most African music is still based on the same principle as the medieval *tactus*. No use whatsoever is made of the

---

82 Arom 1991, p. 189.
83 Arom 1991, pp. 190, 196.

notion of matrices of regular contrasts of strong and weak beats. African music is thus based, not on measures in the sense of classical musical teaching, but on *pulsations*, i.e., on a sequence of isochronous temporal units which can be materialised as a beat.[84]

This kind of music represents or embodies the measurement of time only in a weak sense. To use again the analogy of length measurement, its ongoing series of neutral pulses might be regarded as equivalent to a ruler with only one unit of measure, marked with only one kind of mark. Without a system of larger units into which the smaller units are integrated, such a ruler would not be particularly effective; it would signal the possibility of measurement without any great measuring capability. Mensural music, therefore, might be regarded historically within the Western tradition as a step on a path from rhythmically free music, such Gregorian chant, and musics such as medieval secular song whose rhythm is derived from that of speech, towards the fully metrical music of later centuries. This step was accomplished by adapting the natural rhythms of speech such that the lengths of all syllables became a multiple of the shortest, sometimes referred to as the *chronos prōtos*, a term which indicates the influence of ancient Greek verse on musicians of this time.[85] This generated a system somewhat more measured than that of poetic feet but still far from the modern conception of musical meter.

If we are correct in conceiving measured music of this type as an 'intermediate stage', the next step in the metrication of European music, according to Emmanuel, occurred with the new fashion for structural symmetry which emerged from the dance craze of the late sixteenth century in the European courts. The bar, and its marker, the barline, which had hitherto existed purely as a notational convenience, at this point took on a central role in rhythmic organisation. I would argue that the fully hierarchical metrical schemes of much twentieth-century popular music represent a still further stage in this process, one whose explanation is more likely to be found in shifts in the experience of, and attitudes towards, temporality in general on the part of whole societies as they entered the period of modernity. These transformations will be examined in Chapter 6. Such a historical conception need not entail a normative element; that is, it need not involve a judgment of progress or improvement. Chailley argues that the rise of the bar resulted in a loss of rhythmic subtlety, jeopardising the rhythmic advances of the mensural system, and resulting in the dogmatic tyranny of the barline. But once established, the die was cast and great composers like Bach were forced to strive to achieve

---

84   Arom 1991, p. 180.
85   Arom 1991, p. 198.

rhythmic flexibility from within the confines of meter by bending it to their will. Adorno, as we shall see, makes a remarkably similar argument about the stultifying effect of the 'beat' in early jazz.

Meter has become so deeply entrenched in Western musical culture that it requires an effort of will to appreciate music which is organised differently. There is of course modern non-metric Western music, but it overwhelmingly eschews isochronous pulse as well as rejecting meter. The conception that has become ingrained in Western musical culture is that pulse and meter are inseparable. Old, non-metric folk tunes are metricated in modern performances, and often harmonised as well, in a process which is regarded as improving them or bringing them up to date. It is not simply the case that Western music notation is ill suited to capturing traditional African rhythms; there is a tendency for the Western ear, as well as the eye, to attempt to impose a metrical scheme on those rhythms. We are conditioned to want to know where the first beat of the bar is, whether or not we have the musical vocabulary to formulate the question in those terms. But if the modern Western ear struggles to appreciate music which has regular pulse but no meter, we should remember that 'there was a time when European music worked more or less in this way'.[86] The difference between traditional African music and modern Western music is not primarily one of geography, still less of culture conceived in ethnic terms, but one of history.

Once we have adopted that perspective, we may be able to put to some use Merriam's discussion of African and Western conceptions of time, by putting it on a historical footing which it otherwise lacks. Merriam suggests that differences in the temporal features of African and Western music may be accounted for in terms of the differences in the conception of time which pertain in African and Western societies. Summarising what he terms the Western conception of time, he says:

> Time for us is essentially linear; that is, it is viewed as a series of equally spaced pulses which are thought to extend infinitely both backward and forward from the particular time point at which we are thinking.[87]

He makes the familiar argument that we in the West spatialise time – we conceive of time in terms of distance – and that, in addition, we tend to hold a reified conception of time:

---

86   Arom 1991, p. 180.
87   Merriam 1982, p. 447.

We in Western Europe have elicited an idea, or a medium, which we call 'time' – or better, 'chronology' – and have calibrated it into a standard gauge against which we associate single events or a series of events. The presence of such a time gauge means that we measure time.[88]

According to Merriam, African conceptions of time are quite different. The famous anthropologist E.E. Evans-Pritchard testifies:

> Strictly speaking, the Nuer have no concept of time and, consequently, no developed abstract system of time-reckoning.... there is no equivalent expression in the Nuer language for our word 'time', and ... they cannot, therefore, as we can, speak of time as though it were something actual, which passes, can be wasted, can be saved, and so forth. Presumably they have in consequence a different perception of time to ours. Certainly they never experience the same feeling of fighting against time, of having to co-ordinate activities with an abstract passage of time. There are no autonomous points of reference to which activities have to conform with precision. Also the Nuer has ... few, and not well-defined, units of time. They think much more easily in terms of activities and of successions of activities ... than they do in units of time.[89]

Even in those African languages which do possess a word for it, the concept of time does not take on the attributes of a substance in its own right. Leach suggests that in some African societies,

> the time process is not experienced as a 'succession of epochal durations' at all; there is no sense of going on and on in the same direction, or round and round the same wheel. On the contrary, time is experienced as something discontinuous, a repetition of repeated reversal, a sequence of oscillations between polar opposites: night and day, winter and summer, drought and flood, age and youth, life and death. In such a scheme the past has no 'depth' to it, all past is equally past; it is simply the opposite of now.[90]

---

88 Ibid.
89 Merriam 1982, p. 445.
90 Merriam 1982, p. 456.

Overall, Merriam argues that in general in African societies, time reckoning is non-linear and takes places by reference to either natural phenomena, or more particularly, social activity. Rather than a linear conception, time is thought of variously as discontinuous, reversible, cyclical, or spiral. He concludes, 'Time is not reckoned as distance, it is not epochal, and it is not measured with special apparatus.... Plus, the smallest time divisions are rough divisions of the day e.g. sunrise, noontime, sunset, night etc.'.[91]

The problem that arises from this is that, contrary to this description of the features of African time reckoning, African music does appear to demand both a linear concept of time and the measurement of time in small units. Merriam attempts to solve the problem by arguing that the small time units are not relevant because African musicians learn their parts within the context of the ensemble; they do not learn them individually by counting against an abstract master pulse as commonly happens in Western music. This gestalt notion of African rhythm is corroborated by Chernoff and others, but it does not adequately deal with the problem of the small units, since a genuinely gestalt-based process of teaching and learning multi-layered rhythm would not necessitate any underlying regular pulse whatsoever. Merriam rejects the suggestion that a dual time reckoning system is at work: one for social life in general and another, involving small units, which operates in connection with music. But dual time reckoning is surely a feasible explanation, or at least it becomes one provided we accept that the isochronous units of music, whether they are small or large, have nothing to do with time measurement. The beats of traditional African music provide a temporal continuum, but without a system of larger units into which they can be determinately integrated, they fall short of a time measurement system. Nor is the fact that they are isochronous an indication of a measuring purpose. Temporal regularity can be explained by the needs of the dancers or by the evenness of physical activities such as walking. Indeed, a type of African rhythm is known to have emerged in East and South-eastern Africa from the mortar pounding of millet in which the participants plays each successive stroke in turn which may be represented diagrammatically in this way:[92]

```
1   -   -   2   -   -   3   -   -   4
    1   -   -   2   -   -   3   -   -
        1   -   -   2   -   -   3   -
```

---

91   Ibid.
92   Kubik, 'Africa', *Grove Music Online, Oxford Music Online*.

This results in a 'multiple main beat' such that, from their own point of view, each participant is playing on the beat. The lack of a single main beat rules out any unitary measuring capability. The pulse generated is nonetheless isochronous due to the demand for efficiency in the work task from which it is derived.

Even where there is a unitary reference beat, as with the continuous undifferentiated beat of European mensural music, the African pulse indicates the potential for music to be a measure of time, without being a sufficiently developed system to achieve it. It requires the development of meter, with its hierarchies of levels, to realise that potential.

The real problem with Merriam's formulation is its ahistorical nature. Presenting the alternative conceptions of time as inherently African or Western assumes, ironically, that these are timeless conditions, and in so doing also precludes the possibility of any explanation as to why such differences exist. It ignores the fact that the 'Western' conception of time arose historically and was preceded in medieval Europe by conceptions of time which bore some similarity to those described by Merriam as 'African', conceptions which gave rise, as they did in Africa, to non-metric, or pre-metric, music.

Musical meter emerges under certain historically determined conditions, conditions which developed first in Europe and which are often subsumed under the umbrella term, 'modernity', but perhaps should be identified more specifically as associated with the rise of capitalism, or at least of 'bourgeois society'. That this development is an urban-led phenomenon that impacted only slowly and weakly on rural folk musics confirms such an analysis, as does the fact that the indigenous popular styles which have emerged in urban Africa during the twentieth century are fully metrical. Agawu fails to make this historical distinction when he discusses genres such as highlife, *jùjú* and *fújì*. Highlife, like many other African popular styles, is not evidence, as he believes, that the differences between traditional African and Western musics have been exaggerated as part of a process of 'othering' similar to that identified by Edward Said in *Orientalism* as 'the denial of nonuniqueness to Africa'.[93] Highlife does indeed use a traditional African time-line or *topos*, but because it is a thoroughly twentieth-century genre, emerging first in 1930s Ghana, the traditional rhythm is subsumed within a strongly metrical framework.[94] Similarly, the *clave* of Latin American music is a metricated version of an African *topos*, or a 'truce' between (traditional) African and (modern) European concepts, as Small prefers to put it.[95] Modern Cuban styles, along with highlife, Nigerian

---

93   Agawu 2003, p. 94.
94   'Highlife', *Encyclopedia of Popular Music*.
95   Small 1987, p. 270.

Afrobeat, Congolese *rumba*, Cameroonian *makossa*, South African *mbube*, and many others are all musics of the African city, products of the urbanisation and industrialisation of those countries, patchy though that process has been. Agawu recognises the emergence of these non-traditional musics and attributes it to direct Western influences: 'African popular music may be understood historically as a direct outgrowth of colonialism'.[96] He says:

> The formal arrangement of highlife songs may reproduce the protocol of big bands of the swing era. ... Calypso, Cuban rhythms, and other idioms of New World music are found in highlife. And in more recent times, American rock, African-American gospel, and, perhaps most spectacularly, rap have made their way into African popular music.[97]

All this is true, and the influence of, for example, American funk on *Afrobeat* and jazz on South African township styles is strong and explicit. But to conceive African popular music solely in terms of Western cultural influence is to take an idealist view which misses the material transformations that created the conditions for such syncretism and hybridity to proliferate. Agawu points out that nineteenth century colonialism influenced African music-making in important ways. There were concerts of European classical music in the colonial capitals and Christian hymns were spread by proselytising European missionaries.[98] But this was a fragile and superficial influence which had little effect on the traditional forms of music-making of the continent except for those small circles of Africans in direct contact with the colonial populations. In general, colonialism is often recognised as having retarded the more fundamental economic and social development of Africa. It is with the ending of colonialism that the great transformations have taken place, driven by endogenous factors as well as being shaped by exogenous ones. What has been transformed is not simply a thin veneer of culture on the surface of a more or less static society, but conditions of life as a whole amounting to nothing less than a process of transition from traditional societies to modern ones, albeit in patchy and contradictory ways.

It is primarily because the conditions of life in the megacities of Africa are now close to those that obtain, especially for the poor, in the advanced societies of the West, that African music now shares more fundamental characteristics with that of the West. Chief among these characteristics is the particularly

---

96   Agawu 2003, p. 15.
97   Agawu 2003, p. 146.
98   Agawu 2003, pp. 12–13.

intense form of metrical organisation I have been calling groove. To argue this is not to deny the huge influence exerted on American music by forced migrants from Africa, or even to deny that a component of that influence was rhythmic. The argument that the syncopation central to groove music derives at least in part from the staggered cross-rhythms of traditional African music is a persuasive one, as long as it is recognised that staggered cross-rhythms only become syncopations in the context of meter. But since the musical culture transported to America by Africans was a non-metric one, we must reject the argument that groove arrived in Western music from this source.

CHAPTER 3

Bergsonism and Unmeasurable Time

In the Introduction to this book, we began to explore the contested terrain of the nature of the intimate relationship between music and time. Few would contest the statement that music is an 'art of time', but there are various ways to interpret such a view. At one extreme is the position of Philip Alperson, who argues that music's temporality is no different from that of any other type of occurrence. Music is 'an art whose method of presentation is progressive in time'; it has a determinate period of duration and involves an irreversible succession of events which is perceived as temporal through the use of memory and expectation.[1] This position is consistent with Kant's understanding of time as the form of intuition by which we are able to make temporal sense of perception. Music is temporal for us in exactly the same way that everything else we perceive is temporal. Here, music simply takes place *in* time.

In the more or less opposite camp are those who argue that music's relationship to temporality goes much deeper. Joan Stambaugh insists that music is not a structure *in* time, but is itself a temporal structure.[2] 'The time that bounds music is not outside music itself, enclosing it as a container holds its contents'.[3] Rather, time 'constitutes the concrete stuff of music'.[4] Time is not merely form, that which organises temporally the musical content. Rather, what is unique about music is that time is both content and form:

> Time ceases to be a form in which something happens when the 'content' of this form is not separable from the form itself. When the content itself is 'time', time becomes the 'happening' itself. It is not that *in which* something happens, but rather the very process of this happening.[5]

Stambaugh is among those who argue that musical time is time made audible. Similarly, Suzanne Langer maintains that in the same way that the 'plastic arts' such as sculpture make space visible, '*music makes time audible, and its form*

---

1 Alperson 1980, p. 411.
2 Stambaugh 1964, p. 266.
3 Stambaugh 1964, p. 277.
4 Stambaugh 1964, p. 271.
5 Stambaugh 1964, p. 273.

and continuity sensible.[6] Music is capable of doing this because it is a symbolic form, albeit one whose symbols are not completely distinct from that which they symbolise. Others go still further and express the notion the central purpose of music is to present 'the image of time'; that rhythm, the organisation of events in time and the motion that results, comprises music's very essence.[7] Composer Roger Sessions writes:

> It seems to me that the essential medium of music, the basis of its expressive powers and the element which gives it its unique quality among the arts, is *time*, made living for us through its expressive essence, *movement*.[8]

But what kind of time is it that music presents or is symbolic of? Langer answers by arguing that:

> The realm in which tonal entities move is a realm of pure *duration*.... it is something completely different from the time in which our public and practical life proceeds. It is completely incommensurable with the progress of common affairs. Musical duration is an image of what might be termed 'lived' or 'experienced' time – the passage of life that we feel as expectation becomes 'now', and 'now' turns into unalterable fact. Such a passage is measurable only in terms of sensibilities, tensions, and emotions; and it has not merely a different measure, but an altogether different structure from practical or scientific time.[9]

This kind of time differs from commonsense time, from scientific, practical, clock time. Clock time measures change only as two contrasting states, before and after, the outcome of change rather than its content.[10] The rhythm of music is like the rhythm of life: it is not a rhythm of equal measurements of time, of regular ticks of the clock or metronome, which are not genuinely rhythmic at all. Rather:

---

6   Langer 1953, p. 110.
7   Langer 1953, p. 104.
8   Quoted in Langer 1953, p. 111 (fn).
9   Langer 1953, p. 109.
10   Langer 1953, p. 112.

the essence of rhythm is the preparation of a new event by the ending of a previous one ... Rhythm is the setting up of new tensions by the resolution of former ones. They need not be of equal duration at all.[11]

That is why breathing is rhythmic even when irregular. 'The concept of rhythm as a relation between tensions rather than as a matter of equal divisions of time (i.e. meter)' means that all the elements of music can be considered rhythmic as they prepare the future and generate expectation, 'including the expectation of sheer continuity'.[12]

All this is something of a challenge to the existence of meter in music, and still more so to groove, understood as an aesthetic of measured time. The argument that measurement, or temporal regularity, fails to capture the true essence of time – or *durée* – derives from the critique of conventional understandings of time made by Henri Bergson. It is a position which underpins much of the hostility to groove music and which informed the modernist sensibility in relation to the aesthetic representation of time. It is, therefore, to Bergson's ideas that we must now turn.

Bergson's Metaphysics of Time

Bergson's philosophy of time begins with a critique of the objective, commonsense concept of time which is informed by the physical sciences. Physics and astronomy in particular, Bergson argues, have spatialised time, they have failed to recognise the fundamental difference between space and time. Space is necessarily thought of as homogeneous and infinitely divisible. Objects are conceived as existing at certain spatial points or moving a measurable distance between identifiable positions. These conceptions and methods have been uncritically transferred from space to time, with the result that time is thought of in spatial terms, and expressed in terms of extensity as a line capable of being divided into equal subdivisions. Our very language – 'length of time', 'at this point in time', 'in the distant past', etc. – reflects this way of thinking.

Such a way of dealing with time is the inevitable product of the pragmatic concerns of life, but is nonetheless erroneous and inadequate, according to Bergson. It results in the destruction of the very essence of time itself: succession. Time cannot be expressed as a line or as a chain of discrete moments:

---

11   Langer 1953, p. 127.
12   Langer 1953, p. 129.

Note that the mental image thus shaped implies the perception, no longer successive, but simultaneous, of a *before* and *after*, and that it would be a contradiction to suppose a succession which was only a succession, and which nevertheless was contained in one and the same instant.[13]

Spatialising time involves presenting it all at once, reducing its inherent successive quality, its dynamic, to lifeless simultaneity:

[One should not] admit the possibility of giving an adequate representation of time in space, of the successive by the simultaneous.[14]

The spatialised conception of time is intimately bound up with quantification, with the demand for measurement associated with the modern scientific method. It fragments time into a series of equivalent instants which can then be numbered, an atomistic methodology which seeks to dismantle everything in order to understand it.[15]

The evidence, for Bergson, that time is of a different order than space is initially provided by psychology. Mental states are not discrete entities, following one another in a chain, or like beads on a thread, touching without penetrating one another. Since our mental experiences flow into one another, permeate and melt into one another, a true conception of temporal succession should reflect this:

We can thus conceive of succession without distinction, and think of it as a mutual penetration, an interconnection and organization of elements, each one of which represents the whole, and cannot be distinguished from it except by abstract thought.[16]

Bergson uses the term *durée* for this succession without distinction, time without division, 'the form which the succession of our conscious states assumes when our ego lets itself *live*, when it refrains from separating its present state from its former states'.[17] *Durée* is genuine temporality, boundless, whole, the

---

13 Bergson 2002b, p. 60.
14 Bergson 1996, p. 114.
15 Moore 1996, p. 56.
16 Ansell Pearson and Mullarkey 2002, p. 60.
17 As Moore points out, *durée*'s usual translation as 'duration' imparts the sense of a measured time-span which Bergson was anxious to avoid. Moore prefers 'durance', but I will stick with the French word (Moore 1996, p. 58).

condition of life and evolution. Spatialisation sacrifices the qualitative heterogeneity of *durée* for a homogeneous web of temporal points, it reduces genuine temporal flow to a series of snapshots. As a result, science fails adequately to comprehend movement or change. It produces a 'cinematographic' model of the world which attempts to capture movement through a succession of immobilities, stationary moments, 'virtual stopping-places'. This 'cinematographical character of our knowledge of things is due to the kaleidoscopic character of our adaptation to them' – our attention is not on the movement produced by shaking the kaleidoscope but on the new stationary arrangement of the pieces. Time is thus treated by science merely as an 'independent variable', marking the interval between two distinct states but playing no role in what happens in between.[18]

In short, Bergson's conception of *durée* is time as flux, as unfolding, as Becoming, as a boundless, indivisible whole, in which past and present coexist in an interpenetrating multiplicity of rhythms and tensions. It is not difficult to see how such a view might be attractive to those attempting to formulate an understanding of musical time, especially as Bergson himself drew musical parallels with *durée*:

> When we listen to a melody we have the purest impression of succession we could possibly have – an impression as far removed as possible from that of simultaneity – and yet it is the very continuity of the melody and impossibility of breaking it up which make that impression upon us.[19]

However, even a melody embodies too much organisation and delineation of form to be true to *durée*:

> A melody to which we listen with our eyes closed and thinking of nothing else, is very close to coinciding with this time which is the very fluidity of our inner life; but it still has too many qualities, too much definition, and we should first have to obliterate the differences between the tones, then the distinctive characteristics of tone itself, retain of it only the continuation of that which precedes in that which follows, the uninterrupted transition, multiplicity without divisibility, and succession without separation, in order at last to find fundamental time. Such is duration immediately perceived, without which we should have no idea of time.[20]

---

18 Bergson 2002a, pp. 27–8.
19 Bergson 2002d, p. 261.
20 Bergson 2002c, p. 205.

Despite these reservations about music's suitability as a model for *durée*, it is usually a Bergsonian concept of time-as-flux which informs, consciously or not, those musicians and critics who wish to reject meter and endorse temporal irregularity in music.

Deleuze and the Multiplicity of Time

Pushing thought about time still further in the direction Bergson began, Gilles Deleuze deserves consideration here because of the relevance of his philosophy to much of the late twentieth-century musical avant garde. Deleuze shares Bergson's critique of spatialised time, and although he does not put the term *durée* at the centre of his thought, he agrees with Bergson that time should be understood *intensively*, as lived flux, rather than *extensively* as homogeneous measure.[21]

What Deleuze sees in Bergson's thought is an openness to times or durations other than our own, and it is this intuition which Deleuze makes foundational to his own philosophical project of completely decentring the human subject. If Bergson's thought represents a subjectification of time through the rejection of a single, uniform time which is held to flow somehow independently of the durations that occupy it, Deleuze uses Bergson's thought as a means to undermine the very concept of subjectivity itself. If there is no 'master time', but instead a multiplicity of durations, then the guarantee of identity or continuity of the self through time upon which subjectivity depends is called into question. Instead of a continuity of sameness, Deleuze emphasises 'virtuality', in Bergson's sense of the word: possibilities, potentialities, differences. Time should be understood not as a unidirectional thread comprised of the repetition of equivalent instants, but as multiplicity, flux, and singular, unique events (haecceities). He insists that we should always be aware that things could be, and will be, other than they are.

Deleuze shares Bergson's emphasis on biology and on evolution but again takes the argument further: not only should the human subject be displaced from the centre of the picture but so should the human species and all organic life. Deleuze puts life itself at the centre of his thought; life not in any of its particular forms or manifestations, but life understood as potential, as force, as the power to differ. To conceive of life as any particular form is already to fall into a rigid way of thinking, to deny the possibility that things could be different.

---

21 Colebrook 2006, p. 21.

Our human perspective is a very limited one, determined by our eye-brain body complex, just as the tick's (to use an example Deleuze takes from the biologist Von Uexküll) is determined and limited by its physical conditions. Thought must try to get beyond its body's limited perspective to perceive other durations, and beyond that to intuit time itself. Modernist cinema can help us do that, first by giving us perspectives that we, as embodied humans, could not hope to have (Deleuze believes technology can perform a liberating function), but also by presenting time as something other than a continuous thread through which we, as integral subjects, travel.[22] Cinema is an art form that can present a non-homogeneous time capable of fluctuation and reversal, especially if, like modernist literature, it avoids the use of teleological narrative as its organising principle.

What kind of music does this philosophical understanding of time imply? How does Deleuze talk about time? He and his collaborator, Félix Guattari, counterpose two kinds of time, two kinds of temporality:

> *Aeon:* the indefinite time of the event, the floating line that knows only speeds and continually divides that which transpires into an already-there that is at the same time not-yet-here, a simultaneous too-late and too-early, a something that is both going to happen and has just happened.[23]

Aeon is the time of the infinitive of the verb rather than any particular tense, 'a floating time against pulsed time or tempo'. The second kind of temporality is:

> *Chronos*: the time of measure that situates things and persons, develops a form, and determines a subject.

Deleuze and Guattari then immediately introduce a musical example:

> Boulez distinguishes tempo and nontempo in music: the 'pulsed time' of a formal and functional music, both floating and machinic [not mechanical – MA], which has nothing but speeds or differences in dynamic. In short, the difference is not at all between the ephemeral and the durable,

---

22 Interestingly, Deleuze does not share Bergson's view, consistent with his overall position, of cinema technology as a prime example of the reduction of time as continuous flux to a series of instants, or snapshots (Colebrook 2006, p. 30).
23 Deleuze and Guattari 1988, p. 262.

nor even between the regular and the irregular, but between two modes of individuation, two modes of temporality.[24]

The temporality of *Chronos* is related to the 'plane of organisation and development', that is, to the development of forms and subjects, which in turn requires a 'punctual system' capable of identifying points in a geometric fashion via horizontal and vertical axes. For Deleuze and Guattari, this system follows an *arborescent* model in which lines are subordinated to points because they are defined by their ends rather than that which exists in between. The plane of organisation and development is like a plan: it is not given with its effects, it can only be inferred from them.

Aeon is the temporality of the plane of consistency or composition, in which there are only speeds and slownesses between unformed elements, and where exist powers without subjects. This is a linear system in which lines are not the result of the plotting of a series of points but exist in their own right. This plane is a plane of immanence: it does not exist separately from its elements. Nothing develops, there are just haecceities and individual affects. Its structural model is the *rhizome* with its non-hierarchical multiplicity of entry and exit points.

It is this latter temporality and the plane of composition associated with it which Deleuze and Guattari regard as a better model both for understanding the myriad forms which life has taken, and has the potential to take in the universe, and for the kinds of thinking and aesthetic responses we should undertake in order to be adequate to it.

What does this mean for music? Music, especially in its notational form, Deleuze and Guattari suggest, can be understood according to a punctual system: melodic lines and bass lines can be seen as horizontals which, when combined, give rise to a vertical or harmonic line or plane which moves along the horizontal.

What great composers must do, and this goes for visual artists as well, is disrupt or go beyond the punctual system of coordinates and free the diagonal, draw a transversal which is not a localised connection between points but rather is a line which has no origin but is always already in the middle, a genuine creation. Deleuze calls this a 'line of flight', a trajectory of deterritorialisation, where deterritorialisation is understood as a breaking away from fixed, established connections and systems, allowing the making of new connections and assemblages characteristic of life.

What moves along this transversal in music is a 'sound block' which exists in '"nonpulsed time": a deterritorialized rhythmic block that has abandoned

---

24   Ibid.

points, coordinates and measure, like a drunken boat that melds with the line or draws a plane of consistency'.[25]

On this basis, we can begin to summarise Deleuze's views on what music should be. First, like all art, it should be deterritorialising; that is to say, it should go beyond what is given, what is established, to make new connections and take new directions. It should break free of formal constraints, preconceived plans or forms, to allow the sonic material to speak for itself and to open out onto the Cosmos. But solidified musical form is not the only 'territorialising' force that must be overcome: the Western tonal organisation of pitch and even tempered scales themselves also represent territorialising punctual systems which limit sound's potential to become expressive. Hence music should not shy away from the use of noise and non-pitched aspects of sound and of the human voice – glissando, timbral effects, and so on.

Most pertinently for the question of time in music, Deleuze argues for the liberation of rhythm, in all its irregularity and multiplicity, from the territorialising straightjacket of musical meter. Rather than conceive of any reciprocal relationship between rhythm and meter, Deleuze and Guattari, not surprisingly given their Bergsonian antipathy towards measured time, regard meter explicitly as the enemy of rhythm:

> It is well known that rhythm is not meter or cadence, even irregular meter or cadence: there is nothing less rhythmic than a military march. The tom-tom is not 1-2, the waltz is not 1, 2, 3, music is not binary or ternary... Meter, whether regular or not, assumes a coded form whose unit of measure may vary, but in a noncommunicating milieu, whereas rhythm is the Unequal or the Incommensurable that is always undergoing transcoding. It does not operate in homogeneous space-time, but by heterogeneous blocks. It changes direction.[26]

Life is rhythmic, its myriad rhythms arising from the milieux that are centred on every living thing. 'Every milieu is vibratory, a block of space-time constituted by the periodic repetition of a component' congealed from the chaos of the surrounding cosmos. 'Rhythm', say Deleuze and Guattari, 'is the milieu's [that is, life's – MA] answer to chaos'.

They then anticipate a possible objection: if rhythm is inherently unequal, how can it arise from vibrations, from periodic repetition? They explain:

---

25   Deleuze and Guattari 1988, p. 296.
26   Deleuze and Guattari 1988, p. 313.

A milieu does in fact exist by virtue of a periodic repetition, but one whose only effect is to produce a difference by which the milieu passes into another milieu. It is the difference that is rhythmic, not the repetition, which nevertheless produces it: productive rhythm has nothing to do with reproductive meter.[27]

In other words, rhythm is produced in the interaction *between* milieus, *between* particular manifestations of life, rather than solely within them. Rhythm is the 'in-between'. That apparent contradiction surmounted, Deleuze and Guattari affirm the essential non-pulsed, non-metric nature of rhythm, and thereby of time itself – or, rather, of the multiplicity of times. As they put it, 'Here, time is not an a priori form; rather the refrain [expressive melody and rhythm] is the a priori form of time, which in each case fabricates different times'.[28]

As has become evident, Deleuze in effect proposes a normative musical aesthetic, one which at one point opposes Eastern music, with its 'speeds and slownesses, movement and rest' to the entire Western tradition of organisation and development.[29] When directing his attention towards Western music, Deleuze's approach is thoroughly avant-gardist in outlook. If rational and regular organisation of pitch and time, planned organisation of musical material, and standard uses of instrumental and vocal timbres are all territorialising restrictions on music's potential to open onto the Cosmos, then all must be challenged and overthrown. Those twentieth-century composers whom he cites with approval include Pierre Boulez, John Cage, Olivier Messiaen, Karlheinz Stockhausen and Luciano Berio. Boulez's views in particular on music seem to coincide closely with Deleuze's and as we have seen, his thoughts on 'smooth' or non-pulsed time form part of Deleuze's argument.[30] Cage and Stockhausen are praised for their processual approach to composition which eschews structural plan, and, along with Berio, for their experimentation with non-traditional sound: electronic sources, unorthodox uses of the voice, and silence used as a sonorous material.

However, it is Messiaen who must take pride of place in any summary of the application of Bergsonian temporal concepts to musical composition. Messiaen follows Bergson directly in theorising two kinds of time – lived duration (*temps vécue*) and abstract or structured time (*temps structuré*) – with the

---

27 Deleuze and Guattari 1988, p. 314.
28 Deleuze and Guattari 1988, p. 349.
29 Deleuze and Guattari 1988, p. 270.
30 Campbell 2010, p. 152.

aim of musically expressing the former.[31] He also shares Deleuze's obsession with birdsong, an index of both an anti-anthropocentrism and an anti-metricalism in music. For Deleuze and Guattari, art is not the privilege of humans, but rather arises from the becoming-expressive of milieus, and is bound up with the marking of territory through colour, odour, sound, or silhouette. The refrain need not be sonic but its paradigmatic form is 'rhythm and melody that have been territorialized because they have become expressive – and have become expressive because they are territorializing', and is exemplified by birdsong. Messiaen shares the view that birds are musicians and much of his work, especially the piano cycle *Catalogue d'Oiseaux*, attempts to invoke the sonic essence of the songs of various bird species which he had painstakingly recorded and transcribed. Perhaps as a result of his attempt to remain faithful to the non-pulsed singing of birds, Messiaen's approach to musical time is ametrical, non-teleological and reversible. His music has been described as 'both timeless and intensely rhythmical', his aim: 'to suspend the sense of time in his music... in order to express the idea of the "eternal"'.[32]

If the music of Messiaen, and perhaps also the other avant-garde composers endorsed by Deleuze and Guattari, is to be taken as exemplary of a philosophic and aesthetic perspective which rejects the homogenising, measured, spatialised form of time in order to release the multiplicity of times of becoming, of the pure event, of difference, then it can be argued that the outcome can often be an attenuation of the sense of time in the music rather than its intensification. For Messiaen, this is the intention: his evocation of the eternal has religious motives, and his attempt to give expression to 'time beyond time' is exemplified by the title of one of his most important works, *Quartet for the End of Time*. But the same might also be true for less spiritually motivated musicians adopting similar temporal techniques. There is a clear tendency that the attempt to do justice musically to the temporal multiplicity of life results instead in conveying non-worldliness. We might be entitled to infer that there is a necessary connection between the expression of 'timefulness' via multiple and irregular temporalities and the resulting impression of *timelessness*, a connection which may have its roots in the ahistorical and quasi-spiritual vitalism at the heart of Deleuze's thought. Griffiths is explicit in identifying this aspect of Messiaen's music with its lack of meter:

> Instead of a metre, which gives each moment in a bar a different significance and hence fosters a sense of orderly progression, Messiaen's music

---

31   Campbell 2010, p. 231.
32   Bogue 2003, p. 28.

is most frequently tied to a pulse, which insists that all moments are the same, that the past, the present and the future are identifiable. Sometimes the pulse is so slow that causal links are sufficiently distended not to be felt: in these extreme adagios the possibility of eternity becomes actually present in the music.[33]

The other school of modern composition which receives endorsement in Deleuze and Guattari's *Mille Plateaux* is the minimalism of Steve Reich, Philip Glass and others, which, though pulsed, seeks, through the use of repetitive micro-patterns with their shifting accents, to avoid the measured regularity of metrical music. But these kinds of minimalist techniques also struggle to express time as becoming or development and instead achieve a sense of static time – what David Kramer calls 'moment time'.[34] The issue of the shortcomings of modernist musical techniques in relation to the ability adequately to express temporality will be revisited in the Chapter 5 in the context of Adorno's writings, and I return to minimalist time in the final chapter.

Despite the distinctiveness of the philosophy and the uniqueness of the terminology, what Deleuze presents us with is a familiar avant-gardist aesthetic, one which argues for the overthrow of all established artistic conventions in the name of innovation, creativity, the rejection of formulae and the pushing of boundaries. It is a position which, despite its very different philosophical pedigree, bears a remarkable resemblance to that of Adorno, a similarity which others have commented upon.[35] In both cases, it leaves its proponents cut off from the vast majority of music-making and listening which takes place in the contemporary world. Adorno's condemnation of popular music is well known and explicitly articulated. It has been claimed that Deleuze held a much more open attitude to Western rock and pop, but the evidence for such a view is limited to his occasional quotation of a song lyric, and a relationship with some musician devotees of his philosophy active at the experimental end of the popular music field.[36] The spirit of Deleuze's and Guattari's argument about music suggests that the essence of popular song is, or is akin to, refrain, that is, the block of content proper to music, but that which is not yet music, and which must be deterritorialised in order to become music. They argue that the refrain 'can as easily develop its force into a sickly sweet ditty as into the purest motif... And sometimes the two combine: Beethoven used as a

---

33   Griffiths 1985, p. 15.
34   Kramer 1988, p. 169.
35   Nesbitt 2004.
36   Murphy and Smith 2001.

"signature tune".[37] On this reading, the answer to the question, 'Is pop music (for Deleuze)?', is an emphatic 'No', because it generally fails to draw the diagonals required to make the deterritorialising leap.[38] From this point of view, Western popular music's chief weakness is its failure to break from its intensive use of regular meter, its adherence to a unitary metronome or clock time, which, perhaps unlike in film, has tended to intensify with recent technological innovations in its production.

Zuckerkandl's Audible Time

If Deleuze represents one direction in which the Bergsonian critique of time-as-measure can be taken in relation to music, the aesthetic theory of Victor Zuckerkandl demonstrates an alternative. In contrast to Deleuze, Zuckerkandl manages to combine elements of Bergson's conception of time with a defence, or even celebration, of meter in Western music.

Zuckerkandl's distinctive thinking is most overtly and consciously Bergsonian in his explanation of motion in music. A melody imparts a sense of continuous movement; to grasp a melody is to follow its dynamic shape and direction, and its meaning to a great extent resides in this quality of movement. Yet there is nothing in a melody which actually moves, there is just a series of tones, each subsequent one replacing the last. Each tone has a definite and steady pitch, and the feeling of continuous movement between each tone and the next does not depend upon small pitch differences between successive tones, still less is it the result of continuous changes of pitch – *glissandi* or *portamenti*. The 'gaps' between tones do not require to be filled; even rests between the tones of a melody do not destroy the continuity of the motion.

Zuckerkandl turns to Bergson for help in understanding this apparent puzzle. Bergson insists that 'all real change is indivisible change. We like to treat it as a series of distinct states which form, as it were, a line in time. This is perfectly natural', but destroys real motion by attempting to comprehend it in term of spatial data.[39] There is such a thing as pure motion, pure dynamism:

> There are changes, but there are underneath the change no things which change: change has no need of a support. There are movements, but there is no inert or invariable object which moves: movement does not imply a mobile.

---

37   Deleuze and Guattari 1988, p. 348.
38   Hainge 2004.
39   Bergson 2002d, p. 258.

And Bergson uses another musical analogy. When we listen to a melody:

> do we not have the clear perception of a movement which is not attached to a mobile, of a change without anything changing? This change is enough, it is the thing itself.[40]

Zuckerkandl enlists the support of psychological theory and experiment to show that motion is perceived as a direct and single sensation rather than as something being successively in successive places.[41] From this he argues that it is not the different pitches of each tone in a melody which generate its movement, but the dynamic qualities they possess which derive from their position in the tonal system:

> The dynamic quality of a tone... is a statement of its incompleteness, its will to completion. To hear a tone as dynamic quality, as a direction, a pointing, means hearing at the same time beyond it, beyond it in the direction of its will, and going towards the next expected tone. Listening to music, then, we are not first *in* one tone, then in the next, and so forth. We are, rather, always *between* the tones, *on the way* from tone to tone; our hearing does not remain with the tone, it reaches through it and beyond it.[42]

This is not simply, for Zuckerkandl, a matter of saying that musical motion is a special breed of motion, or an 'ideal' or 'abstract' motion. Musical motion is paradigmatic of *all* motion, *all* change. Because there are no spatial images to distract and mislead us, in Bergson's words, 'pure change remains, sufficient unto itself, in no way divided, in no way attached to a "thing" which changes'.[43] Music shows us clearly what we struggle to grasp in relation to other phenomena.

Zuckerkandl makes a similar claim concerning time in an equally bold and distinctive treatment of rhythm and meter in music. His starting point is a metaphysical claim about the universality of rhythm which echoes Bergson's vitalism. Melody and harmony are peculiar to the realm of music, but, says Zuckerkandl, 'rhythm is one manifestation of the reign of law throughout the universe'.[44] Moreover, rhythm is not the same as metronomical correctness, it

---

40 Bergson 2002d, p. 259.
41 Zuckerkandl 1973, pp. 129–41; the work of William James, Wertheimer and others.
42 Zuckerkandl 1973, pp. 136–7.
43 Bergson 2002d, p. 259.
44 Zuckerkandl 1973, p. 158.

does not depend on regularity. In the Western music of the last few hundred years it is meter that has imposed a regularity of time on rhythm. However, as we saw in Chapter 1, Zuckerkandl argues that the conventional explanation of meter is wrong. Meter is not produced from a pattern of strong and weak accents as it is conventionally explained, but is much better understood as oscillation. Psychological experiments show that a series of equally spaced pulses are perceived not as 1-2-3-4-5 etc., but as 1-2-1-2 etc. where '2' is not number two but 'away-from-one'. What this implies is that at the heart of meter is a cyclical motion or wave comprising a motion of 'to-fro' or 'away-back', and that the standard understanding of causality in meter must be reversed: 'it is not a differentiation of accents which produces meter, it is meter which produces a differentiation of accents'.[45]

It is tempting to counterpose meter and rhythm, to see them as the embodiments of opposing principles working against each other – meter as mechanical and dogmatic, rhythm as creative and vital.[46] This suggests that meter threatens to stifle the freedom and life from rhythm in the way that the recitation of poetry with mechanical timing destroys its rhythm and fluidity. But what Western music in the modern era has discovered is a way of enhancing rhythm through meter: as Zuckerkandl says, 'not rhythm despite meter, but, on the contrary, rhythm from meter, rhythm fed by the forces dammed up in meter'.[47] The key to this is an understanding of meter as wave, such that 'to put it metaphorically: the ground on which the tones fall is itself in wave motion'.[48] There are forces at work within meter which impart to a tone a different rhythmic impulse depending upon which phase of the metric cycle it falls and which make the counting of beats unnecessary. Metrical order is a dynamic order so that while, as we have seen, for Zuckerkandl, 'melody [is] motion in the dynamic field of tones, rhythm [is] *motion in the dynamic field of meter*'.[49]

This conceptualisation of meter as *field* has important consequences for arguments about the precise sense in which music is a temporal art. Zuckerkandl puts it like this:

> Musical meter is not born in the beats at all, but in the empty intervals *between* the beats, in the places where 'time merely elapses'.... The

---

45 Zuckerkandl 1973, p. 169.
46 See drummer Tony Oxley explaining the destruction of meter necessary for 'free improvisation': 'It was a release from the dogma of the beat' (Bailey 1992, p. 87).
47 Zuckerkandl 1973, p. 160.
48 Zuckerkandl 1973, p. 172.
49 Zuckerkandl 1973, pp. 173–4.

function of time here is, then, no longer that of the empty vessel, which contains the tones, or the bowling alley down which the tones roll; on the contrary, time intervenes, is directly active, in the musical context.... Music is temporal art not in the barren and empty sense that its tones succeed one another 'in time'; it is temporal art in the concrete sense that it enlists the flux of time as a force to serve its ends.[50]

Zuckerkandl recognises that this represents a challenge to the standard conception of time as simply a 'form of experience', a means of ordering events. For him, music shows time as itself active: 'The wave is not an event *in* time, but an event *of* time. Time happens; time is an event'.[51] And in another striking reversal, he argues: 'Change does not create time; time literally creates change'.[52]

In contradiction to the view that only events are experienced, not time itself, Zuckerkandl asserts the opposite: 'through tones, time becomes concrete experiential content; the experience of musical rhythm is an experience of time made possible through tones'.[53] The fact that meter continues to be felt through rests in music decisively proves it. Meter and rhythm themselves are not effects *in* time, but the effects *of* time, or, more specifically, of the temporality of tones: 'time [is] the agent of the forces active in meter and rhythm'.[54] In the same way that magnetic forces cannot be separated from the magnetism that produces them, 'time' as an entity cannot be separated from the temporal forces in rhythm. 'The existence of time is the same as its activity'.[55]

We now come to a crucial element of Zuckerkandl's treatment of time, in which he states, on the basis of music, that 'time knows no equality of parts'.[56] As applied to music, this amounts to the bold and surprising assertion that, contrary to established understanding, meter and rhythm are not based upon a regular pulse which marks out equal divisions of time. What underlies this position is again Bergson's critique of the spatialisation of time in which he maintains that the ways of measuring time developed and used by science are in fact not measurements of time as such, but measurements of space.

---

50 Zuckerkandl 1973, p. 181.
51 Zuckerkandl 1973, p. 184.
52 Zuckerkandl 1973, p. 185.
53 Zuckerkandl 1973, p. 203.
54 Zuckerkandl 1973, p. 206.
55 Zuckerkandl 1973, p. 207.
56 Zuckerkandl 1973, p. 208.

The argument is worth following in some detail because in Zuckerkandl's hands in results in a significant challenge to conventional musical thinking.

For Bergson, all real time is lived time, inner time, the continuous flow of our existence, our *durée*. We do not exist *in* an abstract medium called time, rather our existence *is* time, is *durée*. This does not mean that we are all individually locked up in our private incommensurable times, but it does mean that our *durée* forms our intuitive conception of time and that the outer world only has time for us through its connection with our own *durée*. We arrive at the hypothesis that there is a single, universal, physical time only on the basis of assuming a chain of connections stretching between us and every other individual and element of the universe. This is a kind of 'relay' model in which the conceptualisation of a single *durée* enveloping the universe is accumulated on the basis of the shared experiences of an infinite series of adjacent individuals.[57] There can be no question of time without consciousness, or more particularly, that component of consciousness which pertains directly to time, memory. This is because 'duration is essentially a continuation of what no longer exists into what does exist. This is real time, perceived and lived'.[58]

Bergson insists that *durée* is not measurable, for the simple reason that, unlike other objects of measurement, it is not possible to superimpose successive durations, to lay them side by side in order to compare them. Instead we measure space as a proxy for time – time is spatialised in order to measure it. In Bergson's example, the motion which draws a line on a piece of paper is a continuity of consciousness, pure *durée*, indivisible and unmeasurable. But in the resulting line on the paper 'all is juxtaposition and no longer succession; this is the unfolded [rather than the unfolding], which is the record of the result of motion, and which will be its symbol as well. Now, this line is divisible, measurable.... Time is measured through the intermediary of motion'.[59] But the reason this is possible is that our actions in the world have a dual aspect: in drawing the line, the muscular sensations of our inner *durée* produce a visual trajectory in space and thereby connect our *durée* with it. When we choose to take a motion independent of our own body, such as the earth's rotation, as the measure of time, this counts as time and not space for us only if we think of our own body as potentially being part of it, if 'it *could have been for us* the unfolding of time'.[60]

---

57 Bergson 2002c, pp. 205–6.
58 Bergson 2002c, p. 208.
59 Bergson 2002c, pp. 208–9.
60 Bergson 2002c, p. 210.

Still, according to Bergson, we have not yet measured time in any determinate sense; for that we need simultaneities, and the same approach applies. Our *durée* is a necessary component in the identification of simultaneity: 'We... call two external flows that occupy the same duration "simultaneous" because they both depend upon the duration of a third, our own'. It requires the coming together of three temporal flows – the two under observation plus our own – to identify a simultaneity. We are still talking about the simultaneity of flows rather than instants because 'every duration is thick; real time has no instants'.[61] Instants are the result of turning time into space, they correspond to the mathematical points at the ends of a line, but *durée* has no endpoints, it does not come to a halt. Nevertheless, all time measurement depends on being able to define the simultaneity of instants. Bergson summarises the conditions for measuring time: '(1) it is the simultaneity between two instants of two motions outside us that enables us to measure an interval of time; (2) it is the simultaneity of these moments with moments dotted by them along our inner duration that makes this measurement one of time'.[62] It is as though we ourselves are the only conceivable measuring devices for *durée*.

All of which implies that the faith we place in objective time measurement, both in science and in daily life, rests on rather shaky ground, and does not really get to the heart of the substance of time at all:

> Measuring time consists... in counting simultaneities. All other measuring implies the possibility of directly or indirectly laying the unit of measurement over the object measured. All other measuring therefore bears upon the interval between the extremities even though we are, in fact, confined to counting these extremities. But in dealing with time, we can only count extremities; we merely *agree* to say that we have measured the interval in this way. If we now observe that science works exclusively with measurements, we become aware that, with respect to time, science counts instants, takes note of simultaneities, but remains without a grip on what happens in the intervals.[63]

If time is in essence unmeasurable, and if the notion of equal times is nonsensical, what does this mean for time in music? After all, surely meter is based on beats of equal duration or it is nothing. According to Zuckerkandl, this is erroneous because it:

---

61   Ibid.
62   Bergson 2002c, p. 213.
63   Ibid.

implies a distinction between what occurs and its duration; it regards the metric wave as a process that takes place *in* time. It tacitly assumes that we are confronted with two data: first, the thing that occurs, the [metric] wave; second, a neutral medium, 'duration', which underlies the wave as the empty strip of film underlies the picture that will be taken. Actually we have *not* two data, first the metric wave, or the forces active in the wave, and then a neutral medium 'time' or 'duration' in which the forces work, *in* which the wave pulses; on the contrary, the pulling of the wave is itself already time, is itself already duration. But with this it has become meaningless to talk of an equality of beats.[64]

Like other kinds of wave, metric waves are not about equality but about kinetic impulse. 'The condition that beat two of a duple meter has to fulfill is not that it must be equal in length to beat one, but that it shall close a cycle. To play in time musically does not mean to play tones that fill equal lengths of time, but tones that give rise to the metric wave'.[65]

Again, Zuckerkandl has reversed conventional thinking on this issue. It follows that the research in the psychology of music undertaken to explain how meter continues to be perceived even when there are considerable deviations from clock time in performance, is misplaced. What is required for successful generation of meter is not equal time intervals but an equilibrium, 'a mutual complementing, a mutual interpenetration, a mutual balancing' between the 'one' and the 'two' of the metric wave.[66] This sense of balance will be a more reliable and more real measure of time than a metronome, rigid adherence to which always threatens to destroy the musicality of meter.

This in turn explains the prevalence of repetition in music, which would be meaningless in most other media if it occurred to the extent it does in music. Again, Zuckerkandl takes issue with the conventional wisdom that it is the abstract nature of musical material which necessitates its repeated presentation, but that there is a limit to permissible repetition: over-repetition results in music which is tedious and of little value. Music's temporality means that there can never be exact repetition: the tones may repeat but time cannot. A repeated phrase necessarily takes on new significance due to its new position in relation to the metric wave. Repetition of the tones, far from threatening boredom, is actually the most effective way of generating that wave: 'If time had its way, tones would never say anything but the same thing; as time projects

---

64 Zuckerkandl 1973, 209–10.
65 Zuckerkandl 1973, p. 210.
66 Zuckerkandl 1973, p. 212.

wave after wave, the tones are to do nothing but to reproduce wave after wave in their material'. Repetition is, therefore, for Zuckerkandl, the natural state of music, while the introduction of new material represents a kind of deviation from this norm: 'Every new tonal statement in the course of a composition is, in this sense, made *against* the will of an ever-present urge for repetition, an urge fed by time itself'.[67]

Zuckerkandl claims that the most common kind of repetition, altered repetition, works not because it avoids the potential tedium of exact repetition, but because its minor changes focus attention on the metric wave by highlighting the essential similarity of the material.[68] An alternative explanation, based on the hierarchical conception of meter set out in Chapter 1 might be that when such minor changes are introduced at regular intervals as they often are – say, every second, fourth or eighth time – they generate metric waves at higher hierarchical levels; that is, longer, slower waves subtending the original ones, creating the multilayered, multidimensional metric structure common to much Western music.

In one further aspect of his theorisation of musical time Zuckerkandl demonstrates a debt to Bergson. He argues that music shows time not as transient, not as perishing as it moves from present to past, but as Becoming. Taking the case of the 'one-two' at the heart of the metric wave as an example, he asks: Is the past in music non-existent? He answers in the negative:

> If 'one', once past, were lost in non-existence, extinguished – as, according to the hourglass concept, past time is extinguished – 'two' would simply be a second 'one', and nothing more.

Neither would we feel the new 'one' correctly as 'once-again' if the previous 'one' were not somehow still present in the background. Highly repetitive, metrically organised music, does not, paradoxically, disorient the listener as to how many repetitions there have been. Rather, each repeated bar or period carries with it the number of its repetition, directly given, rendering conscious counting superfluous: 'its entire past is preserved in its present and given directly with it'.[69]

Something similar applies when considering the relation between present and future. 'One' proceeds towards the not-yet-existent 'two', and would not be

---

67   Zuckerkandl 1973, p. 219.
68   Zuckerkandl 1973, p. 221.
69   Zuckerkandl 1973, p. 224.

what it is if the future 'two' were not already part of its existence.[70] In this way past, present, and future are bound together in musical time. So far, this follows the lead set by Bergson as to time's continuous Becoming. But Zuckerkandl appears to depart from Bergson in his insistence that the continued existence of the past in the present of musical time has nothing to do with memory. We do not *remember* 'one' when we feel 'two'; it is not a question of consciousness turning back towards the past. For Bergson, as we have seen, memory is that element of consciousness which guarantees the continuity of *durée* and without which there would be no real time at all. Crucial here is a conception of what constitutes the 'present'. Bergson regards the notion of the present as an instant, like a mathematical point, as an abstraction. The real present has duration; it always necessarily includes some of the past – the words of the present sentence one has already spoken, the portion of the present action one has already completed. For Bergson, the extent of the past which finds itself included in the present is the result of an act of attention:

> The distinction we make between our present and past is . . . , if not arbitrary, at least relative to the extent of the field which our attention to life can embrace. . . . our present falls back into the past when we cease to attribute to it an immediate interest. . . . Consequently nothing prevents us from carrying back as far as possible the line of separation between our present and our past. . . . What we have is a present which endures.[71]

Compare this with his contemporary William James's famous description of the 'specious present':

> The only fact of our immediate experience is . . . 'the *specious* present' . . . the practically cognized present is no knife-edge, but a saddleback, with a certain breadth of its own on which we sit perched, and from which we look in two directions at a time. The unit of composition of our perception of time is a *duration*, with a bow and a stern, as it were – a rearward- and a forward-looking end.[72]

James, in common with other more contemporary psychologists, believed that the scope of the 'specious' or 'perceptual' present is biologically determined, having a length of about twelve seconds. Bergson's present is much more

---

70   Zuckerkandl 1973, pp. 224–5.
71   Bergson 2002d, p. 262.
72   William James, *The Principles of Psychology*, quoted in Moore 1996, p. 63.

elastic but both agree that the inclusion of elements of the past in the present is, to some degree, a function of consciousness or memory. For Zuckerkandl, neither consciousness in general, nor memory in particular, is responsible for recuperating the past into the present; rather the past is given directly with the present in music:

> This is a present from which not *I*, thanks to my particular powers, look backward into the past and forward into the future, but which *itself* thus looks backward and forward.... The past is not extinguished, but not because a memory stores it; it is not extinguished because *time itself stores it*, or, better put, because the being of time is a storing of itself; ... the present of musical experience is not the dividing point that eternally separates past and future; it is the stage upon which, for every ear, the drama of the being of time is played – that ceaseless storing of itself and anticipating itself which is never repeated, which is every instant new.[73]

Zuckerkandl here goes much further that Bergson in attributing to time properties of its own, as opposed to those conferred upon it as a result of the existence of consciousness. This pushes Zuckerkandl to regard the anticipation of the future embodied in musical time as at least as important as its preservation of the past, if not more so; a feature which clearly cannot be explained by consciousness, unless one believes in foresight or premonition. As a result of the dynamic tension inherent in tones, their pointing beyond themselves, we 'face forward' rather than backward when we listen, always anticipating what is to come next. But how is it that a sense of expectation is maintained no matter how many times we have heard a piece, even to the extent that a musical surprise always remains a surprise, and can even be intensified by repeated listenings? Zuckerkandl's answer is that we are not hearing events *in* time, but time itself; we do not anticipate future musical events, but are aware of *futurity*, pure expectation, whose object is time. 'Events that I anticipate in thought are certainly not new when they appear. But time is always new; cannot possibly be anything but new. Heard as a succession of acoustical events, music will soon become boring; heard as the manifestation of time eventuating, it can never bore'. Zuckerkandl describes music as a temporal *Gestalt* in which 'past and future are given with and in the present and are experienced with and in the present; hearing a melody is hearing, having heard, and being about to hear, all at once'.[74]

---

73 Zuckerkandl 1973, p. 228.
74 Zuckerkandl 1973, pp. 233–5.

These formulations position Zuckerkandl as far as it is possible to be from the view of time held by Alperson as the container for events, musical or otherwise; a form for perception whose features include relationships of succession and duration which musicians manipulate in the cause of musical expression. From a starting point informed, at least in part, by Bergson's concept of *durée*, Zuckerkandl has in many ways broken the bounds of Bergson's thought. Time, released from its Kantian conception as mere precondition for perception, is not to be restricted to a metaphysical or even ontological condition for life and evolution, but is itself directly perceivable substance. Zuckerkandl's radicalisation of Bergson is evident in his answer to the question: Are there two times? Do the properties he identifies apply only to the time of music? Does music have its own, different kind of time? His answer is an emphatic 'No'. In music we do not hear musical time as distinct from any other, and musical experiences are not those of another, ideal world. He insists that:

> The audible and the visible belong to the *same* reality; that motion of tones and motion of things take place on the *same* stage; that *one* space, *one* time embrace the world of visible event and the world of audible event.[75]

Music provides the medium, and audition the sense, which allow time to be directly perceived, and which thus furnish the evidence which challenges established conceptions of time. Consequently, Zuckerkandl's philosophy of music represents no less than a critique of the 'concept of reality' which has been assembled by science and philosophy over the last several hundred years. It is an audacious project which regards the relevance of its aesthetic insights not as isolated to music or even to the arts more generally, but as capable of shedding valuable light on the whole of the way we understand the world and of playing a part in correcting the defects, one sidedness and positivism of modern scientific thinking. What it demands is nothing less than the '*musicalization* of thought'.[76]

Whether music is the only, or the appropriate, vehicle for correcting the defects of positivist thinking is debatable, but what Zuckerkandl confirms is that music can be used to explore aspects of the nature of time, or at least conceptions of time, beyond the sphere of music itself. The Bergsonian tradition deploys a concept of time as flux which draws on musical analogies in order to mount a critique of spatialised, measureable notions of time. For Deleuze, the

---

75   Zuckerkandl 1973, p. 364.
76   Zuckerkandl 1973, p. 264.

presence of temporal measure within music renders it less capable of expressing the image of the authentic, vital time of the universe. This results in a position which can only comprehend the majority of the music of our age as somehow false or erroneous, echoing Bergson's own attitude to spatialised conceptions of time. Furthermore, it necessarily reduces the time of music to an image or a representation of the time of the world rather than an articulation of it. For if the time of music is measured, it cannot be the same time as the unmeasureable flux of life and of the universe. Zuckerkandl's unorthodox Bergsonism by contrast allows him to argue that what are generally taken as instances of temporal measure within music – pulse and meter – are nothing of the kind, but are instead a form of tensing of the temporal flux itself. In a radical move, Zuckerkandl effectively reclaims oscillation, which, at least since the invention of the pendulum clock, has been taken as the basis and the justification of measured time, for Bergsonian *durée*. The first gain he achieves by such a move is the ability to address the metrical music of the Western tradition from a broadly Bergsonian perspective without adopting a negative normative position in relation to it. But perhaps more significantly, it allows Zuckerkandl to argue that musical temporality is not simply a picture of time, an artist's likeness, which can be more or less successful in how it captures the truth of its object. Rather, musical time is a sonic manifestation of time itself. Objecting to aspects of it such as meter therefore becomes nonsensical: it would be like objecting to time itself. There is only one kind of time in the world; music is the form in which time makes itself perceptible.

However, the weakness in this theory is its ahistorical nature and its Eurocentrism. Zuckerkandl takes post-Renaissance Western music for music in general and is consequently unable to account for any musics which lie outside this historically and geographically specific zone. This rules out the possibility of making any sense of the temporality of non-metric musics such as the ones we have already considered in previous chapters, except perhaps to regard them as inferior. Nonetheless, Zuckerkandl's insistence that what manifests itself in music is time itself, not merely time consciousness, may be a useful idea when we consider the temporality of capitalism and its relation to music in later chapters.

CHAPTER 4

Schutz's 'Vivid Present' and the Social Time of Music

What can the philosophical tradition of phenomenology offer a materialist investigation of musical time? There are several possible claims for its usefulness. The first is that phenomenology is perhaps the tradition which has most prioritised the study of time. As a philosophy which concentrates on the nature and quality of experience, time is not, for phenomenology, merely one area among others to be explored. Rather, since it is an elemental feature of all experience, temporality holds a central place in all phenomenological investigations.[1]

Secondly, the subject of time is perhaps particularly suited to being addressed phenomenologically, as doing so brackets the thorny ontological questions concerning the reality or existence of time. Arguably, time is best considered as a phenomenon, so that its noumenal status can safely be ignored. Husserl's phenomenological 'reduction' amounts to a 'suspension of judgment' about the real world, while phenomenology aims to be 'an account of our experience of the world which does not presuppose the existence of the world'.[2] Schutz explains that this is not achieved:

> by transforming our naïve belief in the outer world into a disbelief, [or] by replacing our conviction in its existence by the contrary, but by suspending belief. We just make up our mind to refrain from any judgment concerning spatiotemporal existence, ... we set the existence of the world 'out of action', we 'bracket' our belief in it.[3]

Leaving aside the question of whether such a methodology is universally applicable, it is surely an appropriate starting point for all questions about experience, those for which ontological answers do not seem pressing, amongst which time and music are obvious examples.

---

1   As evidenced by the focus of many phenomenological classics, see Husserl 1964; Heidegger 1978.
2   Miller 1984, pp. 182, 196.
3   Schutz 1966, p. 5.

Thirdly, and also in relation to methodology, not only are 'naïve beliefs' and commonsense perspectives about the world bracketed by Husserl's phenomenological reduction, but all aspects of thought which come under the heading of the 'natural attitude', including theoretical and scientific ones. In relation to music, phenomenological thinkers have argued that 'traditional forms of thought that have "visual" tendencies may prejudice an investigation into auditory things'. The primacy of notation in the Western tradition may constitute such a distortion. 'Instead of trying to cast music in a spatial form, which is visually oriented, we [phenomenologists] let it speak in its own form'.[4] Bartholomew suggests that musicological procedures such as Schenkerian analysis may lead us to prioritise structure in our listening and analysis, again relying on spatialised representations which render the music static, effectively denying its temporal element.[5] For Smith, music should be understood as 'a continual *becoming*, in which the modalities of present, past and future are brought together not spatially only but as the emergence (ek-sistence) of the musical phenomenon'.[6] In an argument that has a bearing on the organisation of the temporal aspects of music, rhythm and meter, he notes that what Husserl described as the 'mathematicisation of nature' took place in music theory long before it took hold of the physical sciences, tracing its origins to the Middle Ages with the rise of a metaphysics of number and a preoccupation with proportions, when musical thinking came to be 'based on a mathematical model rather than on an experiential one'.[7] Phenomenology attempts to rectify these distortions by urging a return to the sounds themselves, by making '*sound as such*' primary. In a genuinely phenomenological method, it is claimed:

> only *sound* emerges as a proper *phenomenon* for phenomenological analysis. All else, including 'meaning', is bracketed. Only sound is thematized.[8]

This brings us to the final claim as to why phenomenology can provide unique insights into musical time. Phenomenology regards sounds as phenomena as more immediately and thoroughly temporal than other objects of experience. Husserl described the way in which our experience of a visual object is built: we intend its identity, he argued, from a manifold of perceptions. In visual

---

4 Smith 1979, p. 17.
5 Bartholomew 1985, p. 327.
6 Smith 1979, p. 16.
7 Smith 1979, p. 93.
8 Smith 1979, p. 100.

perception, only one side of an object is given as present. Only one side is fulfilled intentionally while the others are intended emptily. We are often at liberty to move around the object, to fulfill previously unfilled intentions, and to fuse this manifold of intentions into an identity. Bartholomew explains that for Husserl, 'intuition refers to this concept of filled intention. What is intuited is precisely that which is intentionally fulfilled or brought to presence'.[9]

But this perspectival quality does not apply to sound objects. 'The visual object offers an infinite number of sides with no preferred viewing order. The auditory object seems to offer one principal perspective, from beginning to end, and its order is a necessary order'. Hence the question of temporality, though relevant for all objects of experience, is particularly acute for auditory objects because of the unique way they are given in time. This is undoubtedly the reason for Husserl's choice of sound and melody to demonstrate his theory of time-consciousness and, in particular, the notion of 'passive synthesis'. Smith comments:

> We note that throughout his treatment of it he continually refers to musical sound as a temporal phenomenon. He seems to model his conception on the fact of musical experience, where notes *put themselves together* for us in perception and offer themselves as such to consciousness. This putting-together is literally synthesis.[10]

> Time-consciousness is thus the primordial place for the constitution of musical identity and unity.[11]

In this way, the experience of musical tones and melodies, and, by extension, of music, have been regarded by the phenomenological tradition as paradigmatic of time consciousness, and therefore central to an adequate theorisation of it. By suggesting that tones and melody are immanently temporal, Husserl can be seen as adding philosophical weight to the commonsense observation that because music *takes* time, it must be *about* time.

---

9   Bartholomew 1985, p. 341.
10 Smith 1979, p. 110.
11 Smith 1979, p. 112.

Schutz's Phenomenology

Alfred Schutz is probably the most significant thinker to attempt to apply Husserl's insights into time consciousness to music. Schutz is, however, not a straightforward Husserlian, but combines phenomenology with the ideas of Bergson and William James on time, and with Weberian sociology to produce not only an understanding of music as such, but an analysis of the social relations between participants in the practice of music-making. It is the latter which is the more interesting and relevant for our subject, but to discuss it will require addressing both Schutz's general theory of music and the phenomenology of Husserl upon which it builds.

Schutz's temporal analysis takes as its starting point a distinction made by other thinkers between inner and outer time, characterised by Schutz respectively as the realm of individual consciousness and the realm of the real world of our fellow men.

Like Bergson, Schutz regards *durée* as the primary level of time consciousness, an unstructured flux comprising a succession of continuously interpenetrating conscious states, in a condition of pure, heterogeneous, qualitative moments.[12] Schutz endorses the rejection of atomism which may be said to derive from the Aristotelian conception of time as a succession of 'nows'. For Bergson, such a conception results in spatialised, rather than lived, time; for Heidegger in *Being and Time*, it constitutes 'inauthentic' time; while Husserl characterises it 'objective' time. Schutz follows Husserl and James by regarding the source of time as subjective, rooted in the 'stream of thought' or the 'stream of personal conscious life'. His assertion that 'psychical life is not made up of a multiplicity of elements which have to be reunited, it is not a mosaic of juxtaposed sensation, but, from the first, a unity of continuously streaming cogitations', places him firmly in the camp of these thinkers.

From Husserl, Schutz takes the phenomenological explanation for the continuity of subjective time, in particular, how it is possible to have an awareness of temporal succession. Husserl realised that no succession of awareness, that is, a series of perceptions in time, can account for an awareness of their succession. An awareness of duration requires more than a continuity of awareness, which, on its own, can only generate the sense of a perpetual 'now'. So time-consciousness must derive from the simultaneous features of the structure of

---

12   Muzzetto 2006.

awareness itself.[13] Husserl's theory is designed to describe what the temporal structure of awareness must be like in order to produce a consciousness of time.

Using the example of a sounding tone, Husserl calls the element of the perceptual act which results in an awareness of the tone sounding now the 'primal impression' or 'sensation'. But in order to have temporal awareness, more than that is required. As Husserl puts it:

> It pertains to the essence of the intuition of time that in every point of its duration... it is consciousness of *what has just been* and not mere consciousness of the now-point of the objective thing appearing as having duration.[14]

Attached to this primal impression is an element which accounts for an awareness of the tone having sounded in the just-past. Husserl calls this element the 'retention' or 'primal remembrance'.[15] Retention is not a previous primal impression, nor an echo of the previous now-phase of the tone. It is a distinct structural element of awareness at the now-point which presents to consciousness the previous phase of the tone as just-past. As Brough puts it: 'Retention does not transmute what is absent into what is present; it presents the absent in its absence'.[16] In addition, retentions do not present to consciousness the content of an earlier primal impression, but that of an earlier whole perceptual act, complete with its own retentions. Husserl explains it like this:

> The first primal sensation changes into a retention of itself, this retention into a retention, and so on. Conjointly with the first retention, however, a new 'now', a new primal sensation, is present and is joined continuously but momentarily within the first retention, so that the second phase of the flux is a primal sensation of the new now and a retention of the earlier one. The third-phase, again, is a new primal sensation with retention of the second primal sensation and a retention of the retention of the first, and so on.[17]

---

13   Miller 1984, p. 109; Bartholomew 1985, p. 350.
14   Husserl 1964, pp. 53–4.
15   Miller 1984, p. 120.
16   Quoted in Zahavi 2007, p. 463.
17   Husserl 1964, pp. 107–8.

This process gives rise to Husserl's description of the series of retentions as a comet's tail in which the primal impression 'runs-off' into its retentional modifications.[18]

Husserl's theory also posits the existence of an element of awareness, called protention, which is structurally equivalent to retention but oriented towards the future. Protention presents to consciousness in the 'now' the content of a future perceptual act, including that act's own retentions and protentions. Of course, despite their structural symmetry, there is an important difference between protention and retention. The content of protention cannot be an actual experience but rather has the quality of an expectation. As Russell points out, this means that the content of protentions are constantly being revised in the light of actual experience: 'ever-new primal impressions are... continually being greeted *as* fulfilments or disappointments of our expectations or "protentions"'.[19]

It is the structure of our perceptual acts, comprising primal impression, retention, and protention, which constitutes the unity of time consciousness, the continuity of the flux of time. Each now-point, or living present, is connected via retentions to the past and via protentions to the future, synthesising a temporal continuity, or duration. Miller claims that 'Husserl's theory ends up accounting for our sensation of our movement through time *solely in terms of the structure of our temporal awareness*. Consequently, his account *does not entail any metaphysical view of "moving" through time*'.[20]

Husserl does, however, have an explanation for the tendency to think of a now-point as moving through time conceived as an abstract continuum. It is based on the existence of a second kind of memory. Husserl calls retention 'primary remembrance', which although part of the intentionality of perception is experienced passively. It differs from 'secondary remembrance' or 'recollection', which, for Husserl, is an act which places before consciousness a discrete re-presentation of an object of past perception. (Just as protention is the counterpart to retention, 'anticipation' is the counterpart to recollection). Recollection is that form of memory which allows us to return in consciousness to a particular 'now' any number of times. That this is the origin of the idea of 'objective time' is explained by Russell:

> In recalling a past moment to mind at will, it becomes possible to take that moment as a *fixed point* in relation to which the streaming present is

---

18   Muzzetto 2006, p. 8; Russell 2006, p. 133.
19   Russell 2006, p. 133.
20   Miller 1984, p. 162.

increasingly distant. Suddenly, rather than taking the streaming now as a reference point, some particular now-phase is taken up as an 'objective' reference-point. Moreover, this process can be idealized and extended indefinitely. The result is a projection of an infinite plane of now-points existing independently of conscious experience. Thus the idea of 'objective time' is constituted. As opposed to time which is experienced within the form of the living present as an incessant *flowing*, objective time comes to be represented as a *stable* continuum of temporal points at which events may be located in a fixed and unchanging fashion. The now of conscious experience, the living present, is subsequently construed as a pointer moving steadily along the idealized dimension of objective time.[21]

In addition to Husserl's theory of time-consciousness outlined above, Schutz is committed to the notion of the present as temporally extended, a 'vivid present' or 'specious present', rather than a punctual 'now'. He argues:

> The present of our vivid experiences is never a mathematical point, a mere instant, an ideal limit between past and future. The assumption of such a mere instant would be an abstraction borrowed from the geometry of space or its analogue, spatialized time.... The present we are living in is always a specious present, as James calls it, having in itself its structurization, having a before and an after.[22]

Miller argues that Husserl's theory is neutral on the question of whether the living present is punctual or extended. He maintains that Husserl's account had no need to introduce the concept of 'specious present' and treats any limits of retentional and protentional spans, which have emerged through psychological experimentation, as purely contingent factors which have no bearing on the epistemological nature of Husserl's theory.[23] However, it seems that Schutz puts more emphasis than Husserl does on the role of secondary remembrance and expectation – recollection and anticipation – in constituting

---

21   Russell 2006, p. 136. Miller's account of Husserl's theory of time consciousness includes the confusing formulation of 'our sensation of movement through time'. This seems to come close to the concept of 'objective time' that Husserl thought was derivative of genuine time consciousness, in which time does not pre-exist but is *constituted by* the perceiving subject, and may therefore be misleading (Miller 1984, p. 162).
22   Schutz and Kersten 1976, p. 42.
23   Miller 1984, p. 174.

the 'now', leading him to include them in his extended 'vivid present'. As he puts it:

> The vivid present encompasses everything that is actually lived through, it includes elements of the past retained or recollected in the Now and elements of the future entering the Now by way of protention or anticipation.[24]

For Husserl, our sense of time passing, of temporal flux is constituted primarily by retention and protention. Recollection and anticipation are potentially constitutive of a sense of objective or outer time. But for Schutz, 'retentions and reproductions, protentions and anticipations are constitutive for the interconnectedness of the stream of consciousness'. And he goes on to add, 'They are equally constitutive for the experience of music'.[25]

All this is important because, for Schutz, music belongs in the realm of inner time: '[t]here is no doubt that the dimension of time in which the work of music exists is the inner time of our stream of consciousness – in Bergson's terminology, the *durée*'.[26] And since certain kinds of music require the listener to recollect themes and sections which have already elapsed (and to some extent also to anticipate their (re)appearance in the future), Schutz is led to give secondary remembrance equal prominence to retention in his account of inner time without compromising the sharp distinction he makes between inner and outer times. He stresses that the inner temporality of music is quite different from the time a piece of music takes to be played or the length of a track on a recording. The inner time of music, he says, is 'another dimension of time which cannot be measured by our clocks or other mechanical devices. In measurable time there are pieces of equal length, there are minutes and hours. There is no such yardstick for the dimension of time the listener [to music] lives through; there is no equality between its pieces, if there are pieces at all'.[27]

This position would suggest that Schutz's phenomenology is likely to be no more useful to a sympathetic study of measured musical time than Bergsonism. Indeed, like Bergson, Schutz has a problem accounting for any kind of rhythm in music. A temporal realm which is by definition indivisible and unmeasurable is necessarily arrhythmic. Consequently, Schutz claims that 'it is not at all certain that rhythm is essential to musical experience itself'. He goes on to

---

24   Schutz and Kersten, 1976, p. 41.
25   Ibid.
26   Schutz and Kersten, 1976, p. 32.
27   Schutz and Kersten, 1976, p. 37.

suggest that not all musical cultures involve rhythm, arguing that, 'Ambrosian or Gregorian music, even Palestrina's music, is not rhythmical in the same sense as our modern music'.[28] This assertion is perfectly true, and endorses the view argued here in Chapters 1 and 2 that forms of musical temporality have varied widely with cultures and history. But it does in no way prove that such music is not rhythmic or that rhythm is in some way superfluous to music.

Schutz's inclination to attempt to exclude rhythm from pure music can be seen in his treatment of repetition and continuance. He finds that, phenomenologically, the repetition of the same tone is no different from the continuance of that tone. Taking the example of a repeated bass tone, a 'pedal point', he argues that 'the intermittent repetitions of the same tone are brought to coincidence and apperceived as a specious continuance', and concludes that 'repetition ... is merely a special case of the intermittence of a continuance. It is intermittence of a sameness'.[29] Now, it is true, within the context of the Western tradition, that *harmonically* it makes no functional difference whether, for example, a bass pedal tone or a chord in the strings, is sustained or repeated. But the *rhythmic* effect of their repetition is far from inconsequential. On the face of it, the logic of Schutz's argument would suggest that it is of minor significance that the first pitch of Beethoven's famous four-note opening to his Fifth Symphony is repeated three times; arguing that fundamentally, the motif consists of two notes, not four. This is not a position that can seriously be defended.

For Schutz, as for all phenomenologists who take Husserl's theory of time consciousness as their starting point, phenomena are already and necessarily temporal by virtue of the consciousnesses that perceive them. We have seen how this manifests itself in the analysis of a single tone. Consequently, there seems to be a difficulty in accommodating what might be described as the second order of temporality of musical events – the succession of tones of various determinate durations.

This inability to recognise rhythm is clearly a major problem for attempting to apply Schutz's phenomenology in a study of groove music. However, it is his theorisation of 'outer time' and its relationship with inner, musical time that makes Schutz worth persevering with. Outer time, for Schutz as for Bergson, is spatialised time, an objectified, quantifiable time which contrasts markedly with the essentially unmeasurable flux of consciousness. However, Schutz regards outer time not as a false or inauthentic conception of time, but, rather, the form of time which corresponds to our life in the outer, or social, world.

---

28   Schutz and Kersten, 1976, p. 47.
29   Schutz and Kersten, 1976, p. 49.

It is necessarily spatialised because of its implication with dimensions of space and the movements that take place within them. He argues:

> Life requires acting within the outer world, dealing with its objects, mastering the outer world, and performing all these activities in collaboration with others, making fellow-men objects of our acts and being motivated by theirs. This everyday life... is life in space and the spatiotemporal dimension.... The spatialized time of our daily life corresponds to the attitude of full attention to it, to the state of full awakeness.[30]

Unlike Bergson, however, what Schutz finds interesting is the ways in which the physical time of the social world interacts with the continuous flux of consciousness. For him, spatialised, measurable time is not an unfortunate intrusion into *durée*, but the necessary form of time for any kind of action in the world. Though he believes 'all musical experience originates in the flux of inner time', and that the decision to listen to music involves a withdrawal from the world of actions, Schutz is well aware that musical *performance*, the making of music, takes place in the outer, spatial world, and involves the physical co-ordination of bodies with instruments and with each other.[31] Schutz's theory of 'making music together' results from an exploration of the interface between inner and outer times, between continuous, unquantifiable *durée* and spatialised, measurable social time.

Music as Phenomenon

Let us now consider how Schutz uses this broadly Husserlian perspective to elaborate a phenomenological approach to music. We have already noted the fact that Schutz asserts that musical experience takes place in inner time. This is connected to his belief that music is an 'ideal object'. What this means is elucidated by the following statement: 'A phenomenological approach to music may safely disregard the physical qualities of the sound as well as the rationalization of these sounds which leads to the musical scale'. Music is not the sum of all the physical properties of the sound waves, it has nothing ultimately to do with the mathematical proportions upon which pitch temperament systems and theories of consonance and dissonance have been expounded, all of which are entirely culturally and historically specific aesthetic questions

---

30   Schutz and Kersten, 1976, p. 42.
31   Schutz and Kersten, 1976, pp. 43, 46.

rather than phenomenological ones. Neither are the particular instruments or timbres involved relevant to the essence of music. He insists:

> All this is immaterial to the experience of the listener. He responds neither to sound waves, nor does he perceive sounds; he just listens to music.[32]

Schutz's conception of music is far from orthodox and is not universally accepted even by phenomenologists. As we have already seen, for F.J. Smith, music is essentially about sound: '*only sound* emerges as a proper *phenomenon* for phenomenological analysis. All else, including "meaning", is bracketed'.[33] Another writer on the phenomenology of music, Thomas Clifton, seems to agree with Schutz when he argues that 'pitch is "transparentized" in a musical context, which is to say that we experience music *through* pitch, rather than the pitch itself'.[34] However, for Clifton, that 'is not an invitation to treat the piece [of music] as an ideal object', in the way that Schutz does.[35]

Schutz's position on the ontological basis of music can be made clearer by examining what he understands to be the relationship between music and the various means of performing, preserving and reproducing it. The idealism at the heart of Schutz's phenomenology is expressed in the following passage:

> Both the score and the performance have the same relation to the work of music as the printed book or lecture has to the existence of a philosophical thought or a mathematical theory. To be sure, the score, the performance, the book, the lecture, are indispensable means for communicating the musical or scientific thought. They are not, however, this thought itself. A work of music or a mathematical theorem has the character of an ideal object. The communicability of a work of music or a mathematical theorem is bound to real objects – visible or audible objects – but the musical or scientific thought itself exists independently of all these means of communication.[36]

To assert that both musical notation and recording technology are simply means for the preservation of the music which exists independently of them is

---

32 Schutz and Kersten, 1976, p. 27.
33 Smith 1979, p. 100.
34 Clifton 1983, p. 20.
35 Clifton 1983, p. 16.
36 Schutz and Kersten, 1976, p. 28.

an understandable, if not universally accepted, position. To put performance in the same category is contentious, and is arguably a position that reveals a perspective limited, despite Schutz's avowed intentions, by the Western art-music tradition. However, the conception of music as ontologically equivalent to a mathematical or scientific theory allows Schutz to draw one of his more important insights in relation to music's temporality.

A piece of music, he argues, cannot be grasped monothetically, only polythetically. Schutz compares a work of music to Pythagoras's Theorem in order to demonstrate this point. Both are ideal objects in the way that Schutz understands the term. Learning Pythagoras's Theorem involves following the step-by-step process by which it is derived from first principles. However, having once co-performed with her tutor these polythetic steps of constituting the conceptual meaning of the theorem, the student can grasp the resulting conceptual meaning monothetically – with a single ray of thought. There is no need every time to retrace the polythetic steps to their conclusion. The theorem can be summed up monothetically as $a^2 + b^2 = c^2$ and grasped even if those steps have been forgotten.

This is not true of a piece of music. The most we can grasp monothetically are secondary characteristics of a work – that it is a symphony or a fugue, that it evokes a certain emotion in us, and so on. Schutz says, 'The work of music itself can only be recollected and grasped by reconstituting the polythetic steps in which it has been built up, by reproducing mentally or actually its development from the first to the last bar as it goes on in time'.[37]

And he reinforces the point:

> The meaning of a musical work... is essentially of a polythetical structure. It cannot be grasped monothetically. It consists in the articulated step-by-step occurrence in inner time, in the very polythetic constitutional process itself.

The crucial point here is that this involves a synchronisation of temporal fluxes: that of the listener with that of the music, and by extension, its composer:

> The musical content itself, its very meaning, can be grasped merely by reimmersing oneself in the ongoing flux, by reproducing thus the articulated musical occurrence as it unfolds in polythetic steps in inner time, a process itself belonging to the dimension of inner time. And it will 'take as much time' to reconstitute the work in recollection as to experience it

---

37 Schutz and Kersten, 1976, p. 29.

for the first time. In both cases I have to re-establish the quasi simultaneity of my stream of consciousness with that of the composer.[38]

However, Schutz also believes that in order to produce meaning from experience, musical or otherwise, something more is necessary than simply immersing oneself in the flux of inner time. Muzzetto explains that meaning, for Schutz, is 'an operation of intentionality, which ... only becomes visible to the reflective glance'.[39] This reflective aspect of the meaning-conferring process is crucial. Schutz argues that while we are immersed in the flow of *durée*, we experience only undifferentiated experiences which merge into a continuum. Within this flux we live from moment to moment, aware of the passing of time, as Husserl's theory of temporal continuity explains, but nevertheless confined within a stream of experiences which contains no boundaries and which proceeds in an irreversible direction. In this state, the question of meaning does not arise, because it is not possible to direct one's attention at any part of the flux of experience in order to single it out.

However, Schutz continues:

> when, by my act of reflection, I turn my attention to my living experience, I am no longer taking up my position within the stream of pure duration, I am no longer simply living within that flow. The experiences are apprehended, distinguished, brought into relief, marked out from one another... What had first been constituted as a phase now stands out as a full-blown experience.[40]

If experiencing music involves making one's own duration flow with the music's, but the process of attributing meaning requires placing oneself outside of one's stream of consciousness, how is it possible to confer meaning on musical experience? Schutz answers this question by suggesting that the stream of consciousness is not uniform, but should be conceived as a series of impulses, which alternate between movement and rest. He argues that it is not possible to adopt at will the reflective attitude necessary for meaning at any point in the flux of consciousness, but only at resting places between its active phases. He says:

---

38   Schutz 1951, p. 91.
39   Muzzetto 2006, p. 10.
40   Schutz 1976, p. 51.

> We have no power to define the limits of our specious present, to draw its border lines over against the past or the future. Our stream of consciousness is itself articulated. Impulses and resting places, periods of tension and relaxation alternate. Wave follows wave, each wave having its crest and valley.... If we interrupt this development before the impulse comes to an end, if we make this impulse abortive, we cannot grasp our specious present and the relevant sector of our past adherent to it.[41]

The articulation of musical flux into periods of tension and relaxation is called 'phrasing'. It is this structuration of music's inner time which makes meaning possible by gathering elements of the flow into discernible units separated by moments of repose:

> These very short intermittences are the resting places during which the flux of the music comes to a standstill. The listener is invited and incited by them to look from this end-phase back to the initial phase, to return to the beginning still accessible to him by reason of the interplay of retentions....[42]

This description is certainly a very persuasive one which resonates with a musical understanding of the role of phrases. It seems to provide a plausible explanation for the apparently universal requirement for musical ideas to come to a conclusion at regular intervals in order to achieve comprehensibility. By locating its basis in time consciousness it provides a more fundamental explanation than the common conjecture that phrasing is a product of music's origins in the human voice and the consequent need for singers to breathe. The necessity for musical lines to be comprised of distinct phrases can be regarded as analogous to the need for coherent speech to be divided into clauses and sentences, allowing the listener the opportunity to grasp the previous phase of the flux at the moment of its conclusion in order to produce meaning. Like speech without full stops, musical lines that continue indefinitely without points of clear articulation are ungraspable, and therefore meaningless, to their audience, a fact that inexperienced improvisers tend to overlook. Schutz's theory suggests that musical ideas become meaningful only on their completion when they can be grasped as a whole. And the fact that they are grasped as a whole throws light on what we mean by the term 'theme', understood as a discrete unit of musical material. Schutz says of this process:

---

41 Schutz and Kersten, 1976, pp. 65–6.
42 Schutz and Kersten, 1976, p. 66.

'This is the way in which a theme constitutes itself. Once constituted, it becomes a *Gestalt*.... As a unit, it can now be recollected as an entity with particular meaning'.[43] By grasping a group of tones as a 'theme', a 'phrase', a 'melody', or a 'motif', we have effectively conferred meaning upon a phase of musical duration.

Growing Older Together

By far the most productive aspect of Schutz's thought is his attempt to use a Bergsonian/Hussserlian framework to explore social questions, particularly the issue of how meaning arises within the context of social relationships. He develops a theory of intersubjectivity based on the notion of streams of consciousness flowing together, an idea which we have already encountered in relation to the act of listening to music.

Schutz suggests that when we attend to the lived experiences of another person, we are 'simultaneous' with them, 'that our respective streams of consciousness intersect ... We are concerned with the synchronism of two streams of consciousness ... my own and yours'. He goes on to argue:

> The simultaneity involved here is not that of physical time, which is quantifiable, divisible and spatial. For us the term 'simultaneity' is rather an expression for the basic and necessary assumption which I make that your stream of consciousness is analogous to mine. It endures in a sense that a physical thing does not: it subjectively experiences its own aging, and this experience is determinative of all its other experiences. While the duration of physical objects is not *durée* at all, but its exact opposite, persisting over a period of objective time, you and I, on the other hand, have a genuine *durée* which experiences itself, which is continuous, which is manifold, and which is irreversible. Not only does each of us subjectively experience his own *durée* as an absolute reality in the Bergsonian sense, but the *durée* of each of us is given to the other as absolute reality. What we mean, then, by the simultaneity of two durations or streams of consciousness is simply this: the phenomenon of *growing older together*. Any other criterion of simultaneity presupposes the transformation of both duration into a spatiotemporal complex and the transformation of the real *durée* into a merely *constructed time*.[44]

---

43   Ibid.
44   Schutz 1976, p. 103.

The possibility of attending to another's duration in this way is granted primarily by our being able to perceive their physical movements and to attribute meaning to them in terms of the 'field of expression' that they generate. Schutz explains that those bodily movements are taken as expressive signs of the lived experiences of the other person. He says, 'My intentional gaze is directed right through my perceptions of his bodily movements to his lived experiences lying behind them and signified by them'.[45] This does not mean, however, that our streams of consciousness are identical, that I have direct access to the other's experiences. Because I must interpret experiences according to my own standpoint, in relation to my own 'meaning-contexts', which necessarily differ from another's, Schutz says, 'I always fall far short of grasping the totality of [the other's] lived experience, ... [which] is given to me in discontinuous segments, never in its fullness, and only in "interpretive perspectives"'.[46] On the other hand, such simultaneity does not depend on bodily coexistence with the other person or a direct, contemporaneous observation of them. It can also take place across generations or historical time intervals by relying on the 'quasi-simultaneity' produced by attending to another's writings, music or art, all of which are ultimately products of their creators' bodily movements in the outer world and signitive of their lived experiences.[47] It is this quasi-simultaneity which is taking place in the act of listening to music, described above, which can occur even if the composer is long dead.

Schutz regards this flowing together of two streams of consciousness as the basis of all social interaction and intersubjectivity. It is not the product of communication; rather it is the precondition for it – it makes communication and shared meaning possible.[48] It underpins what he calls the 'We-relationship' and his definition of it as 'growing older together'. When I share the same experience with you, such as watching a bird in flight, Schutz says, to say that *we* watched the bird's flight is 'to coordinate temporally a series of my own experiences with a series of yours'. When I attempt to understand the meaning of what you are saying – not just the 'objective meaning', which Schutz defines as the words' meaning in themselves, independent of the circumstances of their utterance, but what is going on in your mind as you speak, what you *mean*:[49]

---

45 Schutz 1976, pp. 100–1.
46 Schutz 1976, p. 107.
47 Schutz 1976, p. 104.
48 Schutz 1966, p. 72.
49 Schutz 1976, pp. 124–7.

> In order to get to your subjective meaning, I must picture to myself your stream of consciousness as flowing side by side with my own. Within this picture I must interpret and construct your intentional Acts as you choose your words. To the extent that you and I can mutually experience this simultaneity, growing older together for a time, to the extent that we can live in it together, to *that* extent we can live in each other's subjective contexts of meaning.[50]

The We-relationship is not the ability to apprehend each other's subjective contexts of meaning itself, but is the basis of this ability. It is the assumption that must be made before it makes sense for me to ask what you mean by your words. Schutz sums it up like this: 'I can live in your subjective meaning-contexts only to the extent that I directly experience you within an actualized content-filled We-relationship'. The We-relationship does not only occupy the medium of inner time; it is spatial as well as temporal because it relies on the perception of bodily movements which take place in the outer world.

Schutz further identifies a curious feature of intersubjective understanding based on the We-relationship. We already know that he holds that the meaning of one's own experiences can only be grasped in retrospect as a result of a reflective glance which amounts to stepping outside of one's stream of consciousness. No such restriction applies to grasping another's lived experience, however. He argues:

> By no means ... need I attend reflectively to *my* lived experience *of* you in order to observe *your* lived experience. On the contrary, by merely 'looking' I can grasp even those of your lived experiences which you have not yet noticed and which are for you still prephenomenal and undifferentiated. This means that, whereas I can observe my own lived experiences only after they are over and done with, I can observe yours as they actually take place.[51]

Schutz concludes, 'Since I can grasp in simultaneity your conscious processing occurring Now, while I can apprehend reflectively only those of my experiences which are, at best, "just past", the consciousness of the Other can be, indeed, defined as a consciousness whose processes the ego can apprehend in simultaneity'.[52]

---

50 Schutz 1976, p. 166.
51 Schutz 1976, p. 102.
52 Schutz 1962, p. 88.

Clearly, the same applies from the point of view of the Other in relation to the experiences of both of us. Zaner comments on this relationship: 'Self is able to be experienced in the present only by the Other but then only by the... "mediation" of symbols. Self can experience its own "Now-Here-Thus", on the other hand, only as "past" '.[53] Schutz emphasises the paradox involved here:

> In one sense each of us knows more of himself than of the Other, yet, in another specific sense the contrary is true. I know more of the Other and he knows more of me than either of us knows of his own stream of consciousness.[54]

This means that what Schutz calls the 'vivid present' is only accessible to us via the experiences of the Other. This distinguishes the 'vivid present' from the present of inner time consciousness, and from Schutz's preferred 'specious present', both of which are centred on the primal impression of perception. The vivid present is not a feature of inner time alone, but a product of consciousness's grasping of other people's activities in the outer, spatial world. And because 'grasping' is an act which attributes meaning, the vivid present is by definition both consciously present and meaningful.

Making Music

How does Schutz apply this thinking to music viewed as an activity in the social world, to music understood not as ideal object but as *music-making*? We have already seen the way in which Schutz theorises the act of listening to music as the synchronisation of the stream of consciousness of the listener with the polythetic steps comprising the music, themselves an expression of the stream of consciousness of the composer. Schutz sums it up in this way:

> We have... the following situation: two series of events in inner time, one belonging to the stream of consciousness of the composer, the other to the stream of consciousness of the beholder, are lived through in simultaneity, which simultaneity is created by the ongoing flux of the musical process.[55]

---

53 Zaner 2002, p. 7.
54 Schutz 1962, pp. 174–5.
55 Schutz 1951, p. 92.

Schutz terms this process of living through a shared vivid present the 'mutual tuning-in relationship', which is simply another way of describing the We-relationship, discussed above. How is this situation modified by the introduction of a performer to the model? Schutz regards the social function of the performer as the intermediary between the composer and the listener. 'By his re-creation of the musical process the performer partakes in the stream of consciousness of the composer as well as of the listener. He thereby enables the latter to become immersed in the particular articulation of the flux of inner time which is the specific meaning of the piece of music'.[56] This description of the performer's role applies equally to situations of live performance and the playing of recorded music. In either case composer, performer and listener all share a vivid present, they are all mutually 'tuned-in' to one another via the same flux, all growing older together.

However, because the performer's contribution to the process involves a series of actions and events in the outer world, namely, the physical production of audible sounds, this is not a process that takes place solely in inner time. This leads Schutz to argue that 'the social relationship between performer and listener is founded upon the common experience of living simultaneously in several dimensions of time'.[57] The element of the time of the outer, spatial world, which is necessary for audible music to exist at all, becomes still more evident when considering the relationship between two or more performers making music together.[58] While the listener's co-performing of the polythetic steps of the music takes place in inner time, each performer is obliged to execute her actions not only in relation to the thought of the composer but in coordination with the inner and outer time of her fellow performers. '[S]he has not only to interpret [her] own part... but [also] to anticipate the other players' interpretations of [their] parts and, even more, the others' anticipations of [her] own execution'.[59] The players share both in the inner *durée* of the music, and in the vivid present of each other's stream of consciousness. 'This is possible', Schutz says, 'because making music together occurs in a true face-to-face relationship – inasmuch as the participants are sharing not only a section of time but also a sector of space'.[60] That the social

---

56   Schutz 1951, p. 93.
57   Schutz 1951, p. 94.
58   The only possible exception to this is if one takes the concept of music as ideal object to its extreme, for which the reading in one's head of a musical score is as satisfactory a musical experience as a performance, if not a better or purer one.
59   Schutz 1951, p. 94.
60   Schutz 1951, p. 95.

relationship required for music-making is founded on the collective living through of different dimensions of time is equally true for orchestral performances, a congregation singing hymns, people sitting around a campfire, or improvising jazz musicians. All involve the synchronisation of two dimensions of time:

> On the one hand, there is the inner time in which each performer recreates in polythetic steps the musical thought of the (eventually anonymous) composer and by which he is also connected with the listener. On the other, making music together is an event in outer time, presupposing also a face-to-face relationship, that is, a community of space, and it is this dimension which unifies the fluxes of inner time and warrants their synchronization into a vivid present.[61]

The elements of face-to-face interaction between performers in outer time which Schutz identifies are facial expressions and the movements and gestures associated with the playing of instruments. Since inner time is by its nature unmeasurable, there being 'no equality between its pieces, if pieces there [are] at all...', it is also the case that any counting, beating by a conductor, or use of a metronome takes place in this outer realm. But it is clear that Schutz has a very restricted view of the role of such practices, regarding them as beyond the scope of musical performance as such. When he speaks of the outer time 'that the musician "counts" in order to assure the correct "tempo"', he is clearly thinking of a 'count-in' that takes place before the commencement of the music, rather than during it, and the inverted commas convey his doubt as to whether there can properly be counted time or measured tempo.[62] Elsewhere he describes beat counting and conducting as devices which co-performers may have recourse to 'when for one reason or another the flux of inner time in which the musical content unfolds has been interrupted'. The role of the conductor is to 'establish with each of the performers the contact which they are unable to find with one another in immediacy' because of the size of the ensemble. 'He does so by action in the outer world, and his evocative gestures into which he translates the musical events going on in inner time, replace for each performer the immediate grasping of the expressive activities of all his coperformers'.[63]

---

61 Schutz 1951, p. 96.
62 Schutz 1951, p. 89.
63 Schutz 1951, p. 95.

The problem with this is the rigid separation that Schutz maintains between the activities apportioned to outer time and the inner time of the music. Beating and counting-in only take place, for Schutz, 'outside' the music in order to get it started, or to restart it if it has broken down. Once the 'flux of inner time' of the music is under way, there are no beats, nor can there be because inner time is unmeasurable. But if a count-in or a metronome is to be of any use at all, even if only for rehearsal purposes, it must reflect and coincide with some element of the music itself. A successful count-in is not the same as the count used to coordinate two people lifting a heavy object. In that case, all that is required is the synchronisation of a single impulse. The speed of a musical count-in, however, must not only coordinate the initial moment of the music, but, more importantly, give a precise indication of the tempo of the pulse around which the music will be organised once it has begun.[64] Schutz's description of the conductor's movements as 'evocative gestures' ignores the fact they remain, in most cases in the Western tradition, even when at their most florid and expressive, movements which mark the occurrences of the beat. They are gestures which measure time into more or less regular intervals, so if they are indeed translations into outer time of musical events going on in inner time, as Schutz maintains, those regular intervals must also be present in the inner time of the music.

As Epstein argues, referring to the measured time of music as 'objective time' is misleading because 'it implies a time outside of music, somehow not experienced', yet beat and meter are not purely abstract but are manifested concretely and sonically in music. Epstein recognises two orders of musical time but prefers to term them chronometric and integral rather than objective and subjective. Meter and beat are the principal elements of chronometric time while rhythm and pulse are those of integral time. For Epstein, the temporal processes in a musical work result from 'the conflicts and coordinations between meter and rhythm, between beat and pulse at many levels of the music'.[65]

The core of Schutz's position appears to be that all the manifestations of time measurement that take place in the outer world as part of the process of music-making are purely expedient practices for the purposes of coordination between performers. That they are entirely extraneous to the music itself follows logically from the theory that the latter unfolds exclusively in inner time. It is noteworthy that Schutz only discusses counting and beating in relation to the question of multiple performers, ignoring the relevance of such practices

---

64 Unpulsed music is generally not counted-in.
65 Epstein 1987, pp. 57, 60.

to individual performers. Obviously the question of a conductor does not arise in the case of a single performer, but solo players do silently count themselves in to the start of a piece, and frequently maintain a count through the piece in order to guide their execution of its rhythm. The purpose here, clearly, is not one of synchronisation with other players; it can only be one of coordination with what Schutz calls 'outer time'. There is a name for the manifestation of 'outer time' within music: it is meter, and Schutz's theory, because of its rejection of rhythm as a necessary element of music, is unable to recognise it. Schutz's analysis of the temporality of music stops with the temporality of the perception of tones themselves, and therefore can tell us nothing about how we perceive the temporal positioning of tones in relation to one another. Consequently, this area of Schutz's thinking does not help us with the musical aspects of our theorisation of groove.

However, Schutz's phenomenological theory of the *practice* of making music, as distinct from the music itself, by addressing the social relations involved in performance and listening, may shed some light on another aspect of groove, namely its apparently collective nature. A phenomenology of groove would seek to explain the powerfully shared sense of temporal unity fostered by such music, the apparent ability of groove music to generate a temporality within which all participants – performers and listeners – become actively bound up. This collective aspect of 'grooving', identified by Allen Farmelo as a 'modified state that people enter into' which produces 'unifying consequences', seems well suited to phenomenological analysis.[66] Schutz's concept of the 'vivid present' within a shared temporal flux may offer a fruitful way of addressing this aspect of the groove experience, provided his theory can be modified to incorporate the rhythmic and metric elements of music that he ignores. As noted already, the most problematic element from this point of view is Schutz's insistence that music takes place in the realm of inner time, and the strict division he enforces between the inner time of the music and the outer time of the world in which music-making takes place. Schutz is very specific about this dichotomy. He writes:

> ... the decision to listen to pure music involves a peculiar attitude on the part of the listener. He stops living in his acts of daily life, stops being directed towards their objects. His attention toward life has been diverted from its original realm.... He lives now on another plane of consciousness.... when the conductor raises his baton, the audience has performed a leap ... from one level of consciousness to another. They are no longer

---

66   Farmelo 1997.

engaged in the dimension of space and spatial time, they are no longer involved in the maze of activities necessary to deal with men and things. They accept the guidance of music in order to relax their tension and to surrender to its flux, a flux which is that of their stream of consciousness in inner time.[67]

The listener described here is of a very specific kind, one who sits in silence attending to the music purely mentally. Since this listener has left the world of space and spatial time, she does not respond to the music with physical movements, however small, let alone get up and dance. Nor does she take any interest in anyone else's physical movements: not those of her fellow audience members who are equally stationary and atomised, nor those of the musicians as they engage in the music-making. This is a picture of music that could only come from the Western high art tradition, and is an idealised one even by that tradition's norms. It is based on what Small describes as the 'ceremony' of the concert hall, bearing very little relation to the music listening practices of most people in the contemporary West, let alone those of other cultures and other historical periods.[68] The conception of music found, for example, in traditional African societies as participatory and collective, one which does not distinguish between performer and audience or between music and dance, could not produce the inner/outer distinction adhered to by Schutz.[69]

But apart from its unwitting cultural specificity, Schutz's position is puzzling given the weight he accords in his thought to outer time, the time of the world of people and their activities. For Bergson, spatialised conceptions of time resulting largely from the tendency of scientific thought to quantify all phenomena, amount to a distortion of 'authentic' time, the time of life. Husserl's contribution to the study of time is designed to show how it is possible for us to perceive time at all, and his focus remains on internal, subjective, time consciousness. Schutz, though maintaining some of their insights, departs from the largely subjective concerns of these two thinkers by introducing the social realm to the investigation of temporality. Here, the time that derives from the social world, objective time, is given equal status to *durée*. It is spatialised not because of any tendency in thought or science, but because it is the time that pertains to the spatial world, the world of movement and activity. It is not, therefore, to be regretted or regarded as somehow inauthentic; rather it is a ineluctable feature of the social life of humans.

---

67 Schutz and Kersten 1976, p. 43.
68 Small 1997, p. 183.
69 Small 1987, pp. 24–8.

The major advance over these other thinkers of acknowledging the importance of 'outer time' in this way is that it posits the existence of collective, or shared, time in a concrete way. Bergson argues that two or more streams of consciousness can flow together, but Schutz makes this concrete by identifying the mechanism by which this is possible. It is only as a result of movement or activity in the spatial realm that such synchronisation can be achieved. The possibility of shared meaning rests on the resulting common temporality. Schutz's conception of the 'vivid present' is a particularly striking product of this way of conceiving temporality. Arguably, the present or 'Now' does not play a crucial role in Husserl's theory of time consciousness except as a useful explanatory device. In one sense Now can be regarded as the moment of the primal impression, but in another, the concept of Now is irrelevant to Husserl's description of time consciousness since, for him, temporality is *constructed* by consciousness, not *detected* by it.

Though committed to the essentials of Husserl's explanation of time consciousness, Schutz introduces a powerful notion of the present which results from a fusion of inner and outer times. The vivid present is a consciousness of the Now which is anchored in activity in the outer world. This means that it has two important features. Since all activity is social, and at least minimally collective in nature – by virtue of the fact that even the most individual of acts are potentially witnessable and leave traces in the world – Schutz's vivid present breaks out of the subjective constraints of Bergson's and Husserl's conceptions. It is a notion of the present which is inherently collective and social. Indeed, Schutz's insistence that we can grasp other's acts before we can grasp our own, implies that our ability to be conscious of a present derives from our engagement with others. Isolated, we are condemned to live in a world of meaning which is always 'just past'. It is only when we attend to the meaning of others' acts, particularly their acts of communication, that we can achieve any real purchase on the present.[70]

---

70 We might understand this move by Schutz as the recognition of, and the attempt to solve, albeit in a very different way, a problem in Husserl's theory of time consciousness which is also addressed by Derrida. Derrida argues that Husserl's attempt to ground consciousness/ subjectivity in a 'Now' of perception is an instance of the 'metaphysics of presence' which assumes the unproblematic self-identity of the subject. ' "Time" cannot be an "absolute subjectivity" precisely because it cannot be thought on the basis of a present and the self-presence of a present being'. The constitution of subjectivity is always undermined by a 'spacing', which bears some similarity to Schutz's positing of a temporal gap between experience and meaning. However, rather than looking to intersubjectivity to close the gap as Schutz does, Derrida draws the conclusion that all meaning is unstable and subject to continuous deferral (Derrida 1991, p. 27).

Second, as will have already become clear from this description, it is a conception of the present as meaningful. 'Now' is not an abstract mathematical point in time; nor is it the equally abstract extended zone implied by the term 'specious present'. Rather it is the moment at which intersubjective meaning arises. We can now see that Schutz's phrase 'a mutual tuning-in process' has two senses: it is a mutual tuning-in in terms of temporality – a synchronisation of fluxes; and it is a mutual tuning-in to a shared meaning.

This theory has a great deal to offer an understanding of music-making. Musical performance, because it is an activity in the social world and because it always involves a listener as well as a performer, is always a collective activity. Schutz's notion of a vivid present captures what is being aspired to when musicians strive to synchronise their individual parts with each other, and when a listener sets out to grasp, with body and mind, the music that she hears. We might counterpose to this description of performance, music that takes place solely in the mind – music that is only dreamed or conceived, or is 'heard' as a result of the silent reading of a score by someone capable of such an activity. Such music is not part of a vivid present since it involves no element of outer time, no component of action in the outer world. Music that sounds in the outer world, however, is an activity whose participants are focussed on the production of a vivid present, whose essence is intersubjective meaning.

We noted Schutz's assertion that the features of making music while growing older together are in principle the same for all forms of music-making, whether formal or informal, pre-composed or improvised. Cook remarks that this directly contradicts the widely held view, expressed here by Monson, that 'the interactive, collaborative context [of jazz improvisation at the level of the ensemble] ... has no parallel in the musical practice of Western classical composers of the common practice period'.[71] Cook goes on to endorse Schutz's position on the basis that all performance involves an element of improvisation in the sense that performers of 'classical' music do not simply play the notes as written,

> ... because every note in the score is subject to the contextual negotiation of intonation, precise dynamic value, articulation, timbral quality, and so forth. For example, the performers stay in time not because each accommodates his or her playing to an external beat (as when studio musicians record to a click track), but because each is continuously listening to the others, giving rise to a shared, communal temporality – the shared 'inner time' of Schutz's 'mutual tuning-in relationship' ...

---

71   Monson 1996, p. 74.

If there is a temporal difference between improvised and composed music, Cook suggests, it is 'that improvisation takes place on-line (in Schutzian inner time) while composition takes place off-line (in outer time)'.[72]

Is Cook right about this? In the first place, his equating of 'off-line' with Schutz's conception of outer time seems misplaced. Schutz uses the term 'outer time' to refer to the measurable, datable, divisible and collective time of the spatial world. This is the realm in which the social activities of musical performance, including the accommodations of timing between musicians mentioned by Cook, take place. Cook's notion of 'off-line' is more like 'outside' or 'beyond' time, in the sense that the time of 'writing' music does not coincide with the time of playing it. To use a computing term, it is not a 'real time' activity.

Secondly, although there is some validity in Cook's argument that there is a similarity between the musicianship required for performing composed chamber music and that required for engaging in jazz improvisation, it is worth exploring the possible differences too. If the negotiation of timing adjustments within a musical ensemble depends on the ability to anticipate, or protend, what one's coperformers will play next and when they will play it, as it surely does, it must be the case that, all other factors being equal, it is easier to do that when the music is known to the performers in advance. That the performers of a composed piece have access not only to its written form but also to previous playings of it, both others' and their own, serves seriously to limit the degree of spontaneous flexibility required of them in any given performance. And all this is in addition to the fact that the music that Cook is discussing, 'Western art-music of the common practice period', employs a framework of measured time of beats and bars – it has meter, albeit often a relatively flexible one.

By contrast, in the case of music involving a degree of improvisation (in what notes are to be played rather than simply in their timing), at least some aspects of how the music will unfold are not known in advance by the participants. It is not possible to anticipate what each player will play next or when they will play it. One way of dealing with this situation is effectively to forego the aim of direct synchronisation of parts and instead make a virtue of temporal disjunctures and non-coincidences. This is the approach taken by so-called 'free' improvisation. But by far the more common solution is to strengthen the metrical framework of the music to provide some temporal security within which improvisation can take place.[73] Monson explains that in the jazz

---

72 Cook 2004, pp. 5–25.
73 Parallel to this, and concomitant with it, is the tendency to strengthen the harmonic framework with the use of a prescribed chord sequence.

context 'the notion of the groove supplies underlying solidity and cohesiveness to freely interacting, improvising musicians'.[74] This applies not only to jazz, but to the vast majority of twentieth-century popular musics, especially groove musics, which, although not exclusively improvised, largely derive from aural as opposed to written practices.

Schutz's insights provide a possible phenomenological explanation for popular music's stricter adherence than classical chamber music to measured time, a tendency alluded to by Cook's passing reference to click tracks. In both the case of classical chamber music and that of music with improvised origins the interaction between performers produces a vivid present as a result of the coordination of their musical actions in the outer world. In that sense, Schutz is right to say that there is no difference in principle between them. It is also true, as noted above and despite the fact that Schutz ignores it, that both cases typically involve the measuring of outer time – a pulse – which finds its way into the music itself in the form of beats and bars – that is, meter. This in no way compromises the flux of the music since, according to Schutz, music-making already takes place in the realm of outer time, and the difference here is merely one of degree.

But there is a sense in which the character of the presentness thus forged is different in each case. The vivid present of the composed music is determined by its origins in an 'off-line' compositional process which took place some time in the past. Schutz describes the temporal relationship between performers and audience on the one hand, and the composer on the other, as 'quasi-simultaneity' rather than true simultaneity. We might also describe the encounter between the performers in this case as a pre-planned or re-staged form of intersubjectivity. The result is a vivid present which contains a determining element from the past. Non-composed music, on the other hand, has its origins either in the vivid present of its performance (if it is completely improvised), or, more likely, in a vivid present (that is, an 'on-line' or 'real time' process) in the past, or some combination of the two. This is a vivid present which is striving to escape its controlling determination from the past and become a fully present present, or perhaps a more vivid vivid present. This may be a way of accounting for the heightened sense of collective temporal unity associated with groove compared with non-groove musics.

---

74   Monson 1996, p. 67.

Overcoming the Dichotomy of Inner and Outer

Schutz's distinctive application of Husserlian phenomenology to social interaction in the world produces valuable insights into the temporal processes at work in the act of making music. The notion that the practice of 'musicking', to use Christopher Small's neologism, involves the synchronisation of the subjective time consciousnesses of all those participating – composers, performers and listeners alike – into a shared vivid present which has its roots in objective physical activity in the outer world, seems to chime with our experience of enjoying music.[75] In addition, his use of Husserl's theory of time consciousness to construct the basis of an explanation of the function of musical phrasing is equally illuminating and persuasive.

Schutz's inability to deal adequately with the question of rhythm, and his tendency to underplay the extent to which musical time is structured and quantified, derive from his adherence to the notion that music is an ideal object, and from the rigid separation that he maintains between the inner time which music occupies and the outer time of the social world. In this conception, inner time consciousness is entirely individual and subjective, distinct from the temporalities of nature, and prior to intersubjectivity. What is then necessary for any kind of social interaction, music-making included, is for individual, subjective, inner time consciousnesses to be brought together and synchronised through activity that takes place in the outer, physical world. But this conception of time consciousness ultimately rests upon a mind/body dualism which forgets that both the activity of our minds and the actions of our limbs are all features of our physical bodies existing in the world. It suggests that a dividing line between inner and outer runs in a Cartesian manner right through each of us, exiling our bodies to an external world of matter and action which is distinct from that of our thoughts and our selves.

Paul Ricoeur, drawing upon the same phenomenological tradition, theorises the relationship between what Schutz calls inner and outer time in a way which allows for their reconciliation. Ricoeur accuses Husserl, whose insights into the structure of time consciousness he accepts, of 'forgetting nature'.[76] The time of the world, or cosmological time, is not simply 'outer'; nor are conceptions of time based upon its endless succession of instants simply inauthentic or erroneous. On the contrary, cosmological time is connected to our subjective time consciousness through the fact that it is this time to which we must submit as natural beings, and it is to this time that we all ultimately

---

75   Small 1997.
76   Ricoeur 1984, p. 18.

succumb through death. In other words, the apprehension of cosmological time is not solely the product of engagement in the outer, social world. Rather, such temporality is already a component part of the phenomenology of time consciousness through the mortality of our bodies. And because the temporal form that that apprehension takes – the time of calendars and clocks grounded in the measurement of astronomical movement – is a socio-historical product, there must already be an intersubjective component to existential temporality. As Ricoeur argues, calendar time is 'the first bridge constructed by historical practice between lived time and universal time'.[77]

In musical performance, the measured temporality of the social world of collective action is not, therefore, merely an 'outer' link facilitating coordination between the subjective consciousnesses of the performers, but finds expression within the music itself through the presence of pulse and meter, elements of the music which Schutz is forced to deny. Using Ricoeur's argument, we might argue, perhaps over-dramatically, that the presence in music of measured time is the expression within internal time consciousness of cosmological time, mediated through the socially produced mechanisms for tracking it, the phenomenological ground of which is the inevitability of death. Curiously, Schutz's choice of the phrase 'growing older together' points in the direction of this conclusion but he fails to draw it, seeing only the phenomenological aspect of ageing and death and not its 'natural' basis.

Ricoeur's approach, although based in the phenomenological tradition, ends up coming close to a materialist critique of Schutz's position. Any materialist perspective must reject his dualism and insist on both the unity of human beings with the world of matter, and the unity of the human body with its mind or brain. For Marx, for example:

> Nature is man's inorganic body – nature, that is, insofar as it is not itself human body. Man lives on nature – means that nature is his body, with which he must remain in continuous interchange if he is not to die. That man's physical and spiritual life is linked to nature means simply that nature is linked to itself, for man is a part of nature.[78]

Because humans are a part of nature, because they exist in a metabolic relationship, or 'material exchange' with nature, there can be no question of their escaping the cycles and rhythms of the natural world.[79]

---

77   Ricoeur 1984, p. 105.
78   Marx 1975b, p. 276.
79   or *Stoffwechsel*; see Marx 1989, p. 553.

Human beings are both products of nature and part of it; if they have a biological basis when their social existence is excluded from account (it cannot be abolished!); ... and if they live within nature (however much they may be divided off from it by particular social and historical conditions of life and by the so-called 'artistic environment'), then what is surprising in the fact that human beings share in the rhythm of nature and its cycles?[80]

It is not just our bodies – our 'physical life' – that is bound up with nature in this way, but our minds – or 'spiritual life' – too. Marx regards sense perception – the physical interaction between humans and their material surroundings, what he terms *sensuousness* – as the basis of all knowledge:

> Sense-perception must be the basis of all science. Only when it proceeds from sense-perception in the two-fold form of sensuous consciousness and sensuous need – is it true science.[81]

The nature of that sensuous relationship is conceived in inherently temporal terms. In his doctoral thesis, Marx endorses Epicurus's view that because everything in the world is in the process of becoming and passing away, 'human sensuousness is... embodied time, the existing reflection of the sensuous world in itself'.[82]

Such a way of conceiving human temporality is surely less problematic than one which begins from a distinction between inner and outer times. Even if we want to retain the notion of 'inner' consciousness, a materialist perspective insists that such consciousness is always at least partially 'outer' as well, and as such remains connected in some fundamental way to the rest of nature and to other humans. It then becomes the case that music-making is not the objective, outer-world activity which is necessary in order to bring together otherwise isolated inner subjectivities, but rather simply a sensuous (physical and mental) practice in which humans collectively express their shared experiences of the world.

There are many ways in which Schutz's thinking marks a step forward from his intellectual precursors Bergson and Husserl. In his phrase 'making music while growing older', Schutz hints at an almost Epicurean awareness that the roots of time consciousness lie in the inevitable decay and death of human

---

80   Nicolai Bukharin quoted in Foster 2000, p. 227.
81   Marx 1975b, p. 294.
82   Marx 1975a, p. 64.

bodies along with everything else in nature. However, for Schutz, it is the *consciousness* of growing older which is explanatory, his idealism preventing him from seeing the material ageing which lies beneath. In addition, the fact that the category which occupies the role of 'objective' or 'outer' in Schutz's schema is the social world of people and their interactions, rather than the abstract concepts of physical or spatial time, marks the beginning of an understanding of the role of society in shaping time and time consciousness. Finally, the acknowledgement of the central role of activity in music-making – music as practice, rather than merely object – and the concept of the vivid present based upon it, can be regarded as further steps in a direction which increases the tension between his theory of making music and the idealist ontology of music and subjectivist conceptions of time, such as *durée*, to which he continued to cling. What is required is to pursue the direction that these steps indicate, to reject the idea that music exists in a realm which is temporally distinct from the social and natural worlds and to recognise the impact, via rhythm and meter, that socially produced forms of time consciousness have on the temporality of music. In other words, we need to recognise not only the social time of musical performance, but the social time of music itself.

CHAPTER 5

Adorno and Reified Time

Having explored the key idealist conceptions of time and their implications for understanding musical time, we must now begin to assemble a Marxist approach to these questions. Adorno remains the Marxist who has made the greatest contribution to aesthetics, especially in relation to music, and he will be a central reference point for this task for several reasons. First, because few other thinkers have a knowledge of music at a level which is adequate to their philosophical arguments. We have seen in relation to Husserl and Schutz in the last chapter that misunderstandings and confusions about music and music-making impair the positions they attempt to defend. There is no such weakness with Adorno who, in addition to being a significant philosopher in his own right, produced a body of music criticism which is as erudite and insightful as any ever written.

The second reason why Adorno is a touchstone is the intensely critical nature of his work. Neither in his philosophy nor in his musicology is Adorno merely attempting to provide explanations for the way things are. Central to his procedure, and consistent with a Marxist approach, is that critique is a necessary component of any serious analysis. Adorno is frequently taken to task for this, particularly by scholars of popular music, who regularly describe him as elitist and irremediably highbrow, curmudgeonly or out of date. For self-avowed Marxist Adam Krims, 'Adorno is the popular music scholar's scene of primal trauma', whose aesthetic judgments belong to an era now long gone and whose approach marks a dead end in the study of music.[1] What is now urgent is the establishment of a 'Marxist music analysis without Adorno'.[2] Accusing Adorno of letting his personal preferences influence his musical assessment, Max Paddison complains that 'Adorno's work on jazz and popular music is undoubtedly marred by the fact that he himself detested such music'.[3] But why marred? Analysis is surely all the stronger for taking a partisan position. Adorno's contemporary, George Lukács, was scathing about the kind of bourgeois conscientiousness that paraded its 'lack of convictions', regarding it as a submission to capitalist reification.[4] It could equally be argued, contra

---

1 Krims 2007, p. 92.
2 Krims 2003, pp. 131–57.
3 Paddison 2004, p. 113.
4 Lukács 1971, pp. 99–100.

Paddison, that many of Adorno's critics are often compromised by their own enjoyment of popular music and their interest in defending it at all costs. Whether or not one agrees with his judgments, Adorno's refusal to sink into a positivist acceptance of the world as it is reminds us that true knowledge is always committed and critical, and that passivity and a feigned neutrality are the tools of apologists of the status quo. The question is not whether Adorno is too critical, but whether his critique is the right one; and even if it is not, whether his philosophical and aesthetic methodology can lead to conclusions other than the ones he himself drew.

Thirdly, the relevance of Adorno for this study is the attention that he gives to both popular music and the musical modernisms of the early part of the twentieth century. His valorisation of the latter to the detriment of the former encourages some writers to attempt to bridge the gap by claiming to detect in certain kinds of popular music from the 1960s onwards the very modernist aesthetic that Adorno promotes. The sheer depth of the gulf Adorno draws between authentic modernism and popular music would suggest that any defence of popular music which seeks an accommodation with his position by claiming Frank Zappa or Talking Heads for modernism is somewhat misplaced.[5] The fact that such artists represent a only tiny minority of what is taken as popular music renders such an approach less of a refutation of Adorno's blanket condemnation of the popular than a defensive reaction which serves to endorse it. It seems more appropriate to take seriously Adorno's description of modernism and the popular as the 'torn halves of an integral freedom, to which however, they do not add up', halves which both date from the coming to maturity of mass industrial society and seem to represent radically different cultural responses to that historical juncture.[6] In an attempt to explore whether Adorno's aesthetic methodology can yield something other than a wholesale rejection of popular music, this is the starting point that I will adopt here, focusing on the question of time.

Time is a crucial element of the distinction Adorno draws between 'serious' and popular music, and one which sheds a particularly sharp light on just how significantly popular music differs from the self-consciously modernist aesthetic of the early twentieth century. It is my contention that Adorno accepted as the basis for his thought on this question a critique of measured time, often referred to pejoratively as 'objective time' or 'reified time', which was *de rigueur* for virtually all the modernist thinkers of his age. The most explicit philosophical expression of this position is found, as we have seen, in Bergson's critique

---

5 See Paddison 1982.
6 Adorno 1997b, p. 123.

of the spatialisation of time, which was highly influential in the early part of the last century, and to a certain extent, remains so today.

Adorno's remarks on time and the temporality of music are scattered among his musical and aesthetic writings, forming an element of his critique of 'serious' composers such as Wagner, Stravinsky and even Schoenberg. But first it is necessary in the present context to examine the role that arguments about time play in his discussion of popular music and jazz.

The Time of Jazz

In its basic formulation, Adorno's argument about popular music's organisation of time can be regarded as a subset of his general argument concerning the standardised nature of popular music. Expressed most clearly in the 1941 essay 'On Popular Music', this argues that popular song's use of standardised structures (e.g. 32-bar AABA choruses) enforces a dislocation between form and content in which the actual substance of the music merely fills a form which pre-exists it, rather than interacting dialectically with it as is the case in the best classical music. A parallel argument about meter is largely found in his writing on jazz, but since Adorno makes no clear distinction between the terms jazz, light and popular music, we are entitled to take them as applying to popular music as a whole. Adorno speaks of the 'unabating time unit of the music – its "beat"' and 'the undisputed predominance of the beat' that he encounters in jazz, a 'fundamental beat [which] is rigorously maintained [and] ... is marked over and over again by the bass drum'.[7] One might question whether the bass drum's role is a necessary part of the argument, but the central point is that Adorno believes that popular music gives a greater degree of prominence to a regular pulse than does most art music of the Western tradition. He also contends that this temporal regularity often extends to larger periods within the music: 'the principle of symmetry is fully respected, especially in the basic rhythmic structure. The eight-bar period, and even the four-bar half period, are maintained, their authority unchallenged'.[8] That this represents for Adorno an aspect of the standardisation to be found in popular music is made clear by his comments on syncopation. 'Syncopation is [jazz's] basic principle' which 'occasionally in virtuoso pieces yield[s] an extraordinary complexity', but is never allowed to disrupt the basic meter.[9] 'Jazz is music

---

7   Adorno 2002e, p. 460; Adorno 1976, p. 13; Adorno 2002c, pp. 470–1.
8   Adorno 2002c, p. 471.
9   Adorno 2002c, p. 470.

which fuses the most rudimentary melodic, harmonic, metric and formal structure with the ostensibly disruptive principle of syncopation, yet without ever disturbing the crude unity of the basic rhythm, the identically sustained meter, the quarter-note'.[10]

So the basic outline of the argument is clear: in spite of syncopation which can often be quite intricate, the standardised nature of the regular crotchet beat is never overcome. Syncopation here occupies the role played in Adorno's standardisation argument by 'pseudo-individualisation', the presence within popular music of elements like 'improvised breaks' which feign originality and freedom, but which in reality serve only to disguise the rigidity of the standardised form. This rigidity applies as much to performers as to listeners: 'he who is reproducing the music is permitted to tug at the chains of his boredom, and even to clatter them, but he cannot break them'.[11] The underlying schema always dominates:

> In jazz, freedom and rhythmic wealth are illusory from the perspective of musical immanence: metrically the eight-bar structure dominates, making use of syncopation and the interpolation of false beats [by which he means polyrhythmic figures like the 3 + 3 + 2 rumba pattern – MA] only as ornaments. In its harmonic-formal relations, however, this structure asserts itself without challenge, and rhythmic emancipation is restricted to the sustained quarter-notes of the bass drum.[12]

The inadequacy of music organised in this way is that it represents, for Adorno, a renunciation of individual subjectivity in the face of prevailing social conditions. The music displays all the signs of adapting to the reality of the 'machine age'. Jazz shares this impulse with composers like Stravinsky and Hindemith, whose:

> renunciation of dreaming ... is an index that listeners are ready to replace dreaming by adjustment to raw reality, that they reap new pleasure from their acceptance of the unpleasant. They are disillusioned about any possibility of realizing their own dreams in the world in which they live, and consequently adapt themselves to this world.

---

10   Adorno 1983, p. 121.
11   Adorno 2002c, p. 480.
12   Adorno 2002a, p. 430.

Or again:

> The cult of the machine which is represented by unabating jazz beats involves a self-renunciation... The adaptation to machine music necessarily implies a renunciation of one's own human feelings and at the same time a fetishism of the machine such that its instrumental character becomes obscured thereby.[13]

Ironically, it was certain forms of modernist art in the early twentieth century, rather than popular music, which adopted an overt 'cult of the machine'. Adorno sees a mechanisation of music as somewhat inevitable in a society in which subjects 'are appendages of machinery... compelled as they are to adjust themselves and their innermost feelings to the machinery of society, in which they must play their roles and to which they must shape themselves with no reservation'.[14] It is Adorno's argument that music which simply aims to replicate the sounds of industrial society has conceded any aesthetic function and become part of life rather than art: 'at times it sounds as if the music were sacrificing its distance and its aesthetic figurativeness and had stepped over into the physical empirical realm of regulated-arbitrary life'.[15]

For Adorno, there are also deeper and more sinister inferences to be drawn from the regulated time of popular music. Meter, which Adorno understands as prescribed in advance and imposed upon the music, is the manifestation of 'social law' in the music, the authoritarianism of an imposed collectivity. He defines jazz as a fusion of salon music and the march, and for him the latter is irrevocably associated with fascism. That jazz is also a dance music does not lessen its authoritarian nature, because 'insofar as dance is synchronous movement, the tendency to march has been present in dance from the very beginning; thus jazz is connected in its origins with the march and its history lays bare this relationship'.[16]

So, all dance music is tainted by its association with marching, militarism, imposed collectivity and ultimately with fascism. Those listeners who find enjoyment in the regularity of the beat Adorno labels the 'rhythmically obedient type', which is found mostly among the youth. 'They are most susceptible

---

13   Adorno 2002e, p. 461.
14   Quoted from 'Is Marx obsolete?' in Leppert 2002, p. 52.
15   Adorno 2002c, p. 486.
16   Adorno 2002c, p. 489. Another scholar for whom dance and military drill are closely related is the historian William McNeill (see McNeill 1995).

to a process of masochistic adjustment to authoritarian collectivism'.[17] Syncopation creates the impression of freedom from the discipline of meter, but this is a 'caricature of untrammelled subjectivity' whose protestations are futile.[18] Syncopation's superficial rebellion against the regular beat exactly corresponds to the jazz subject's temporary anxiety towards being engulfed in the majority that it had no hand in constructing, until it is ultimately 'received into, or, better, subordinated to the collective as it was predestined to be; until the music indicates...that it was a part of it from the very beginning; that, itself a part of this society, it can never really break away from it....'.[19] This, for Adorno, is very different from the use made of syncopation by a composer like Beethoven. Jazz syncopation:

> is not, like its counterpart, that of Beethoven, the expression of an accumulated subjective force which directed itself against authority until it had produced a new law out of itself. It is purposeless; it leads nowhere and is arbitrarily withdrawn by an undialectical, mathematical incorporation into the beat.[20]

At the heart of the psychological aspect of Adorno's analysis is the notion that, through the rigidity and regularity of its temporal structure, jazz subjectivity willingly collaborates in its own subjugation by authority. It is 'like the sadomasochistic type described by analytic psychology, the person who chafes against the father-figure while secretly admiring him', simultaneously emulating and detesting him, not the image of a 'thriving productive power, but always that of a neurotic weakness', and for that reason, he suggests, jazz is particularly suited to oppressed peoples.[21] Adorno perhaps pushes the psychological argument beyond reasonable bounds when he associates the form of syncopation known as 'anticipation' with sexual dysfunction: this kind of syncopation 'is plainly a "coming-too-early", just as anxiety leads to premature orgasm, just as impotence expresses itself through premature and incomplete orgasm.[22] ... Jazz... integrates stumbling and coming-too-soon onto the collective march-step'.[23] Despite the provocative hyperbole of this argument, what should not be overlooked is that Adorno has correctly identified the

---

17   Adorno 2002e, p. 460.
18   Adorno 1983, p. 126.
19   Adorno 2002c, p. 489.
20   Adorno 2002c, p. 490.
21   Adorno 1983, p. 122; Adorno 2002c, p. 491.
22   Ibid.
23   Adorno 1983, p. 128.

importance of rhythmic anticipation, which, along with polyrhythm of the type alluded to earlier, comprise the two basic forms taken by syncopation in twentieth-century popular music which were analysed in Chapter 1.

Time in Music

It is a truism to say that music is a temporal art. What is at issue in the aesthetic debates about musical time is whether there is anything more to the time of music than the empirical time which a piece of music occupies as a result of its having duration, the time in which its content, its events, unfold. If there is, if music's time involves something beyond real time, a distinct aesthetic temporality, what is this time's relationship to real, empirical time?

Adorno argues that to recognise that musical time and real time are, at root, both manifestations of the same thing, is the correct starting point for a materialist aesthetics of music, but does not tell us very much about the relationship. The ways that music has expressed and organised temporality have varied widely across historical periods:

> Musical time is really musical – in other words not just the measurable time of the duration of the piece – only as time that is dependent on the musical content and in turn determines that content, the concrete means of the transmission of the successive. But this musical time varies so completely from one type to the next that its over-arching idea would have to be limited to the most external aspect – the chronometric unit. ... But just as the temporal form of every music, its inner historicity, varies historically, so this inner historicity also always reflects real, external time. After all, purely musical time, in its differentiation from the other one, always relates to the latter as the echo to the reflected sound.[24]

Musical time is connected to real time, but like other aspects of the external world that find their way into works of art, it has been transfigured aesthetically. It is like a distant reverberation of real time, an aesthetic image of the time of the everyday world. Art is only art to the extent that it undertakes this aesthetic transformation of the empirical world:

> Crude, unmediated space, time, and causality no more exist in art than, in keeping with the idealist philosphem, as a sphere totally apart, art exists beyond their determinations; they play into art as from a distance

---

24   Adorno 2002f, pp. 143–4.

and in it are immediately transformed into something other. Thus, for example, there is no mistaking time as such in music, yet it is so remote from empirical time that, when listening is concentrated, temporal events external to the musical continuum remain external to it and indeed scarcely touch it; if a musician interrupts a passage to repeat it or to pick it up at an earlier point, musical time remains indifferent, unaffected; in a certain fashion it stands still and only proceeds when the course of the music is continued. Empirical time disturbs musical time, if at all, only by dint of its heterogeneity, not because they flow together.... As a musical composition compresses time, and as a painting folds spaces into one another, so the possibility is concretized that the world could be other than it is. Space, time, and causality are maintained, their power is not denied, but they are divested of their compulsiveness. Paradoxically, it is precisely to the extent that art is released from the empirical world by its formal constituents that it is less illusory, less deluded by subjectively dictated lawfulness, than is empirical knowledge.[25]

Thus we have a conception of the relationship between art and reality in which works of art are understood to embody elements of the empirical world, and that it is this connection which grounds art and guarantees its relevance. All materialist conceptions of art must insist on this connection. On the other hand, the objective world does not simply make its appearance undisguised in art: an aesthetic representation is precisely one which makes a transformation of those elements, and in so doing achieves a distance between itself an the empirical world. Music incorporates the time of the world, but not literally:

> It was long held that music must organize the intratemporal succession of events meaningfully: Each event should ensue from the previous one in a fashion that no more permits reversal than does time itself. However, the necessity of this temporal sequence was never literal; it participated in art's semblance character.[26]

It should be clear from what has gone before that in jazz and popular music Adorno believed that this fundamental dialectic between musical time and empirical time is fatally undermined. Before considering exactly how and why that failure occurs, it is worth ascertaining what kinds of musical temporality he considered to be aesthetically adequate or successful.

---

25 Adorno 1997a, p. 182.
26 Adorno 1997a, p. 30.

The first thing that should be recognised is that in his discussions of musical temporality, Adorno's particular emphasis is less the time of immediate, everyday experience, than time as history, which he regards as the ultimate subject matter of music: 'the time that is immanent in every music, its inner historicity, is real historical time, reflected as appearance'.[27] Thus:

> History is the content of artworks. To analyze artworks means no less than to become conscious of the history immanently sedimented in them.[28]

Consequently, musical temporality, if it is to do justice to real time and real human history, should mirror an adequate conception of the processes of history itself, and for Adorno, that means a dialectical understanding of historical movement, one derived from the philosophy of Hegel. Such temporality in music, he argues, first crystallised in the music of the Viennese classicists, Haydn and Mozart, and is a 'time in which being itself is transformed into a process and, at the same time, its result'. Its connection with the society of its day is that it 'is not only genetically but substantively the very same time that constituted the rhythm of emancipated bourgeois society, which interpreted its own play of forces as stability'. This tradition finds its apogee in the music of Beethoven, whose compositional method, Adorno believes, bears a close relationship to Hegel's logic not simply because one may have influenced the other, but because both are rooted in the same socio-historical soil. Beethoven is the model of music's attempt to 'possess the absolute' by achieving the 'intellectual and spiritual sedimentation of real time' within the musical material through the correspondence of its immanent temporal processes with those of society.[29]

What do these 'Hegelian' temporal processes look like when they are manifested in music? They are fundamentally developmental and processual. For Adorno, Beethoven's achievement is to have composed music which moved far beyond a simple juxtaposition of contrasting themes and sections to consist instead of a genuine unfolding of musical material. In the works of the mature Beethoven, it is not so much the themes or the motifs themselves that carry significance, but their transformation and elaboration in a process of continuous development. Adorno praises Beethoven for being able to construct monumental movements from the tiniest fragments which are meaningless in and

---

27 Adorno 2002f, p. 144.
28 Adorno 1997a, p. 112.
29 Adorno 2002f, p. 144.

of themselves. Pure repetition, in music as in life, has no place; where there is a recapitulation of musical material – still an important structural element of the forms used by Beethoven – it has always undergone a transformation under the impact of the developmental passages that precede it. In other words, musical subjects, like their human counterparts, cannot avoid being marked by the effects of time.

In this way, great music sets itself the task of 'draw[ing] the image of abundant time... or, as Beethoven put it, of the glorious moment'. In order adequately to present a 'detailed imagery of the flow of time', it must be a music of change, development, emergence and Becoming.[30]

However, the possibility of a genuine experience of time is threatened by the reification of society. In a passage in his *Introduction to a Sociology of Music*, Adorno draws on Bergson's terminology to describe the effect on temporal experience of the conditions of modern industrial society:

> The more the emphatic concept of experience, the sense of a temporal continuum, dissolves under the conditions of industrial production, and the more time decomposes into discontinuous, shocklike moments, the more nakedly and menacingly will the subjective consciousness come to feel itself at the mercy of the course of abstract, physical time. Even in the life of the individual this time has inexorably separated from that *temps durée* which Bergson still viewed as rescuing the living experience of time. Music calms the sense of it. Bergson knew why he contrasted his *temps espace* with [*durée*]. Abstract time is really not time any more when it confronts the content of experience as something mechanical divided into static, immutable units; and its gloomy, unstructured character becomes the opposite of [*durée*], something spatial and narrow at the same time, like an infinitely long, dark hallway.[31]

Bergson's formulations on the spatialisation of time had become an influential reference point for many thinkers and artists of the modernist heyday of the early part of the twentieth century. In some ways, Adorno's use of them is surprising, given Bergson's distance from his own Marxian framework, but in this passage Adorno appears to accept what underpins them: the duality of, on the one hand, an *a priori* continuity of time as experience, or lived time; and, on the other, an abstract time composed of instants. And although Adorno's

---

30   Adorno 1976, pp. 48–9.
31   Adorno 1976, pp. 47–8. The Ashton translation uses 'permanence' instead of *durée*, but that is clearly an error based on a lack of familiarity with Bergson.

materialism means that he sees the disintegration of real time into reified instants as having been produced by processes unleashed by the industrialisation of society, rather than simply as an intellectual error which could be corrected by adopting an appropriate mode of thought, he nonetheless articulates the notion that a 'real', continuous time exists prior to its decomposition by industrial capitalism.

So, for Adorno, as for Bergson, measured time with its series of identical instants represents a neutered, mortified image of what time, in its 'abundance', should be. For that reason, there is nothing more destructive in music to an adequate image of the flow of time-as-Becoming than an overt manifestation of clock time – the beat. 'Functional music', (by which we can assume Adorno means popular and dance music), instead of using its temporality to 'go against time' in order to 'dispel the sadness of ticking time from our psychological landscape', only confirms it by participating in its reification. As he puts it:

> it parasitically clings to time and ornaments it. It 'beats time', copying the chronometric beat, and in so doing 'kills time', as the vulgar but entirely adequate phrase has it.[32]

Thus it is clear that what underpins Adorno's critique, encountered earlier, of music organised around a prominent beat and metrical regularity, is something very close to Bergson's belief that duration, the 'real' time that is continuous and flowing, cannot be adequately grasped or represented by reducing it to a series of instants. The measuring out of time into regular parcels effectively destroys temporality – it literally 'kills time'.

'Serious' Music and Time

Despite the praise he heaps on Beethoven, Adorno is well aware that the compositional procedures he employed to great effect in the mid-nineteenth century are no longer appropriate or even possible in the twentieth. The problem now facing composers is how to resist the reifying forces emanating from the structures of industrial mass production and create music that does not simply imitate or normalise the debased temporality of capitalism. Adorno is of course well-known as a leading advocate of musical modernism, having had a close association with the Second Viennese School of composers led by Arnold

---

32   Adorno 1976, p. 49.

Schoenberg, one of whom, Alban Berg, was for a time his composition teacher. Although Adorno does not make this argument explicitly, it worth noting that in the music of Schoenberg and Berg, any sense of rhythmic regularity is undermined both through the extended use of the nineteenth-century technique of *rubato* and through the avoidance of symmetry in the thematic material itself. The third composer of this school, Anton Webern, is recognised as having been responsible for the inception of a method of composition taken up by many of the later avant-gardists in which any sense of pulse or beat is deliberately effaced.

Adorno, like other modernists working in a range of art forms, regards the purpose of art not so much to recuperate a lost temporal unity or continuity, but rather steadfastly to refuse to endorse a falsely coherent or positivistic one. Many artists of this period were developing ways to express the fractured and dislocated nature of subjective experience in the face of a rigid, objectified social order. This helps to explain why the Bergsonian critique of the spatialisation and objectification of time was able to assert its relevance and exercise considerable influence within many of the modernist artistic movements.

As befits the methodological negativity that he espoused in all his writings, the grounds for Adorno's endorsement of the Second Viennese School emerge most clearly in the context of his critiques of other composers of 'serious' music, notably Wagner and Stravinsky. Their treatment of time comprises an important part of his discussions of the work of both of them. Despite the ostensibly historical nature of the subject-matter of Wagner's operas, Adorno regards Wagner's music as inherently unhistorical and atemporal. In contrast to Beethoven's technique of continuously developing variations of thematic material, Wagner's themes remain essentially static. As Witkin comments, 'motives in Wagner are not thematically developed so much as repeated and transposed. The expectation that something is about to happen is conveyed, but it is an expectation that is frustrated ...'.[33] Adorno puts it like this:

> Eternal sameness presents itself as the eternally new, the static as the dynamic, or, conversely, intrinsically dynamic categories are projected onto unhistorical pre-subjective characters.[34]

It is Wagner's use of the *leitmotif*, elements of thematic material that recur throughout an opera to signify particular characters or situations in the drama, that best encapsulates the stasis that Adorno identifies. A leitmotif, by

---

33   Witkin 1998, p. 83.
34   Adorno 2005, p. 51.

definition, does not develop, but simply repeats, a fact that induces Adorno to agree with Nietzsche's comment that in Wagner all sense of rhythm and hence time collapses.[35] Adorno regards Wagner's leitmotifs as 'having pretensions to a "Beingness" "in and for themselves" much more than was ever the case with Beethoven': Wagner deploys them allegorically rather than developmentally, 'stringing them together like discrete objects' in a way that defies their integration into a totalising form.[36] Not only is Wagner's music static in the sense that it 'fails to create any new qualities and constantly flows into the already known', but, in addition, suffers, like jazz, from domination by an abstract beat, indicating a 'spatial' conception of time:[37]

> Giant packages of his operas are divided up by the notion of striking, beating time. The whole of the music seems to have been worked out first in terms of the beat, and then filled in ... Wagner's use of the beat to control time is abstract; it is no more than the idea of time as something articulated by the beat and then projected onto the larger periods.... the measure to which he subjects time does not derive from the musical content, but from the reified order of time itself.[38]

The spatialisation of time is again Adorno's concern in his consideration of the music of Stravinsky, whose admirers, Adorno notes, celebrate the restoration of rhythm, hitherto marginalised in the Western art music tradition by melody and harmony, to full prominence in his music. Adorno concedes that in Stravinsky the rhythmic element is prominent, but, he argues, only at 'the expense of all other aspects of rhythmic organisation'.[39] Adorno's analysis is organised around the conceptual pair, 'expressive-dynamic' and 'rhythmic-spatial', two modes of listening (and by extension, it seems, two corresponding types of music), whose relative prominence in Western music is historically determined. The expressive-dynamic type derives from singing, and has a relationship to time such that it 'transforms the heterogeneous course of time into the force of the musical process'. The rhythmic-spatial type 'obeys the beat of the drum. It is intent upon the articulation of time through the division into

---

35   Rampley 2000, p. 226.
36   Paddison 1997, p. 247.
37   Adorno 2005, p. 33.
38   Adorno 2005, pp. 22–3.
39   Adorno 1973a, p. 155.

equal measures which...virtually abrogates and spatializes [time]'.[40] The rhythmic-spatial is also associated with dance, to which, as we have seen, Adorno is hostile, regarding it '– in contrast to mature music – [as] an art of static time, a turning in a circle, movement without progress'.[41]

Adorno suggests that though the great music of the past achieved a 'mutual penetration of both modes of listening', there may be a historical tendency towards the dying out of the expressive-dynamic, a decline which Stravinsky does nothing to resist.[42] Rhythmic-spatial music seemed to be 'sprout[ing] forth everywhere...as though it were rooted in nature'.[43] Adorno charges Stravinsky's music with an absence of 'any subjectively expressive flexibility of the beat', against which he sets 'irregular, jolting accents, without being diverted from the order of the ever-consistent underlying meter'.[44] Stravinsky largely eschews the principle of motivic development or thematic evolution as the binding force of musical form, relying instead upon techniques of juxtaposition and superimposition of harmonies, textures, orchestral colours and rhythms. This is a type of montage which short circuits temporal succession in the interest of presenting a simultaneity of experience; its elements are torn from any organic process and employed for their immediate sensational qualities. Adorno describes this style as 'infantilism', arguing that 'Stravinsky's music is devoid of recollection and consequently lacking in any time continuum of permanence. Its course lies in reflexes'. Despite all its pretensions to the contrary, this is music that is thoroughly lifeless:

> [The] lack in Stravinsky's music is, in the narrowest sense, a lack of thematic material, a lack which actually excludes the breath of form, the continuity of the process – indeed it excludes 'life' itself from his music.[45]

What is notable is the extent of the similarity between the way Adorno criticises the temporality of jazz and popular music on the one hand and that of Wagner and Stravinsky on the other. The critique comprises two basic elements. The first, which applies to both the popular and serious music that Adorno criticises, and might be summarised as the 'rigid beat' critique, sug-

---

40   Adorno 1973a, pp. 197–8. The original translation reads '...division into equal measures which time virtually abrogates and spatializes', which I take to be an error.
41   Adorno 1973a, p. 196.
42   Adorno 1973a, p. 198.
43   Adorno 1973a, p. 200.
44   Adorno 1973a, p. 154; Adorno 1973a, p. 200.
45   Adorno 1973a, p. 164.

gests that any genuinely subjective sense of temporality in music is stifled by the abstract time of chronometry. This reification of time, in the form of a regular pulse, rigidly adhered to, amounts to the destruction of temporality, since the reduction of time to a series of instants, to the counting of beats, destroys the dynamic quality that time must retain if it is to be time at all. It is in this critique that we feel the influence of Bergson: the notion that there is a real time – *durée* in Bergson's terminology, a 'time continuum of permanence' in Adorno's – which flows and is bound up with the succession of events, which is betrayed and annihilated when it is represented by abstract measurement. The temporal succession of duration is transformed into simultaneity: time becomes space. In the context of Adorno's aesthetics, this temporal reification is just one aspect of a situation in which the relationship between musical form and content has degenerated irrevocably. There is no longer a healthy dialectic whereby form not only provides the necessary structure for the articulation of content, but is also shaped by it, or, in Adorno's phrase, sedimented from it. Rather, content has become completely subordinated to an objectified form which pre-exists the content it is destined to contain. Adorno's comments about the 32-bar structure of popular song are identical to his critique of Wagner's use of 'beating time': in both cases the form is set out in advance and is simply 'filled in' with musical material.[46] If Adorno is right about how these structures come about, the term spatialisation appears an apt one to describe it.

The second kind of criticism is related but slightly different. It concerns the elaboration of musical material in the compositional process, and is not directed by Adorno at popular music but only at the art music composers he criticises. We might call this the 'development' critique on the basis that it is deployed against music which is constructed using little or no thematic or motivic development. Adorno believes that the great achievement of the autonomous music of the Western tradition was its ability to represent the movement of history through its immanent musical processes. Central to this is the treatment of musical subjects (themes) so that they undergo a process of variation, interaction and transformation throughout the course of a work, a process which might be regarded as analogous to the development of human subjectivity in the world. The advantage of these compositional procedures from the perspective of temporality is that they supersede repetition as a structural device, so that even where the recapitulation of material occurs, such as in nineteenth-century sonata form, it becomes transformed by the ongoing processes of development and variation at work throughout the piece. The

---

46   See Adorno 2002e; Adorno 2005, Chapter 2, respectively.

philosophical ideas that might be said to underlie this element of Adorno's critique are Hegelian, dependent as they are on the concept of the dialectic in the form of continuous progress and change driven from within; indeed, we have seen how Adorno regards Beethoven as the Hegelian composer *par excellence*. Adorno does not level this criticism at popular music perhaps because he takes it for granted that such developmental processes can never be incorporated into popular idioms. However, there would seem to be no reason why such a critique could not in principle be applied to popular music.

In opposition to the musics and composers he attacks, Adorno endorses modernism. Not any modernism – as, for Adorno, some incarnations of modernism are equally guilty of crimes against temporality as Stravinsky or jazz – but specifically the modernism of Schoenberg and his school. As was noted earlier, it is certainly true that the music of the Second Viennese School cannot be accused of succumbing to a metronomic beat. But in addition, Adorno regards the works of Alban Berg along with Schoenberg's early output as exemplary for their commitment to the organic development of thematic material, their generation of logical musical form through a process of progressive variation. In this respect they stand in the tradition of Beethoven, albeit having jettisoned his – by then historically obsolete – language of tonality in favour of an atonal idiom.

However, Adorno's attitude to this form of modernism is not as unequivocal as that. Schoenberg, in his search for new compositional procedures to replace the framework previously supplied by the tonal system, is led to devise the twelve-tone serial technique. Adorno believes that on the one hand Schoenberg deserves credit for grappling with the historical problems that beset musical material in this period and forging a new solution which avoids the regressive pitfalls of neoclassicism or primitivism. On the other hand, it becomes clear to Adorno that serialism produces as many problems as it solves, and again, temporality is at the heart of his analysis.

Modernism and the Trend towards Stasis

In order to understand Adorno's argument, it is necessary to return to the relationship between form and content and its implications for music's relationship to time. We have seen that Adorno credits the principle of thematic development with the breakthrough by which musical organisation comes under the control of autonomous subjectivity. Prior to this discovery, music was largely constructed through the principle of repetition, possibly with an element of variation, but essentially the material comprising a piece was 'all the same thing'. This kind of music Adorno regards as 'indifferent to time'; it fills an otherwise empty passage of time but does not attempt to shape time. With the arrival of the principle of development, 'music is no longer indifferent to time, since it no longer functions on the level of repetition in time, but rather on that of alteration'.[47] The thematic material is transformed by the course of time; time has been made meaningful as a result of the transformations that it has wrought. However, for this to be the case requires that there is a limit to the transformation of thematic material. There must be a degree of sameness against which the alteration can be measured: a situation of total difference would be as atemporal as one of total sameness. Adorno refers to this as the principle of 'non-identity of identity' under which 'music does not simply surrender to time, because in its constant alteration it retains its thematic identity'. Thus there is a paradoxical relationship to time in the music of the classical period:

> This relationship involves ... the limitation of the principle of development. Music through its powers of evocation is able to hold the pure force of time at a distance only as long as the development is not absolute, only as long as it is something not totally subjected to music, but rather – in Kantian terms – an *a priori* musical '*Ding an sich*'.[48]

Beethoven finds it necessary to retain, alongside the most concentrated passages of logical thematic development, the conventional reprise of the themes in a recapitulation section. This represents the static moment within the dynamic form. Following Beethoven, these conventions are eroded, according to Adorno, by the increasing force of subjective expression. 'The subjective moments of expression liberate themselves from the continuum of time. They can no longer be held in check'.[49] To counter this, Brahms, coming later in the nineteenth century, extends the principle of variation over the entire form, rejecting conventional formulae and generating unity by ensuring that 'there is no longer anything which is unthematic; nothing which cannot be understood as the derivative of the thematic material, no matter how latent it may have become'.[50]

This is the historical condition of musical material which Schoenberg inherits, a state in which overt repetition has become unbearable and yet 'wherever

---

47   Adorno 1973a, p. 56.
48   Ibid.
49   Ibid.
50   Adorno 1973a, p. 57.

music articulates itself meaningfully, its inner logicality is tied up with overt or latent repetitions'.[51] Schoenberg initially addresses this by employing a technique of continuous development, by composing in a quasi-Brahmsian manner but without the convention of tonality. Later, he famously adopts the serial technique, in which a fixed row of twelve pitches provides the basis for an entire work. This departure is normally explained as a procedure designed to guarantee atonality and avoid any subconscious emergence of key centres in the music by ensuring that all twelve pitches recur regularly within the musical texture. Adorno sees it slightly differently, regarding it a means of solving the recurring problem of the balance between repetition and difference, between identity and non-identity. The tone row effectively becomes a kind of *Ur*-theme for the piece, supplying all the thematic and motivic material which is subjected to a continuous and varied process of 'working-out'.

Adorno has serious misgivings about the musical temporality that a reliance on a pre-composed series embodies. The ever-presence of the tone row means that identity predominates in its relationship with non-identity. Of serialism's ability to generate melody he says:

> The true quality of a melody is always to be measured by whether or not it succeeds in transforming the spatial relations of intervals into time. Twelve-tone technique destroys this relationship at its very roots. Time and interval diverge. All intervallic relationships are absolutely determined by the basic row and its derivatives. No new material is introduced into the progression of intervals, and the omnipresence of the row makes it unfit in itself for the construction of temporal relationships, for this type of relationship is based upon differentiations and not simply upon identity.[52]

More seriously, the fact that the progress of the composition is determined by the tone row, as it were, from the outside, results in temporal stasis:

> The continuum of subjective time-experience is no longer entrusted with the power of collecting musical events, functioning as a unity, and thereby imparting meaning to them. The resulting discontinuity destroys musical dynamics, to which it owes its very being. Once again music subdues time, but no longer by substituting music in its perfection for time, but by negating time through the inhibition of all musical moments by

---

51 Quoted from 'Form in the New Music' in Paddison 1997, p. 178.
52 Adorno 1973a, pp. 74–5.

means of an omnipresent construction.... Late Schoenberg shares with jazz – and moreover with Stravinsky – the dissociation of musical time. Music formulates a design of the world, which – for better or for worse – no longer recognizes history'.[53]

Given the centrality of the category of history to Adorno's aesthetics, and indeed his entire thought, the words 'for better or worse' are surprising here. But it should also be pointed out that, despite Adorno's bracketing of Schoenberg with Stravinsky in this passage, he regards their motivations very differently. While Stravinsky is accused of deliberately aiming for temporal standstill in his music, Adorno believes there is a sense in which 'in the twelve-tone technique stasis is produced almost against the will of the composer through the density of the material'. Schoenberg is constantly attempting to break out of this stasis, but Stravinsky is 'trying to ordain it as the immutable and obligatory law of the new musical language'.[54]

In the hands of the successive generation of avant-garde composers who adopted it, the techniques of serialism were extended to apply not only to pitch, but also to every other musical parameter including rhythm and note duration, instrumentation and timbre. This inevitably compounded the tendency of these 'totally integrated' works to a condition of temporal standstill. Adorno uses the concept of 'equidistance from the centre' to describe the suppression of the dynamic progression of the music through time he detects in much of the avant-garde:

> If it is at all possible to point to something like a [basic] 'idea' underlying the shaping of form in the new music, then one would have to put forward the idea of a static form: that is, of a form in which each single event is equidistant from the centre, in which concepts like development and progression ... increasingly lose their meaning and in which in a certain sense the music relates indifferently to time.[55]

Thus, the modernist tradition, espoused by Adorno in part because of its ability to resist the destruction of temporality by the forces of reification which had afflicted popular music, finds itself incapable of expressing time at all. Form holds sway over content, the universal has primacy over the particular,

---

53   Adorno 1973a, p. 60.
54   Quoted from 'Neunzehn Beiträge über neue Musik' in Paddison 1997, p. 177.
55   Ibid.

'complete integration is harshly imposed on its object – as dominion, not as reconcilement', and

> The dimension of time, whose formation was the traditional task of music and within which correct listening moved, is virtually eliminated from the art of our time.[56]

Music and the Empirical World

It seems that, for Adorno, there is no form of music in the twentieth century that is capable of an adequate relationship to, or representation of, time. Popular music has succumbed to the abstract time of the clock or metronome which denies temporality by reducing time to space. The procedures of modernism and the avant garde have produced temporal stasis by strangling all movement under the weight of total formal integration. And those musics which make use of the outdated styles and techniques of earlier times are condemned for turning their back on history. What are we to make of a historical juncture whose music seems incapable of addressing such a fundamental element of subjective experience? Short of drawing a Fukuyama-esque conclusion that there is no longer any temporality that can find expression in music because history has stopped, Adorno has led us to a place which apparently has no exit. It is tempting to draw the conclusion that Adorno's thought is fundamentally compromised, and reject his entire system of aesthetics. That would be a mistake, however, since we would lose the large number of significant insights that it provides. Better to explore ways in which some of the central concepts of Adorno's thought might be redeployed in the interests of theorising the relationship of time to the vast majority of the music circulating in the world today.

At the heart of the way Adorno understands the historical development of artforms is the dialectic of mimesis and rationality. Mimesis is the element of art inherited from myth; it has its origins in the traditional functions of art in magic, in ritual and in religious ceremony, before art achieved its autonomy. To behave mimetically is to 'make oneself like' an aspect of the world, to adapt oneself to one's environment as a means of defence against it. Mimesis is a practice which follows the 'logic of the object' and in the process of reflecting it, one criticises it, and frees oneself from its domination. Thus, the practice of artistically representing nature in landscapes has its roots in a need for inocu-

---

56 Adorno 1976, p. 180.

lation against a natural environment more threatening than beautiful. Adorno argues that though the element of mimesis plays a diminished role in the autonomous art of the bourgeois era, it nonetheless lies at the core of all art: 'Every work of art still bears the imprint of its magical origin. We may even concede that, if the magical element should be extirpated from art altogether, the decline of art itself will have been reached'.[57]

However, the process of Enlightenment is, in part, one of artists gaining increasing control and mastery of their artistic material. Art is, as Adorno puts it, 'a stage in the process of what Max Weber called the disenchantment of the world, and it is entwined with rationalization'.[58] On the one hand, under the impact of the progressive rationalisation of artistic creation, mimesis shrinks to occupy a much less prominent position in the artwork, and much more of the content of the artwork is to do with the technical elaboration of the artistic material. We have already encountered Adorno's assessment of the way Beethoven subjects his musical material to the overwhelming force of developmental logic: here rational compositional procedures dominate over any moment of pure inspiration or the musical imitations of nature found in, say, his *Pastoral Symphony*. More generally, the process of rationalisation in music accelerated hugely with the rise of bourgeois society and music's autonomous status. Of considerable influence on Adorno's thought is Max Weber, whose concept of means-end rationality as repressive and restricting is the model for Adorno's notion of instrumental rationality, and who also undertook a study of the rationalisation of music. Like Adorno, Weber sees a connection between the process of rationalisation and the development of the aesthetic realm opened up by art's winning autonomy status. He writes: 'Rationalization proper commences with the evolution of music into a professional art ...: that is reaching beyond the limited use of tone formulae for purely practical purposes, thus awakening purely aesthetic needs'.[59]

For Weber, the rationalisation of music comprises a number of features, starting with the subjecting of the basic sounding material of tones to logical organisation with the development of the tempered scale. This allowed for the creation of the fully symmetrical tonal system upon which the entire edifice of the Western art music tradition is built. Weber regards modern Western temperament as having been achieved in theoretical terms by Rameau and in practical ones by Bach's *Well-Tempered Klavier* at the start of the bourgeois era, opening up the possibility of developing the wholesale rationalisation of

---

57   Quoted from 'Theses on Art and Religion Today' in Paddison 2004, p. 77.
58   Adorno 1997a, p. 70.
59   Weber 1958, pp. 41–2.

compositional procedures and forms, from sonata form through to serialism.[60] But musical rationalisation more broadly also includes the development of musical instrument technology and of performance technique, both of which subject the means of sound production to ever greater control, as well as the increasing encroaching of capitalism's dynamic of efficiency into the production, distribution and consumption of music.

On the other hand, Adorno regards rationality not simply as a process which gradually marginalises mimesis, but as itself becoming the object of mimesis. Instrumental rationality, which has come to transform society in its own image, and is responsible for the increasing domination of nature ostensibly in the interests of progress, efficiency and development, but which in fact produces the ruthless domination of man over nature and of man over man, has become the threatening entity against which human subjectivity wishes to protect itself. Paddison writes, 'art uses the rationality of the world of empirical reality *mimetically* as a means of freeing itself from the repression of means-ends rationality.... Adorno suggests that, in internalising the rationality of the external world to an extreme degree, the art work sets up resistance to it and at the same time goes beyond it'.[61]

Adorno puts the relationship between mimesis and rationality like this:

> Art works oppose domination by mimetically adapting to it. If they are to produce something that is different in kind from the world of repression, they must assimilate themselves to repressive behaviour. Even those works of art which take a polemical stance against the *status quo* operate according to the principle they oppose. This principle deprives all being of its specific qualities. In sum, aesthetic rationality wants to make amends for the damage done by instrumental rationality outside art.[62]

Here rationalisation in art is understood as the mimesis of the instrumental rationalisation of society, rather than simply an instance of it.

It may be possible to apply this dialectic of mimesis and rationality specifically to the issue of time in a way that produces different assessments from those arrived at by Adorno. Weber's discussion of the rationalisation of musical material focuses almost exclusively on the aspect of pitch, only addressing rhythm in reference to the emergence of mensural notation. But in order to produce a complete account of the process of rationalisation it would seem

---

60   Weber 1958, p. 100.
61   Paddison 1997, p. 141.
62   Adorno 1997a, p. 403.

necessary to consider rhythm much more systematically. Let us start with the following discussion of pitch intervals by Weber:

> The harmonically perfect intervals, the octave, fifth, and fourth were distinguished by the recognizability which made them paramount for the development of a primitive tonality. They are distinguished for the musical memory from tone distances near them by their greater clarity. As it is easier correctly to remember real as contrasted to unreal events and clear as contrasted to confused thoughts, a corresponding condition is present for distinguishing right and wrong rational intervals. The analogy between musically and logically rational relations may be extended at least this far.... The phenomenon of measurability of the perfect intervals, once recognized, has been of extraordinary influence on the imagination....[63]

The Western system's foundations on certain intervals (in place long before the bourgeois era) is due to the rationality – in the mathematical sense – of the number relationships involved (octaves, fifths and fourths are the result of the simplest ratios of the frequencies of the pitches that comprise them – 2:1, 3:2 and 4:3 respectively), and on the ability for these to be accurately reproduced. The rationalisation of pitches is thus predicated on the ability to discriminate between the 'correct' version of intervals and those that fall outside an agreed degree of tolerance. It is the basis upon which it becomes possible for the adequate tuning of instruments to permit ensemble playing, and for precise notation systems which in turn allow for the development of new, rationally-based compositional procedures such as polyphony and extended forms. Adorno makes no argument against the pitch system which he, like everyone else in the West, has inherited. He does not follow Ernst Bloch in counterposing dialectical to mathematical organisation and arguing that the latter has no place in music, so he presumably accepts the necessity of the mathematisation of pitch which resulted in the tempered scale.[64]

If the Western pitch system is the result of the progressive application of rational principles to every aspect of society, as Weber believed, it would be surprising if musical temporality had not undergone an analogous process to the rationalisation of pitch. A key moment in this process was the emergence of meter as the temporal structural principle of Western music. The subjugation of melody to a definite, more or less unchanging pulse has a very long

---

63 Weber 1958, p. 39.
64 Bloch 1985.

history, as we have seen, but the development of meter as regular groupings into bars of such pulses, (best understood as the superimposition of pulses at rates a half, a third or a quarter the speed of the main pulse), is contemporaneous with the beginnings of the pitch rationalisation process described by Weber. Clearly, meter involves the same elements of rationality as pitch: simple number relationships which permit easy recognisability and reproducibility; and a level of measurability or discrimination underpinning the rhythmic concepts of being 'in time' or 'out of time' which parallel those of being 'in tune' or 'in the wrong key'.

Adorno does not refer directly to meter as it is found in the art music tradition. We can infer that it falls, for him, under the concept of the 'rhythmic-spatial' and therefore always has a deleterious influence unless held firmly in check by the expressive-dynamic. He speaks of 'Viennese classicism crystallising the dynamic developmental time of music', but fails to acknowledge the strong metrical organisation underlying the music of Haydn and Mozart.[65] When it comes to pitch, he recognises that such developments represent progress to the extent that they allow a greater productive control over the artistic materials. He writes:

> Artistic production cannot escape the universal tendency of Enlightenment – of progressive domination of nature. Throughout the course of history the artist becomes more and more consciously and freely the master of his material....[66]

Indeed he goes do far as to say that the rigorous application of rationality is the only way to save the 'spell' of art, that irrational core of all art that makes it art. But on the other hand those very innovations produced by rationalisation can harden into rigid conventions which ultimately constrain creative freedom and threaten subjectivity. Rationalisation, therefore is simultaneously both a good and a bad thing.

When it comes to rhythm, Adorno chooses to view the rationalisation process through the lens of notation. He argues that notation does not emerge simply as an *aide-memoire*, but has a disciplinary function. Again, the Bergsonian charge of spatialisation is at the heart of the argument:

> The first units of musical writing are the rigidly even drumbeats of the barbarians, and perhaps musical writing per se is originally an imitation

---

65   Adorno 2002f, p. 144.
66   Quoted from 'Theses on Art and Religion Today' in Paddison 2004, p. 77.

of those rhythmic-disciplinary systems which themselves already *spatialize* temporal relations in music through the 'atemporal' regularity of their divisions. Every written note is the image of a beat: the objectification of music, the conversion of the temporal flow into a spatial one, is not only formally a spatialization, but according to its original *content*, namely the spatialization of experience for the purpose of controlling it.[67]

The writing down of music is literally spatialising, and cannot avoid regulating, inhibiting and suppressing its content. But Adorno recognises that it is also necessary: '[t]he reification and independence of the musical text is the precondition for aesthetic freedom'. In this case, as in others, '[a]utonomy and fetishism are two sides of the *same* truth'.[68]

On the face of it, Adorno again presents a dialectical position, but it is dialectical in relation to notation rather than rhythmic rationalisation. Notation is regarded as a necessary development for the existence of the autonomous artwork despite its deleterious reifying effects. Rhythmic rationalisation, which we can sum up as meter, is not viewed in the same way: it is held to have no positive effects and is placed wholly in the negative column. The problem stems from regarding meter simply as an effect of notation. In the first place, this does not accord entirely with the empirical facts since the intensely metrical musics we are considering are largely non-notated (or are only notated after the event), as are the 'rigidly even drumbeats of the barbarians'. The Western notation system proves itself rather clumsy at representing the syncopations of popular music. Secondly, Adorno fails to comment on the fact that notation spatialises, or at least rationalises, pitch just as much as it does rhythm. But most importantly, it leads to a blindness to the benefits that meter brings. For it seems logical to argue that, just as with pitch rationalisation, rhythmic rationalisation enhances aesthetic control of the musical material in its own right. The obverse of its undoubted drawbacks is an enhanced subtlety of discrimination in relation to duration and temporal placement which increases musical expressivity.

As we saw in Chapter 3, there is an alternative way of conceiving the relationship between rhythm and meter, other than seeing it as simply the oppression of the former by the latter. Zuckerkandl denies that meter or strict timing results in the curtailing of rhythmic freedom:

---

67 Adorno 2006, p. 53.
68 Ibid.

rhythm bound to the law of meter... finally proved to be nowise inferior in subtlety and power to the affect of free rhythm. And it is not rhythm despite meter, but, on the contrary, rhythm from meter, rhythm fed by the forces dammed up in meter. Antithesis has become synthesis. Voluntary subjection to a strict constraint has, in the course of evolution, led to a victorious advance into a new freedom.[69]

For Zuckerkandl, there is a dialectical relationship between meter and rhythm, one in which the restrictions imposed by meter on rhythm have the productive effect of enhancing the rhythmic power of music. Unmuddied by the issue of notation, this provides the more fruitful way of understanding syncopation. For Adorno, popular music's syncopation always remains inferior to that found in the best serious music. He writes:

> Even in the techniques of syncopation, there is nothing that was not present in rudimentary form in Brahms and outdone by Schoenberg and Stravinsky. The practice of contemporary popular music has not so much developed these techniques as conformistically dulled them.[70]

As we have seen, this is the case because in popular music, syncopation fails to break free of the meter. Even when Adorno is at his most accommodating to jazz, it is clear that he sees a fundamental antithesis between meter and syncopation:

> What it was possible to learn from jazz is the emancipation of the rhythmic emphasis from metrical time; a decent, if very limited and specialized thing, with which composers had long been familiar, but which, through jazz, may have achieved a certain breadth in reproductive practice.[71]

What Zuckerkandl correctly shows is that this antithesis is false and that Adorno's demand that syncopation should obliterate meter is misplaced. Syncopation is the paradigmatic example of the dialectical relationship between meter and rhythm. Because, as we have seen, its essence is the presence of rhythmic emphasis which contradicts the stresses of the meter, syncopation has no meaning or existence independent of meter. Syncopation's

---

69 Zuckerkandl 1973, p. 160.
70 Adorno 2002d, p. 313.
71 Adorno 2002b, p. 499.

prominence in popular music goes hand in hand with an increased metrical sense and 'tightness' of the pulse. The degree of syncopation can be greater than was possible for Brahms and Schoenberg precisely because of this increased adherence to a strictly regular beat. It is only this metrical strictness which allows accents close to the beat to be heard as syncopations rather than mistaken for early or late versions of the beat itself, as would be the case in conditions in which a flexibility of the beat, such as *rubato*, were the norm. As with other instances of rationalisation, however, there is a price to be paid for this enhanced power of syncopation. Just as a rationalised pitch system reduces all key centres to a standardised uniformity and prohibits any expressivity to be gained from the use of pitches that fall 'between the cracks' of precisely regulated pitches, so a strict pulse and a deeply regular meter tend to stifle rhythmic flexibility. Adorno understands this dialectic of rationalisation in relation to pitch, but, because he views metrication as a product of notation, he sees only the negative aspects of the same process as it affects musical temporality.

The foregoing analysis has taken the development and intensification of meter as an aspect of the rationalisation of musical materials which itself is an element of a more widespread process of 'disenchantment', to use Weber's term. Returning now to Adorno's conceptualisation of the dialectic of mimesis and rationality, what is the relevance of mimesis to a discussion of musical time? Again, it appears that there may be an inconsistency in the way that Adorno applies the notion of mimesis in relation to his critique of temporal regularity in popular music.

We have seen how Adorno attributes what he calls the 'decomposition of time into discontinuous, "shocklike" moments' to modern industrial society, which affects not only the temporality manifested in music but the prevalent time consciousness of society as a whole. Similarly, the repetition found in popular music is ultimately to be explained materialistically as an echo of the iterative processes of industrialism:

> The form of labour in industrial mass production is virtually that of always repeating the same; ideally, nothing new occurs at all. But the modes of behaviour that have evolved in the sphere of production, on the conveyor belt, are potentially ... spreading over all of society, including sectors where no work is performed directly in line with those schemata.[72]

---

72   Adorno 1976, p. 49.

The rhythmic features of the most prevalent kinds of twentieth-century music are not, therefore, surprising. This is consistent with the profound way in which Adorno understands the notion that art is a product of its society. The structures and history of the empirical world become sedimented in the artistic forms and materials which are available at any particular period. Adorno, however, regards music which emulates the temporal reification of industrial society as thoroughly ideological. He continues:

> With respect to a time thus choked off by iteration, the function of music is reduced to making believe that – as Beckett put it in *Endgame* – something is happening at all, that anything changes.[73]

Repetition in music naturalises the ever same processes of capitalist society, painting the measured, repetitive course of time as meaningful, and ruling out any genuine change or development. It encourages identification with social power, reconciling its listeners to the existing social order:

> It fulfils men in themselves, to train them for consent. It thereby serves the status quo, which could be changed only by people who, instead of confirming themselves and the world, would reflect critically on the world and on themselves.[74]

For Adorno, music has a duty to resist an ideological role which naturalises the dominant features of the existing social order. It must avoid falling into the rhythmic patterns set by a society increasingly under the domination of instrumental rationality, it must eschew the discipline of measured time in the form of meter and repetition. This, after all, is the basis of his advocacy of artistic modernism, even though the forms taken by that modernism often failed to live up to their utopian promise.

It is possible to use Adorno's own aesthetic theory to take a different view: that a process of mimesis is involved here. Adorno suggests that the dissonant atonalism of the Schoenberg school is, at least in part, a representation of the condition of suffering to be found in the world. Tonality is a worn out mode of expression because its consonant triads and 'perfect' resolutions cannot be reconciled with the oppression and alienation of the world as it is. Part of what modernism does, then, is accurately reflect the reality of social conditions, because to do otherwise would be ideological. However, it follows from the

---

73   Adorno 1976, pp. 47–8.
74   Adorno 1976, pp. 50–1.

previous discussion that with respect to the dominant forms of temporality and time consciousness of industrial capitalism, it is popular music which has the more mimetic relationship to the world. Modernism and the avant-garde can be accused of picturing a more integrated and dynamic temporality which no longer matches the reality of most people's experience. It is either anachronistic, or utopian (in the worst sense of the word), or both.

Of course, Adorno's notion of mimesis involves far more than presenting the world as it appears to be. The process of adapting to the world as it is, is the precondition for pointing beyond it. This is what he means by works of art 'tak[ing] a polemical stance against the *status quo* [by] operating according to the principle they oppose'.[75] Mimesis is a 'making oneself like' an aspect of the world in order to make it less threatening, to control it. Mimetic representation is not simply a mirror to the world, but a mediation between subject and object which results in an interpenetration of the two, diminishing the polarity between them. In the mimetic act of making oneself like the object, the object is humanised.

It is feasible to argue that temporal regularity found in the best instances of groove music qualifies as genuine mimesis because it displays both of the necessary criteria. First, it takes as its starting point the temporal reality of the world as it is, complete with its mechanised, industrial processes, its positivist scientific thinking whose culture of measurement seeks to subsume quality under quantity, and its generalised time consciousness of regularity inculcated by the infiltration of the clock into every facet of life. Music has little choice in this; indeed, to turn one's back on this aspect of reality as it has come to be sedimented in musical materials is, following Adorno, to approach music unhistorically. Second, however, the best popular music does not simply incorporate clock time into its forms, but through a process of mimesis seeks to humanise a temporality which has become rigid and reified. The very rigidity and regularity of the modern time experience is turned against itself through the techniques of syncopation to generate flexibility and unpredictability, and the dislocated instants that Adorno saw as having shattered time's essential flow are woven into a new temporal continuum. On this basis, the groove-based temporality of the best of Western popular music can be recognised as a mimetic response to the highly measured temporality of the contemporary world, capable of effecting a critique of it.

---

75   Adorno 1997a, p. 403.

Subjectivity and Collectivity

The intimate connection between the evolution of meter in Western music and the origins of polyphony has often been commented upon. Zuckerkandl remarks on the coincidental historical arrival of these two important phenomena which he regards as unique to the Western tradition. The Western music of the second millennium

> alone has imposed the shackles of time, of meter, upon itself, and indeed at the same moment when it was preparing to take the momentous step into polyphony. So long as only a single voice is involved, it is free to give each of its steps whatever duration it pleases. But if several voices, voices saying different things, are to proceed side by side and together, their motions must, for better or worse, be regulated by some time standard.[76]

Likewise Weber, although he discusses temporal measurement solely in terms of notation, also points to the connection:

> Mensural notation permitted the planning of many-voiced art compositions.... Only the elevation of many-voiced music under notational art created the composer proper and guaranteed the polyphonic creations of the Western world, in contrast to those of all other peoples, permanence, aftereffect, and continuing development.[77]

These passages suggest a pragmatic impetus for the development of musical meter: to facilitate the coordination of music in which more than one thing is happening simultaneously. Adorno's approach suggests a slightly different explanation. It is not that meter is simply the necessary practical precondition for polyphonic music. Rather, both developments are driven by a deeper logic: the need for a musical expression of a new kind of subjectivity emerging under the impact of the Enlightenment – what Adorno calls the bourgeois Subject.

For Adorno, the Subject, as it is manifested in music, is not the composer, speaking in the language of music to his audience. It is to be found as much in the musical material as in the particular form it takes in an individual piece. 'The subject in a work of art is neither the viewer not the creative artist nor some absolute spirit. It is spirit (*Geist*), to the extent to which it is embedded in,

---

76 Zuckerkandl 1973, p. 159.
77 Weber 1958, p. 88.

and mediated and preformed by, the object'.[78] There is a dialectic of subject and object at the heart of the process: musical material results from the historical 'objectification' of the bourgeois Subject. In other words, Adorno believes that all that appears objective in terms of musical language and structures was once subjective, but has forgotten its subjective origins.

What takes place in the musical process is an interplay between the subjectivity of the composer and the objectified subjectivity of society. This way of conceiving the process means that even the composer is ultimately not an individual subject: 'The compositorial Subject is not individual but collective. All music, even that which is the most individualistic stylistically, has an inalienable collective content: each single sound already says "We"'.[79] Nevertheless, despite this element of collectivity comprising the musical material, the Subjectivity which is under threat from the process of reification is, for Adorno, explicitly individual. Thus he writes: 'The liquidation of the *individual* is the real signature of the new musical situation'.[80] Hence, he draws a distinction between the 'We' of the material and the false, repressive collectivity manifested in the 'beat' of popular music. The fact that he detects in works of Stravinsky, such as *The Rite of Spring*, a similar enforced subsuming of individual subjectivity under the weight of a pre-existing collective, appropriately encapsulated by the motif of sacrifice in that ballet, suggests that the difference between these two kinds of collectivity has much to do with the nature of the temporality in each case. It would appear that for there to be a genuine dialectic between Subject and Object (musical material), the subjectivity of particular themes and motifs (the musical subjects) must be free to bring their own temporality with them, as it were, rather than be required to adapt themselves to the objectivity of a preordained time frame in the form of meter. It is a difference which can be summed up in the distinction between *objectification* – the sedimentation of previous subjectivity in musical materials – and *reification* – the hardening of musical structures to a point where they inflexibly dominate the musical content of a piece.

Adorno understands musical form as a homologue of society: the ultimate source of the tendency towards reified musical forms was the reification of society as a whole in the twentieth century. In that sense, there is a kind of inevitability to the contemporary condition of music in which form is increasingly imposed 'from above' leaving no space for it to emerge from the 'inner necessity' of the content. It is this that led Adorno to propose in 1961 *une*

---

78   Adorno 1997a, p. 238.
79   Quoted from 'Ideen zur Musiksoziologie' in Paddison 1997, p. 115.
80   Adorno 2002d, p. 293 (emphasis added).

musique informelle – a formless music – a compositional practice which deliberately refuses both the 'bad universality' of pre-given, handed down forms from the past and the positivism and false totality of serialism.[81] Here, Adorno is clearly turning his back on any kind of collectivity, even the aspiration to retrieve the relatively benign relationship between the 'I' of musical content and the 'We' represented by the objectified subjectivity of musical form. The project for *une musique informelle* is an openly individualistic one that asserts the independence of the freedom of the Subject in the face of a hostile collective.

Nowhere, as far as Adorno was concerned, was the malign supremacy of the collective over individual subjectivity to be found more brazenly expressed musically than in the march, a form in which there is no place for deviation from the strict dictates of a regular beat, imposed on musical content from above. As we have seen, Adorno, more tendentiously, regards dance music as also embodying the same properties on the grounds that its rhythmic outline is determined in advance of its particular content. However, in an early essay, Adorno suggests a different relationship from which it is possible to sketch out an alternative way of understanding this dialectic. He argues that the 'rupture between self and forms', increasingly afflicting composers as the bourgeois era progresses, has its effect on the interpretation of music (i.e. its performance). In earlier historical periods, musical forms had a socially-endorsed authority which endowed the quality of 'being understood' on the composers working within them, while at the same time affording the performer a greater level of freedom of interpretation, even improvisation. He writes:

> The greater the structure of acknowledged objectivity in the musical work, the greater the freedom available to its interpreter. With the fading away of the objectively-given 'form world' there also fades away with it the freedom of interpretation.[82]

This is an attempt to explain the progressive diminishing of interpretative freedom in the Western art music tradition, from the considerable amount of improvisation required of performers in the Baroque era to the totally prescriptive scores of the twentieth century. But it also suggests that objectivity of form and subjective freedom need not be in inverse relationship, indeed that highly objective forms may be the precondition for subjective expression. Adorno's concept of a 'rupture between self and forms' applies to the individual

---

81 Paddison 1997, p. 182.
82 Quoted from 'Zum Problem der Reproduktion' in Paddison 1997, p. 197.

composer grappling with the handed down musical material at his disposal. But the argument he makes about interpretation may be relevant to music whose genesis comes about through forms of improvisation or 'jamming', practices which are inherently collective in nature; that is, those in which the distinction between composition and performance that Adorno took for granted appears blurred. This applies to a large part of popular music; not only to jazz, a music in which improvisation takes place during its performance, but also to other forms of popular music, in which much of the division of labour between composers and performers normal in the art music tradition has often given way to a compositional process involving a degree of collective practical experimentation by the performers.[83]

There is an obvious practical reason why music constructed in this way should require a strong temporal framework. Just as the initial development of meter (and the notation associated with it) was the precondition for polyphonic composed music, so the tighter, deeper meter of twentieth-century groove-based popular music allows for the temporal coordination of polyphonically improvised music. But this has a relevance beyond purely practical considerations to the question of collectivity and subjective freedom, as others have noticed. Anthropologist John Szwed has remarked that musical improvisation suggests 'social principles which reward maximal individualism within the framework of spontaneous egalitarian interaction'.[84] The objectivity of meter in such music is not so much imposed 'from above' or 'in advance', as Adorno characterised it, but is entered into by those participating in the creative process. It is not only collective in the sense of being the sedimentation of past subjectivity (though it remains that), but is collective in a much more present sense too. The nature of the relationship between each individual subjectivity and the objectivity of the form in which they are participating recalls Marx's comments on the society and the individual in *Grundrisse*:

---

83 Adorno was scathing about jazz improvisation, regarding it as merely the reiteration of clichés in order to achieve the 'pseudo-individualisation' of otherwise identical commodities. Many writers have commented on Adorno's distorted view of jazz due to his apparent ignorance of everything but the most commercial and mainstream music performed by white dance bands, a form in which indeed genuine improvisation is largely non-existent. He also appears to be completely unaware of the wider issue of collective compositional processes in non-jazz popular music.

84 Quoted in Belgrad 1998, p. 191.

> The human being is in the most literal sense a *Zwon politikon*, not merely a gregarious animal, but an animal which can individuate itself only in the midst of society.[85]

Terry Eagleton comments along similar lines on the concept of individuation:

> We are, by nature, sociable animals who must cooperate or die; but we are also individual beings who seek our own fulfilment. To be individuated is an activity of our species-being, not a condition at odds with it.[86]

Eagleton goes on to suggest a jazz group as a model of this relationship, where 'the free musical expression of each member act[s] as the basis for the free expression of the others'.[87] Actually this formulation is not specific enough as it does not emphasise each individual's responsibility to the maintenance of the objective structures which guarantee the free expression of others. We might reformulate it as 'the objectivity of the agreed musical form – chord sequence and especially meter (groove) – acts as the basis for the free expression (individuated subjectivity) of all'.

Presentness

Adorno's privileging of a model of music creation – a strict division of labour between composer and performers – peculiar to the Western art music tradition has further implications for the issue of temporality. It is a model of composition which, even if it produces music which embodies what Adorno would recognise as an adequate temporal logic by virtue of the dialectical development of its subject matter through time, nevertheless takes place, in a sense, outside of time. While the content of the work may be thoroughly processual, the work itself, once completed, enters the world as a static object, as a monad, as Adorno termed it. Indeed Adorno believed that it was only because of its 'thingness' that a modernist work was in a position to offer a critique of the reified world of commodities.

Not only do the composer's generation of temporal musical processes, and the objective nature of the work itself, take place beyond real time, or 'off-line',

---

85 Marx 1973, p. 84.
86 Eagleton 2007, p. 167.
87 Eagleton 2007, pp. 171–2.

as Cook puts it, Adorno also expects the listener to be similarly situated.[88] He posits as an ideal 'structural listening' which he contrasts with the distracted, superficial listening demanded by commodified popular music. He is highly critical of the phenomenological notion of experience as immediately given, as 'lived experience', believing that such experience (*Erlebnis*) could only be atomistic and ultimately meaningless. Instead, he advocates an interpretative and reflective form of perception (*Erfahrung*) which aims to penetrate the surface appearance of the work of art, to comprehend the 'inner structure' of the work which is not accessible to immediate perception. Paddison explains that *Erfahrung* 'implies for [Adorno] a mode of experience which can both follow the "events" of the work from moment to moment as they unfold through time, but which can also transcend this level to relate the individual moments in terms of the past, present and future within their total context, "out of time", so to speak'.[89]

Arguably, what Adorno is doing here is simply raising the kind of listening demanded by the Western art music tradition to an ideal type. John Shepherd argues that Western classical music's concept of form is unique in requiring the use of long-term memory to facilitate an ability to relate what one is hearing to what one has already heard, and means that 'in order to understand tonal music, industrial man must stand outside time and music'.[90]

Christopher Small attributes the cause of this phenomenon to the representational character of Western music, a mode which 'requires a certain detachment from what is being presented, a certain analytical frame of mind.... Just as the spectator stands outside the picture, looking into it, so the listener looks into the piece from the outside'.[91] This has implications for the 'presentness' of the music:

> The music does not exist purely in the present tense, taking each moment as it comes, but leads the listener forward to coming events, often in passages which are themselves of no great intrinsic interest... much of a classical movement exists simply to space out and point attention

---

88   Cook 2004.
89   Paddison 1997, p. 214. This position is in line with Adorno's somewhat idiosyncratic view that the silent reading of a musical score is – for those capable of it – the most rewarding way to experience a musical work.
90   Shepherd 1977, p. 111.
91   Small 1997, p. 154.

towards important events; these are, so to speak, not fully present, only those elements we call themes existing fully in the musical present.[92]

He compares improvised and composed music in this way:

> Western composed music resembles an account of a journey of exploration that has been taken by the composer, who comes back, as it were, from 'Out There', and tells us something, as best he can, of what it was like. The journey may have been a long, arduous and fascinating one, and we may be excited, moved, even amused, by it, but we cannot fully enter into the experience with him because the experience was over and he was safely home before we came to hear of it.... In improvising, in the other hand, the musician takes us with him on his journey of exploration; we negotiate with him every twist and turn, every precipice and danger.[93]

It would be wrong to infer from these remarks that non-Western and non-classical music do not involve the presentation in some way of the unfolding of time, or that they exist in a kind of perpetual present. Most kinds of music require the use of memory for their appreciation just as the comprehension of a sentence requires that the beginning of it is held in the memory while its end is being spoken. However, they point to the possibility that the temporal dynamic of even those works which Adorno holds to be the most temporally satisfactory may be limited by both their mode of creation and the mode of listening required for their appreciation. To the extent that theirs is a *representation* of temporal processes rather than a participation in them, they necessarily distance themselves from the present temporality of the world.

Related to this is Adorno's conception of the structure of historical time, one derived from Hegel's dialectic. From this conception flows his endorsement of Beethoven's techniques of thematic development, transformed recapitulation, and the interpenetration of form and content. According to Adorno, this is the form that the unfolding of time (as history) takes, and music which fails to incorporate this model into its temporal processes has turned its back on history and has consequently succumbed to the existing order. The strength of this view is a conception of time as immanent, and of change as emergent from the possibilities, or the negativity, of the existing situation rather than being determined from the outside by fate, destiny or deity. Its weakness in

---

92   Small 1977, pp. 88–9.
93   Small 1977, p. 176.

Adorno's hands is a tendency to ontologise time, to raise this model of time's unfolding to the level of a metaphysic of time which is held to be universally valid, for all of history. Whether Adorno, in so doing, is faithful to Hegel is debatable; but such a position certainly represents a departure from Marx's conception of history. As Bensaïd explains, contrary to the distorted interpretations of 'orthodox Marxism', Marx's 'new way of writing history' broke with all universally applicable models of time, even supposedly dialectical ones, to assert the inherent unpredictability of historical change. As Bensaïd puts it:

> Non-contemporaneity, non-linearity. Discordance of spheres and times. Time punctuated by alternation and intermittence. The broken time of politics and strategy. Open to the rhythmical contradictions of cycles and genealogies, this 'historical materialism' cannot be confused with 'naturalistic materialism'. Every individual is involved in a multiplicity of times in which economic cycles, organic cycles, ecological cycles, and the deep trends of geology, climate and demography intervene. Swaying this way and that, time is replete with the opportunities and auspicious moments once foreshadowed by the *kairos* of the Sophists. Duration no longer acts in the manner of a cause, but of a chance.... Chance is no longer an accident or parasitic on causality, but the direct correlate of 'necessary development', the other of necessity, the chance of *this* necessity, just as freedom is not caprice, but freedom from a constraint. Determinate, historical development remains full of junctions and bifurcations, forks and points.[94]

This is a temporality in which 'politics attains primacy over history', decisions and chance play a role in shaping the future, albeit always within limits set by the present, and 'historical laws' are restricted in their application to particular historical conjunctures.[95] Adorno was a trenchant critic of historicist conceptions of history, but there is a sense in which his dialectical model of history, though more sophisticated than those which invoke 'universal progress' or 'the inevitability of a socialist future', by claiming universality, represents a kind of historicism nonetheless. Once freed of it, we may allow that Beethoven's temporal procedures are not as normative as Adorno claims.

---

94 Bensaïd 2009, p. 23.
95 Bensaïd 2009, p. 55.

Adorno's Contribution

What are the strengths of Adorno's discussion of time in music? First, the insight that temporality, or, more particularly, the form that temporality takes, within music is a crucial part of its aesthetic constitution is of extreme importance; and, in addition, the suggestion that the temporality of a work of art has a relationship to the prevailing circumstances in the 'empirical world' is a crucial element of any materialist understanding of music. Adorno's thinking on this is incomplete: apart from the argument that in a reified society in which music has become thoroughly commodified, time is also bound to appear in reified form, Adorno seems undecided as to the extent that the time of music is the same time as that of the empirical world. He is generally hostile to all attempts to posit 'natural' bases for music, whether mathematical or physical, and wonders whether time should be considered an invariant. On the one hand, the musical time is an echo of real time; on the other, in relation to modernism, he argues:

> Today, music rebels against conventional temporal order; in any case, the treatment of musical time allows for widely diverging solutions. As questionable as it is that music can ever wrest itself from the invariant of time, it is just as certain that once this invariant is an object of reflection it becomes an element of composition and no longer an a priori.[96]

Adorno's second important contribution is to notice that there is something different about the temporality of popular music as compared with 'serious music', or at least with the highpoint of the Western art music tradition, and to pursue a comparison between them. How is such a difference to be explained? Not by positing the existence of an alternative aesthetic, one derived either from peoples of non-European descent, or from a 'return to the body', or both. Adorno sees the terms 'African' or 'black' as little more than brand names when applied to jazz, and any characteristics which may have been derived from African music have long since been transformed by the logic of commodification. He writes, 'today, in any case, all of the formal elements of jazz have been completely abstractly pre-formed by the capitalist requirement that they be exchangeable as commodities.... the skin of the black man functions as much as a coloristic effect as does the silver of the saxophone'. As for the supposed naturalness of jazz, he says:

---

96   Adorno 1997a, p. 30.

It is not old and repressed instincts which are freed in the form of standardized rhythms and standardized explosive outbursts; it is new, repressed and mutilated instincts which have stiffened into the masks of those in the distant past.[97]

In other words, what is different about the temporality of popular music is very much the product of developments that have taken place in the urban centres of the advanced capitalist world, rather than the effect of influences from other parts of the world. The fact that it is the product of history, not geography, means that some of the same features can be detected in serious music also, exposed as it is to the same historical forces, rationalisation chief among them. Here we have a dialectic of continuity and difference: one the one hand, popular music is marked out as different from both the art music tradition and folk music; on the other, it is produced by the same society as art music, it does not in any sense originate from outside.

This, then, is the problematic within which popular music is to be understood. The question remains as to the precise way that dialectic of continuity and difference is to be articulated. Popular music is a product, for better or worse, of the same process of rationalisation that has affected all music since at least the beginning of the bourgeois era. I have argued that one of the problems with Adorno's critique of metric regularity in popular music is that he overlooks the extent to which meter had already developed as part of that process as a central element of the autonomous music of that era. At one level, then, meter represents an element of continuity between the 'classical' tradition and popular music. However, its degree of intensification in much popular music marks a qualitative difference from its manifestation in other kinds of music. Adorno sees the difference but not the continuity. The main reason for this is that he accepts a Bergsonian analysis of time which posits the *a priori* existence of a continuously flowing, integrated temporality that is fundamentally irreconcilable with measurement. Though criticising it for being crude and undialectical, he argues that 'the crass dichotomy of Bergson's two times does [nevertheless] register the historic dichotomy between living experience and the objectified and repetitive labor process'.[98] This ill-advised borrowing from a philosophical tradition at odds with his Marxist materialism leads him to fail to apply his own dialectic of rationalisation consistently: he recognises the benefits to the composer's power over the musical material that accrue from the rationalisation of pitch, while ignoring the shrinking of expressive

---

97   Adorno 2002c, pp. 477–8.
98   Adorno 1973b, p. 334.

range that such rationalisation also brings. Conversely, because he does not regard the analogous processes of the measurement and systematisation of musical time as rationalisation, he sees only the harmful results, discounting any possibility that there may be a positive side to such developments.

Underlying all this, we have the problem of what music's role should be. Without a dialectical conception, Adorno's insistence that art involves both mimesis of the empirical world and a rejection of it seems on the face of it to be thoroughly contradictory. But, in fact, Adorno is arguing, plausibly enough, that art's ability to mount any kind of critique of the world is dependent upon a degree of similarity with it. However, within that general principle there are as many positions that can be taken as there are concrete artistic examples to discuss. Adorno argues strongly that the regularity and repetition of popular music's time represents a capitulation to the reification of time and of society in general. I have suggested that if Adorno can argue that it is only by adopting the form of an objectified thing, a monad, that a work of art can be a critique of the world of reified things, then it is also arguable that only by incorporating reified time within its structure can music begin to offer a critique of that reification. Indeed, the alternative, the conscious avoidance by music of reified temporality, can only lead to a failure to articulate any kind of temporality whatsoever. This is the position that Adorno recognises that avant garde music has arrived at.

Paradoxically, given his hostility to it, Adorno provides us with an original set of conceptual tools for the understanding of popular music and its relationship to other musics. His theorisation of the ways in which the rationalisation processes at work in society impinge on art, and his dialectical understanding of the confrontation in the creative process between individual subjectivity and the objectivity of handed down musical material, itself the sedimented product of subjectivity that has forgotten its origins, are both major contributions to aesthetic theory. He offers us ways of thinking about how art and music are rooted historically and materially in the world but are not simply passive reflections of it, being capable at the same time of offering a critique and resistance to it. Adorno's thought is, however, weakened by the presence within it of Bergsonian conceptions of time which fall short of the thoroughly historical and materialistic standards of the much of the rest of his aesthetic theory. But because his is a philosophy that resists straightforward application and positive answers, even this weakness can be used to provide insights into the relationship between the time of society and of the world and the time of music. The potency of Adorno's thinking on these issues requires that it will be necessary to return to some his positions in the concluding chapter.

CHAPTER 6

Meter, Groove and the Times of Capitalism

Any materialist account of changes in the temporality of music must examine not simply variations in the ways time has been conceived and theorised, but must also trace the transformations in material circumstances which have produced historical shifts in the experience of lived time. The materialist assumption is that certain lived circumstances at particular conjunctures of history and geography are sufficiently generalised to produce a shared experience of time which finds itself reflected, largely unconsciously, in the music of those conjunctures. We are, of course, particularly interested in the emergence of a new musical temporality in Western music – groove – around the turn of the twentieth century. But our conception of this transformation is dependent on the development of meter in Western music some three hundred years earlier. As we have seen, one way of characterising groove is as a particularly extreme or intensified form of meter. We might say, using the language of dialectics, that groove is an example of the transformation of quantity into quality, an intensification of pre-existing metric practices in music to the point where a distinct phenomenon emerges. Because of groove's dependence on the considerably older musical practice of meter, we must begin with an account of the material circumstances which led to the development of meter.

In fact, the emergence of meter as a universal organising principle for musical temporality is a much more significant development than the emergence of groove. It is part of the wholesale transformation of every aspect of life – material, intellectual, cultural – wrought by the inception of capitalist modernity whose effect on consciousness, thought and art has been investigated by numerous writers, perhaps most notably by Marshall Berman in his *All That Is Solid Melts Into Air*. For our investigation into the temporal aspect of this wider transformation, the key development is the spread of the clock in European society during the seventeenth and eighteenth centuries and the way in which it, and the practices which depended upon it, inaugurated for the first time a conception of abstract, or chronometric, time. It is difficult to overstate the scale of the impact of this development. David Landes calls it a 'revolution in time', one in which, as Lewis Mumford puts it: 'the categories of time and space underwent an extraordinary change and no aspect of life was left untouched by this transformation'.[1]

---

[1] Landes 1983; Mumford 2000, p. 121.

In order adequately to grasp the extent of the transformation Mumford is talking about, we must attempt to reconstruct something of the nature of time consciousness in the pre-clock world. Or perhaps we should say the non-clock world, as the influence of clocks was barely felt in rural areas even during the period during which it was intensifying its grip in the industrialising towns. According to Jacques Le Goff, the mass of the population living on the land had no interest and no desire for measuring time: '[Agricultural] labour time was still the time of an economy dominated by agrarian rhythms, free of haste, careless of exactitude, unconcerned by productivity – and of a society created in the image of that economy, sober and modest, without enormous appetites, undemanding, and incapable of quantitative efforts'.[2] For rural populations living in this way, time is not determined by the clock but by natural events which take place according to daily, seasonal and annual rhythms. The time to get up is set by sunrise or the demands of animals and thus varies with the time of year. Work time is the time taken to complete concrete tasks, not a predetermined clock measure to be subsequently filled with activity. Thompson describes such a conception of time as 'task-oriented', one born out of necessity rather than rule, part of a situation in which there is neither a single, unifying time shaping every individual's activity, nor a sharp demarcation between work and life.[3]

As an alternative to the familiar distinction encountered earlier of cyclical versus linear time, Postone proposes the terms 'concrete' and 'abstract' time. He argues:

> Before the rise of modern, capitalist society in Western Europe, dominant conceptions of time were of various forms of concrete time: time was not an autonomous category, independent of events, hence it could be determined qualitatively, as good or bad, sacred or profane.[4]

So concrete time is not defined by reference to any particular, non-linear directionality. Rather it is time which is dependent upon the events which comprise it: 'In the traditional Jewish and Christian notions of history, for example, the events mentioned do not occur within time, but structure and determine it'. Consequently, even when such time is measured or reckoned, the temporal units used are not of invariant size but alter with the length of the period of

---

2 Landes 1983, p. 58.
3 Thompson 1967, p. 60.
4 Postone 1993, p. 201.

daylight. This was true, for example, of the ancient Islamic world but also of the system of 'canonical hours' of the medieval church in Europe.

By contrast, abstract time is uniform, continuous, homogeneous, 'empty' time which is conceived independently of events. Abstract time forms a framework within which events take place and can be situated. This is Newton's 'absolute, true and mathematical time [which] flows equably without relation to anything external', whose parts are 'equal, constant, nonqualitative units'. According to the China scholar, Joseph Needham, this notion of time was exclusive to modern Western Europe, and was not found in ancient Greece, the Islamic world, early medieval Europe, India or China.[5]

The first individuals to have their lives systematically subjected to the control of clock time were members of monastic communities. The Western churches' 'canonical hours' were temporal rules based around a series of services named after numbers of the clock such as *tierce, sext* and *none*, which in turn gave their names to the offices being recited at those hours.[6] Monks 'lived and worked to bells' which rang according to this system of variable, that is, unequal, hours.[7] Part of the motivation for this was religious: praying simultaneously was held to increase the potency of prayer; but partly it was economic too, in a way which prefigured the productivity goals of the early industrialists:

> The bells, in short, were drivers – goads to effective, productive labor. It is this larger role, going far beyond reveille, that may account for the higher standard of punctuality enforced by the new monastic orders of the eleventh and twelfth centuries. The Cistercians in particular were as much an economic as a spiritual enterprise... Their agriculture was the most advanced in Europe; their factories and mines, the most efficient.[8]

Religious communities aside, an increasing divergence developed in the late Middle Ages between the time consciousnesses of town and country. In the countryside time marked by hours was received and perceived whereas in the growing urban areas time came to be tracked and used. Landes relates that in the towns of this period,

---

5 Postone 1993, pp. 201–2.
6 Landes 1983, p. 61.
7 Landes 1983, p. 68.
8 Landes 1983, p. 69.

bells sounded for start of work, meal breaks, end of work, closing of gates, start of market, close of market, assembly, emergencies, council meetings, end of drink service, time for street cleaning, curfew, and so on through an extraordinary variety of special peals in individual towns and cities.[9]

The first time signals deployed to regulate labour were of entirely natural origin: in Paris, tanners worked in winter as long as it was light enough to tell two similar coins apart, other trades started when it was light enough to recognise someone in the street. Further signals were based on the church's temporal hours and hence varied with the seasons. In the same city, carpenters stopped work on Saturday when the big bell of Notre Dame sounded *none*. But time signals took on an especial importance in the early textile manufacturing towns where the small workshops and the putting-out system began to be superseded by larger scale production involving the gathering together of workers in a single factory. In these circumstances, natural and seasonal measures of time gave way to time measured by the mechanical clock with its time measurements which remained constant irrespective of the season.

The major breakthrough in clock technology came with Christiaan Huygens's first pendulum clock in 1657 and improvements in accuracy and reliability followed rapidly.[10] The new mechanical clocks were bound up with manufacturing generally in more ways than one. Not only did factory owners require a level of punctuality and synchronisation from their workers to match the newly mechanised industrial processes, but the clock was itself a machine, very often manufactured by the same people engaged in the invention and manufacture of industrial machinery. Mumford argues that it was the clock, rather than the steam engine, which was the 'key-machine of the modern industrial age', marking 'a perfection toward which other machines aspire'.[11]

However, to regard the increasing spread of abstract time as arising solely from the technological development of clocks capable of measuring equal hours accurately would be a mistake. Postone cites several pieces of evidence which undermine a purely technological explanation of the emergence of abstract time. In the first place, the water clocks that preceded mechanical clocks required intricate mechanisms to turn constant flows of water into hours that varied with the seasons. Clearly, marking regular hours is much more straightforward than marking variable hours, so water clocks were in this

---

9   Landes 1983, p. 72.
10 Landes 1983, pp. 83–187.
11 Mumford 1963, p. xix.

respect technologically more complex than the clocks that followed. Secondly, China provides an example of a society which until the industrial revolution was more technologically advanced than Europe, but which did not fall under the sway of abstract time. China had astronomical clocks capable of measuring equal hours, and by the late sixteenth century also had access to mechanical clocks from Europe. However, these systems of time measurement made no impact on social life in China which remained resolutely traditional. Indeed, the European mechanical clocks presented to the Chinese court were regarded as little more than ingenious toys. In Japan the story is similar: European mechanical clocks were often adapted to mark variable hours by moving the position of the numerals on the clock face. In other words, in the East the technological advances of the mechanical clock were recognised and appreciated but shorn from the concept of abstract time with which they were associated in Europe. Postone concludes: 'The mechanical clock, then, does not, in and of itself, necessarily give rise to abstract time'.[12] Technological developments are not irrelevant but social and cultural factors must be primary in any explanation of the emergence of abstract time consciousness.

The spread of clock time, then, is not simply a product of industrialisation, but of *capitalist* industrialisation. Its impetus did not just derive from the needs of the new manufacturing techniques for more exact time routines, but, as we shall explore more deeply later, from the centrality of labour time as a measure of exploitation in capitalist competition.[13] Its introduction provoked a huge amount of resistance and struggle on the part of those who found themselves subjected to it for the first time. The time discipline required by the new working practices could only be introduced by breaking centuries-old habits and behaviours, of which Saint Monday – the extension of weekend revelry into the following week – is the most well known.[14] In addition to their being entirely alien to those who moved from rural timescales into the cauldron of the early industrial cities, Thompson speculates that these practices are also in some sense unnatural ways of working. On the basis of the evidence provided by today's artists, freelance writers and students, he argues that when people exercise control over their own labour schedule, its patterns are characterised by bouts of intense labour interspersed with periods of idleness.[15] Such a view rests on an assumption about raw human nature that may be unsustainable,

---

12   Postone 1993, pp. 204–6; see also Landes 1983, ch. 1.
13   Thompson 1967, p. 80.
14   Thompson 1967, p. 78.
15   Thompson 1967, p. 73.

but what is undeniable is that from this point onwards, time became the central term in the class struggles waged by the new proletariat:

> In the cities time became the nexus of class struggle, being invested now with not just a use value but an exchange value. With the recasting of the worker's time sense assured by a new labor process relying on the all-pervasive clock, time became a formal, measurable quality able to become a commodity. The increasing division of labor and associated deskilling allowed labor power to become a commodity measurable in units of clock time.[16]

Once the initial resistance to regularised working hours was defeated, as was perhaps inevitable, workers increasingly fought their employers over clock time rather than *against* it. 'A new terrain of class struggle was formed based upon the arrangement and length of work time and the rates for the job but not on the existence of [clock] time itself'.[17] Or as Thompson puts it:

> The first generation of factory workers were taught by their masters the importance of time; the second generation formed their short-time committees in the ten-hour movement; the third generation struck for overtime or time-and-a-half. They had accepted the categories of their employers and had learned to fight back within them. They had learned their lesson, that time is money, only too well.[18]

In this way, the struggle over the length of the working day became 'the most direct expression of class conflict in the capitalist economy'.[19] The sphere of work may have been the driving force for the spread of clock time, but there were profound implications for every area of society. As Thrift argues, gearing human activity to the machine required a process of entrainment in two dimensions: instrumental action and symbolic interaction.[20] Every sphere of life came to be regulated by clock time, either as part of a conscious effort to instil the new values in the existing and the next generations of labour, or by a less directed process of colonisation. In keeping with a concept of time as a commodity to be 'spent' rather than 'passed', a new ethos of time thrift

---

16   Thrift 1996, p. 554.
17   Thrift 1996, p. 558.
18   Thompson 1967, p. 86.
19   Giddens 1981, p. 120.
20   Thrift 1996, p. 555.

emerged, which, by the nineteenth century, formed a major part of the moralistic propaganda directed at those held to be using their time wastefully or unproductively.[21] Schools, especially those run by Methodists, saw their role as inculcating this ethos in children. As Foucault noted in *Discipline and Punish*, in the new Sunday schools, 'the division of time became increasingly minute; activities were governed in detail by orders that had to be obeyed immediately', while recreation came to be dominated by activities of fixed lengths taking place in defined spaces.[22]

In all these concrete ways, life, especially of those working in the new industrial towns, came to be regulated by the ever more precise measurement of time. As those subjected to it became habituated to its ways, time came to be understood in a way which would have been unfathomable to previous generations. As Adam puts it:

> The clock, we can state quite categorically, changed the meaning of time. The machine supplanted ... the experiential understanding of time as change ... and shifted the experience and meaning of time towards invariability, quantity and precise motion expressed by number. With the mechanical clock, time became dissociated from planetary rhythms and seasons, from change and ageing, from experience and memory. It became independent from time and space, self-sufficient, empty of meaning and thus apparently neutral.... As an invariable measure of length, time was amenable to mathematical use, infinite division and precise calculation. As a quantity it became not only an essential parameter in scientific investigation but also an economic resource that could be allocated, spent or saved. As abstract value it could be exchanged with other abstract values such as money.... As time became naturalized as time per se, it became, in Mumford's words, 'the new medium of existence'. Although the shift to clock time relations occurred slowly over a period of some four hundred years, the radical nature of the change cannot be overestimated: the machine time seeped deeply into the fabric of social life and spread like a spider's web across the globe, leaving those who resisted the new time defined as backward and old-fashioned.[23]

The sense that time is a substance to be put to use instead of squandered was reflected ideologically in a number of ways. It is a central feature of the

---

21   Thompson 1967, pp. 84, 90–1.
22   Foucault 1977, p. 150; Thrift 1996, p. 558.
23   Adam 2004, pp. 113–4.

'Protestant ethic' that Weber posited as the precondition of the rise of capitalism, and is expressed in Benjamin Franklin's famous 'time is money' passage of 1748 which equates passing time unprofitably with throwing away money.[24] Whereas in the early stages of industrialisation the new strict temporal habits had to be forcibly imposed on the growing urban workforce, over time they became increasingly internalised. Punctuality became a highly prized social attribute, and the extent to which individuals aspired to achieve it in their own personal behaviour was a sign of a shift from time *obedience* to time *discipline*, motivated from within rather than imposed from without.[25] This transformation was greatly aided by the development of personal timepieces, first portable clocks, then watches, in the late sixteenth and early seventeenth centuries. Landes argues that this privatisation or personalisation of time 'was a major stimulus to the individualism that was an ever more salient aspect of Western civilization'.[26]

The spread of a new set of social practices and values based on a new concept of abstract time may be understood as a political and ideological project driven by a newly powerful bourgeois class in the interests of capital. Such an explanation is not unreasonable and certainly forms part of the analysis. However, there is a further dimension that must be explored: the extent to which abstract time is a necessary product of the structural mechanisms of capitalism as an economic system itself, not simply an ideological byproduct of it.

Such an exploration may proceed on a number of levels. At the most superficial, it can be argued that the valorisation of punctuality, discussed above, signifies an orientation on the future. This was associated ideologically, as Weber notes, with Protestant asceticism, its futurity expressed in terms of the ultimate goal of salvation of the soul.[27] Adam argues that it fits into a picture, taken as characteristic of modernity, in which people moved away from seeing themselves in the hands of fate and at the mercy of unknowable and uncontrollable forces.[28] We might argue that this shift in consciousness is driven by the emergence of modern science and the development of productive forces to a point where humans really did have more control over their collective future than ever before in history. In these circumstances, the concept of a ribbon of rationally measured time stretching ahead like a path providing a sense of

---

24   Franklin 1748.
25   Landes 1983, p. 7.
26   Landes 1983, p. 89.
27   Weber 2003, ch. 4.
28   Adam 2004, pp. 44–5.

predictability and the basis for calculated actions designed to control and affect the future is the product in consciousness of these material developments. But at a deeper level of analysis, future-orientation can be seen as the product not simply of modernity, but of capitalist modernity. As Le Goff explains, even capitalism in its early, mercantile, form involves a temporality quite distinct from that of the church or of feudal society: 'The merchant's activity is based on assumptions of which time is the very foundation – storage in anticipation of famine, purchase for resale when the time is ripe...'.[29] In other words, there is a kind of futurity built into the very economic practice of mercantilism which necessarily generates a particular kind of temporality. The arrival of mature industrial capitalism embodies this futurity in intensified form, dependent as it is on investment decisions being made on the basis of expectations about future returns. The economic mechanism that encapsulates this abstract futurity in its clearest form is that of credit, which relies on assumptions about the future paying off of debt.[30] The temporality entailed by borrowing and lending money is one of a future conceived as a continuation of the present, or as an extension of the present along an axis of abstract, measured time. Viewed this way, the rise of a concept of abstract time is not explained merely on the basis that it functions in the interests of capital and those who own it, or even that it is structurally homologous with aspects of a capitalist economy, though both of those are true. At the deepest level, abstract time is to be understood as structured into capitalism, as the temporality *of* capitalism, because capitalism is temporal in a way in which previous economic formations were not. It is as though, as Adam puts it, 'capital has a built-in clock that is constantly ticking away'.[31]

Abstract Labour and Abstract Time

We have already seen the extent to which the spread of clock time was predicated upon the emergence of new labour practices arising from industrialisation. We can now take the analysis of labour's role in the abstract time

---

29 Adam 2004, p. 125.
30 Jameson draws on this idea in arguing that the futures markets of the contemporary global finance sector have achieved 'a structural reorganization of time itself' (Jameson 1998, p. 43). In fact, this temporal quality of futurity is a product not simply of 'late capitalist' (postmodern) financialisation but of capitalism itself.
31 Adam 2004, pp. 125–6.

consciousness to a deeper, more structural, level, using Moishe Postone's interpretation of Marx's concept of abstract labour.

Marx begins his analysis of the commodity as the basis of the capitalist productive system by distinguishing between a product's use value and its exchange value. He argues that the system of exchange at the heart of capitalism depends upon consideration of the exchange value of commodities alone, disregarding their concrete, material properties as well as their concrete, determinate uses. It follows that commodities must also be considered independently from the concrete forms of labour that produced them, 'the labour of the joiner, the mason, the spinner, or of any other definite kind of productive labour'. He argues that commodities exchange on the basis of the one element that is common to them all, 'human labour in the abstract'. Capitalism operates according to a system of value based on 'homogeneous human labour, of labour power expended without regard to the mode of its expenditure'. He concludes:

> A use value, or useful article, therefore, has value only because human labour in the abstract has been embodied or materialised in it. How, then, is the magnitude of this value to be measured? Plainly, by the quantity of the value-creating substance, the labour, contained in the article. The quantity of labour, however, is measured by its duration, and labour time in its turn finds its standard in weeks, days, and hours.[32]

It is important to understand that, for Marx, it is not the labour time of this or that particular worker or group of workers that determines the value of a product under capitalism. If that were the case, then an object made by slow, inefficient workers using obsolete tools would have more value than that made by efficient workers using the most up-to-date techniques. Rather, the labour that forms the substance of value is 'homogeneous human labour', each unit of which, insofar as it contributes to the value of the product, must be no longer than is 'socially necessary'. Marx explains that socially necessary labour time is 'that required to produce an article under the normal conditions of production, and with the average degree of skill and intensity prevalent at the time'.[33] According to Postone, abstract labour, measured with respect to time, acts as a general social mediator under capitalism, a mechanism which is enforced by the competition between capitalist firms. Each capitalist is engaged in a struggle continually to reduce the value of his products by reducing the quantity of

---

32   Marx 1977, p. 46.
33   Marx 1977, p. 47.

abstract labour embodied within them. He must maximise the output of each worker for the time period that they are employed by any method available to him, such as by increasing the intensity of labour and by investing in labour-saving technology. The overall effect is a tendency for the productivity of labour to increase, or, put another way, for the amount of socially necessary labour required for the production of an object to decrease. Marx gives the example of the introduction of powerlooms in England in the nineteenth century which reduced by half the amount of labour required to produce a given quantity of cloth, thereby reducing the value of the product of an hour's labour in the weaving industry to half its former level. The hand-weavers felt the discipline of the introduction of a new norm for what constituted 'socially necessary labour time' and were put out of business as a result.[34]

Postone believes that the workings of the law of value in this way have profound implications. Social production takes on a quasi-objective quality which comes to dominate individuals. Because, as Marx puts it, the law of value operates according to 'a social process that goes on behind the backs of the producers, and, consequently, appear[s] to be fixed by custom', social life is no longer the totality of interpersonal relations but becomes a system of dependence on an objective framework of social production.[35] 'These *objective* dependency relations also appear ... in such a way that individuals are now ruled by *abstractions*, whereas earlier they depended on one another'.[36] Key among these abstractions, because of its function as a measure of abstract labour, is time. Capitalism, therefore, produces a situation in which individuals find themselves subject to the domination of abstract time as it makes itself felt as an objective standard through the imposition of the law of value. Though capitalism is a system in which, unlike previous systems, individuals are free from relations of personal domination, it is a system in which, Postone argues, labour 'becomes the central element of a totality that dominates individuals':

> As a category of the totality, socially necessary labor time expresses a quasi-objective social necessity with which the producers are confronted. It is the temporal dimension of the abstract domination that characterizes

---

34   Marx 1977, p. 47.
35   Marx 1977, pp. 51–2. McNally argues that the picture presented by Postone here is too one-sided: 'capital never manages to entirely instrumentalise labour, to liquidate its qualities of sentient, desiring, thinking beings'. Concrete time continues to exist alongside abstract time, just as use-value can never be totally obliterated by exchange-value (McNally 2004, pp. 202–3).
36   Postone 1993, p. 125.

the structures of alienated social relations in capitalism. The social totality constituted by labor as an objective general mediation has a temporal character, wherein *time becomes necessity*.[37]

Or as Marx puts it, '[l]abour, thus measured by time, does not seem, indeed, to be the labour of different persons, but on the contrary the different working individuals seem to be mere organs of this labour'.[38]

Postone highlights a particular feature of the interrelationship between value, abstract labour and time in Marx's analysis. As we have seen, according to Marx, 'The value of a commodity, therefore, varies directly as the quantity, and inversely as the productiveness, of the labour incorporated in it'.[39] Postone points out that this means that changes in the productivity of labour do not affect the value created in a given period of time. In the example cited above, the doubling of the productivity of labour achieved by the introduction of power looms halved the value of each unit of woven cloth by allowing twice as many units of it to be produced per hour. The total amount of value yielded each hour remained the same after mechanisation as before. 'However then productive power may vary, the same labour, exercised during equal periods of time, always yields equal amounts of value'.[40] Or again: 'A working day of given length always creates the same amount of value, no matter how the productiveness of labour, and, with it, the mass of the product, and the price of each single commodity produced, may vary'.[41] Increases in productivity simply result in the total value being distributed between a greater mass of products. Postone comments: 'The only determinant of value is the amount of abstract labor time expended, measured in constant temporal units. It is, therefore, independent of changes in productivity.... In capitalism, abstract temporal measure rather than concrete material quantity is the measure of social wealth'.[42] This confirms that the terms value and time are in a fixed relationship to one another such that each can be adequately expressed in terms of the other. Under capitalism, value effectively is time, and, moreover, is so in a way that does not vary historically.

How can it be that over the course of the history of capitalism, the impressive advances in the productivity of human labour achieved with each

---

37 Postone 1993, p. 191.
38 Marx 1981, p. 30.
39 Marx 1977, p. 48.
40 Marx 1977, p. 53.
41 Marx 1977, p. 487.
42 Postone 1993, p. 195.

successive wave of technological innovation has multiplied the quantity of goods produced to an almost unimaginable extent, 'accomplish[ing] wonders far surpassing Egyptian pyramids, Roman aqueducts, and Gothic cathedrals',[43] but has had not the slightest effect on the quantity of value produced per worker per hour? The answer lies in an important distinction that must be made between 'wealth' and 'value'. For Marx, material wealth refers to the fruits of the entire capacity of the human species to produce what it needs from nature. Wealth is therefore a category which is a function of concrete, use-producing labour. It refers to the concrete achievements of humanity, the wants that have been satisfied, the capabilities that have been developed. Value, by contrast, only expresses the relations between people as mediated by abstract labour. It is indifferent to the overall productive capacity of humans, taking no account of the changing relationship of humans to nature, and effectively disregarding the contribution of nature to productive output.[44] The distinction between wealth and value allows Marx to argue that capitalism's application of science and technology does nothing to increase the amount of value yielded per unit of time, even though it does increase the amount of material wealth produced.[45]

Since capitalism operates according to a law of value, rather than one of wealth, time, as abstract measure of homogeneous human labour, has the character of an ever-present, totalising constant, imposing its law on all productive activity. Labour time 'is transformed into a temporal norm that not only is abstracted from, but also stands above and determines, individual action'.[46] The important aspect of this analysis for the issue of time consciousness, is that the transformation that a system of generalised commodity production – capitalism – effects in changing time from 'the result *of* activity into a normative measure *for* activity' is not an illusion.[47] It is not a misunderstanding or a misconception of the 'true' nature of time, but is real in the sense of being intrinsic to the social processes generated by capitalism. The abstract character of time is not confined to thought; it is a 'real abstraction'. As Toscano points out, when, in the *Grundrisse*, Marx says that under capitalism, 'individuals are now ruled by *abstractions*, whereas earlier they depended on

---

43 Marx and Engels 1960, p. 17.
44 Nature was regarded by classical bourgeois economists as a 'free gift' to production (see Ricardo 2004, pp. 61–2).
45 Postone 1993, p. 195.
46 Postone 1993, p. 214.
47 Postone 1993, p. 215.

one another', he is addressing primarily the structures of society, not habits of thought:[48]

> The Marxist elaboration of the idea of abstraction permits us to appreciate the limits of any (voluntaristic or idealist) attempt to transform our practices of abstraction which does not fully grasp their embeddedness in mechanisms of social reproduction and the formidable political, and not merely epistemic, challenges that dislodging them might entail.[49]

Toscano is challenging here other theorisations of culture derived from Marx in which abstractions such as money and, especially, fictitious capital are posited as having somehow detached themselves from all social materiality to become 'free-floating'.[50] Postone's exposition of Marx's analysis of the functioning of labour time in capitalism is consistent with the position that, as Paci puts it, 'The abstract, in capitalist society, *functions concretely*'.[51] Abstract time, then, is not to be understood as an epiphenomenon of capitalism, but as the temporality of capitalism itself.

Postone, however, does not halt his analysis at the point where abstract time has been identified as rooted in the innermost workings of capitalism. He goes on to suggest that there is an additional, concrete component to capitalism's temporality. Although the level of productivity does not determine the value of total output for a given time period, it does, as we have seen, set the standard for the value of each commodity. Through the mechanism of 'socially necessary labour time', changes in productivity affect the norm for the length of time required to produce a commodity. Postone identifies a paradox:

> Productivity – the use value dimension of labor – does not, then, change the total value yielded per abstract time unit; it does, however, determine the time unit itself. We are thus faced with the following apparent paradox: the magnitude of value is a function only of labor expenditure as measured by an independent variable (abstract time), yet the constant

---

48 Marx 1973, p. 164.
49 Toscano 2008, p. 59.
50 Jameson 1997, p. 251. Explanations of certain characteristics of 'late capitalist' or postmodern culture and aesthetic sensibility as a product of 'generalised abstraction' became quite fashionable at the height of the speculative financial boom of the late 1990s and early 2000s. cf. also Jameson 1998. They have become rather less so since the financial crash of 2007–8 (see the critique in Day 2011, ch. 4).
51 Quoted in Toscano 2008, p. 274.

time unit itself apparently is a dependent variable, one that is redetermined with changes in productivity. Abstract time, then, is not only socially constituted as a qualitatively determinate form of time, but it is quantitatively constituted as well: what constitutes a social labor hour is determined by the general level of productivity, the use value dimension. Yet although the social labor hour is redetermined, it remains constant as a unit of abstract time.[52]

Postone describes the dynamic produced by this interaction between the purely quantitative aspect of time as abstract measure of human activity, and its qualitative aspect deriving from the concrete level of productivity at a given stage of the development of the productive forces, as the 'treadmill effect'. The initial effect of innovations which enhance productivity is to increase the amount of value produced in a given period of time. However, as the innovation becomes generalised across the economy, the level of value produced per unit of time, 'because of its abstract and general temporal determination, falls back to its previous level'. Thus, there is a continual ratcheting up of the productivity norm which determines the 'social labor-hour'. Postone argues that it is this treadmill effect, driven by the drive for ever-increasing levels of productivity, which is the source of capitalism's directional dynamic, its immanent historical logic.[53]

So, although the abstract temporal measure of value remains constant, its hidden social content is continually changing:

> not every hour is an hour – in other words, not every hour of labor time counts as the social labor hour that determines the magnitude of total value. The abstract temporal constant, then, is both constant and nonconstant. In abstract temporal terms, the social labor hour remains constant as a measure of the total value produced; in concrete terms, it changes as productivity does.... It has become clear that, with increased productivity, the time unit becomes 'denser' in terms of the production of goods. Yet this 'density' is not manifest in the sphere of abstract temporality, the value sphere: the abstract temporal unit – the hour – and the total value produced remain constant.... This paradox cannot be resolved within the framework of abstract Newtonian time ... the process whereby the constant hour becomes 'denser' ... remains nonmanifest in terms of

---

52   Postone 1993, p. 289.
53   Postone 1993, pp. 289–91.

the abstract temporal frame of value. It can, however, be expressed in other temporal terms, with reference to a form of concrete temporality.[54]

If abstract time provides the framework or axis against which productivity is measured in order to determine socially useful labour time, it cannot provide the framework for measuring changes to the social labour hour as it is itself progressively redetermined by variations in the level of productivity. Generalised increases in productivity produce changes in the quality of each measured unit of time which cannot be grasped by a purely quantitative, abstract scale. Postone argues that the frame of reference required to grasp these substantive changes in the social labour hour is one of concrete, rather than abstract, time; that is, time as a dependent, not an independent, variable:

> Productivity, according to Marx, is grounded in the social character of the use value dimension of labor. Hence, this movement of time is a function of the use value dimension of labor as it interacts with the value frame, and can be understood as a sort of concrete time. In investigating the interaction of concrete and abstract labor, which lies at the heart of Marx's analysis of capital, we have uncovered that *a feature of capitalism is a mode of (concrete) time that expresses the motion of (abstract) time*.[55]

This second aspect of capitalism's temporality is both concrete, because it derives from the use-value component of human labour, and directional, because it is driven by cumulative increases in the level of productivity. As such it is, Postone believes, nothing other than the 'flow of history' or 'historical time'. This form of time, unlike the static time-as-measure generated by labour as social mediation, is not an abstract continuum independent of human activity within which events take place, but is dynamic, concrete and qualitative. 'It is the movement *of* time, as opposed to the movement *in* time', and consequently cannot be expressed in terms of the frame of reference of abstract time which knows only value or quantity as measure. Postone continues:

> Historical time in capitalism, then, can be considered as a form of concrete time that is socially constituted and expresses an ongoing qualitative transformation of work and production, of social life more generally,

---

54 Postone 1993, p. 292.
55 Postone 1993, p. 293.

and of forms of consciousness, values, and needs. Unlike the 'flow' of abstract time, this movement of time is not equable, but changes and can even accelerate. *A characteristic of capitalism, then, is the social constitution of two forms of time – abstract time and historical time – that are related intrinsically.*[56]

The outcome, for Postone, of the discovery of this second form of time operating behind the more clearly visible abstract time of capitalism is the possibility of a critique of positions, such as those of Lukács and Adorno, which equate capitalism straightforwardly with static bourgeois relations and counterpose the dynamic of history to it. On the basis of Postone's analysis, this position is wrong on two counts. In the first place, the temporality of capitalism is not simply the abstract time most clearly visible at its surface, but, as we have seen, also comprises a dynamic, qualitative time which interacts with it. Secondly, it undermines any conception of history as external to, and at odds with, capitalism. The view that capitalism is a social formation that has arisen *within* a broader historical time frame is erroneous, and commits the mistake of attributing to historical time the kind of abstract quality which, by definition, it should not have. Historical time is an authentic temporality of capitalism itself, generated by the same social processes responsible for abstract time. In fact, according to Postone it is entirely consistent with Marx to argue that this kind of historical time is specific to capitalism and that to endow pre-capitalist social formations with historicity of this type is falsely to project back onto them a temporal characteristic unique to capitalism. He argues that Marx showed that:

> there is indeed a form of logic in history, of historical necessity, but that it is immanent only to the capitalist social formation, and not to human history as a whole.... Marx's mature critical social theory does not hypostatize history as a sort of force moving all human societies; it does not presuppose that a directional dynamic of history in general exists. Rather it seeks to explain the existence of the sort of ongoing directional dynamic that defines modern society, and to do so in terms of historically determinate social forms constituted by labor in a process of alienation.[57]

The identification of historical necessity with capitalism seems consistent with the view, associated in one form with Hegel, but popularised by many

---

56   Postone 1993, pp. 293–4.
57   Postone 1993, pp. 304–5.

others, that only with the onset of modernity does a genuinely historical consciousness emerge in human societies.[58] But this is a historical consciousness

---

58 Of course, Postone is suggesting more than this – that history itself (at least as progress and development) is specific to the capitalist era. Whether this is consistent with Marx's understanding of history is questionable; it certainly seems at odds with the formulation of historical change found in the Preface to a *Contribution to the Critique of Political Economy* which is usually understood to be intended to apply to all societies, or at least all class societies. Miller has correctly commented that restricting the scope of history in this way precludes an explanation for the historical emergence of capitalism (Miller K. 2004, p. 221). Postone argues that the dialectic between the two forms of time – abstract and historical – is nothing other than a temporal manifestation of the dialectic between forces and relations of production. His motivation for this is his desire to insist, *contra* Engels's formulation in *Socialism: Scientific and Utopian*, that the contradiction in capitalism is not a 'rebellion of the mode of production against the mode of exchange' (Engels 1960, p. 136), but lies entirely within the sphere of production. It therefore cannot be overcome simply via changes in the mode of distribution alone, as was attempted in the USSR (Postone 1993, p. 124). Postone also believes that the contradiction between forces and relations of production, or between abstract time as measure of value and historical time as concrete development of human productivity, is sharpening due to the increasing materialisation of scientific knowledge in production. As capitalism develops and the use-value aspect of human labour – socially productive knowledge – comes to predominate in relation to simple labour time, 'production increasingly becomes a process of the objectification of historical time rather than of immediate labor time' (Postone 1993, p. 298). However, the system necessarily continues to operate on the basis of the objectification of labour time – value. Clearly the contribution of scientific knowledge to production does increase as capitalism develops. But it would be a mistake to believe that such knowledge can manifest itself as a component of production independently of human labour. Increases in productivity may rest on advances in scientific knowledge but in general take effect through the deployment in the productive process of ever-more sophisticated machinery, which itself is the product of human labour. That is why Marx refers to this element of capital as 'dead labour'. Its proliferation does not represent a tendency for capitalist production to depend more on knowledge and less on labour, but a tendency for it to depend more on the congealed labour of the past in relation to the living labour of the present. It is this tendency, expressed by Marx as an increase in the organic composition of capital, which perhaps has a better claim to be a candidate for the source of the historical temporality of capitalism identified by Postone than his unmediated concept of accumulated scientific knowledge. This is particularly the case as Marx also believed that this tendency has serious implications for the long-term rate of profit and therefore for the onset of economic crises, aspects of Marx's analysis of capitalism which do not feature in Postone's account. Viewed in this way, increases in productivity are, at root, increases in the density of labour time, that is, increases in the total amount of labour (living and dead) that can be mobilised by living workers.

which, because of the abstract time of capitalism, also puts a peculiar emphasis on the present. He writes:

> In [a] sense, ... *value is an expression of time as the present*. It is a measure of, and compelling norm for, the expenditure of immediate labor time regardless of the historical level of productivity.[59]

The centrality of this temporality of capitalism produces a strong sense of the present which is not undermined by the accumulation of historical time. However, the latter does change the concrete presupposition of that present, continually reconstituting it through changes in the level of productivity. Capitalism is marked by an immanent historical dynamic, but this historical time is constantly translated into the framework of the present. Thus, 'present necessity is not "automatically" negated but paradoxically reinforced; it is impelled forward in time as a perpetual present, an apparently eternal necessity'.[60]

This is what Postone means by capitalism's 'eternal present'. The temporality of capitalism is a product of a particular mode of interaction between the presentness of abstract time as measure of value and the historical accumulation of labour productivity such that the present is continually projected forward into the future. Without the historical aspect, the presentness of abstract time would be perceived as eternal in the sense of stasis, rendering the present indistinguishable from the past and future and making the concept of 'now' meaningless.[61] However, the historical temporality generated by technological development has the effect of making the present meaningful by locating it within the context of qualitative change. The result is abstract time projected into the future, and historical time reduced to a constant present. As Postone puts it, capitalism is revealed 'to be a society marked by a temporal duality – an ongoing, accelerating flow of history, on the one hand, and on ongoing conversion of this movement of time into a constant present, on the other'.[62] As we shall see in the next chapter, this formulation chimes with cultural analyses of the temporality of modernity made by a number of thinkers, Benjamin among them.

Postone's view represents a powerful challenge to the position, argued most forcefully by Adorno, that music marked strongly by the abstract temporal

---

59 Postone 1993, p. 298.
60 Postone 1993, pp. 299–301.
61 See Chapter 5 where I discuss Husserl's phenomenological account of time consciousness.
62 Postone 1993, p. 301.

framework of meter is incapable of adequately expressing historical time. Rather than being mutually exclusive, the one abstract and spatial, the other dialectical and emergent, the two temporalities are revealed to be the necessary products of the same social processes. The description of 'eternal present' understood as the projection of a heightened sense of 'now' being continually projected into the future might be regarded as capturing the essence of the temporality of groove music. Postone's analysis might explain why music which eschews a sense of meter entirely runs the risk of failing to articulate any kind of temporality and can only express eternity, and why even the music which Adorno regarded as exemplary in its encapsulation of dialectical, historical time – Beethoven's – also required meter to do so.[63]

Exchange and Abstract Time

Postone's is not the only significant theoretical attempt to account materialistically for the emergence of a concept of abstract time. An earlier contribution to this field is Alfred Sohn-Rethel's 'critique of epistemology' which seeks to give a historical materialist explanation of the basis of abstract thought in general, of which abstract time is merely one component.[64] Sohn-Rethel's ambitious aim is to produce a critique of bourgeois epistemology which parallels Marx's critique of political economy, and is capable of undermining the claim of timeless universality generally made for abstract, logical thought as it is found in modern science and especially mathematics. Forms of cognition are just as timebound and historical as other modes of thought such as religion, Sohn-Rethel reasons; they are far from universal to human society considered over its entire history, and therefore the task is to locate such thought in the concrete historical conditions of its emergence.

Like Postone, Sohn-Rethel seeks to expose the 'real abstraction' in society which gives rise to abstraction in thought. Abstraction, he argues, 'does not originate in men's minds but in their actions'; it is the product of human social interactions.[65] Unlike Postone, however, he believes that abstract thought 'does not spring from labour, but from exchange as a particular mode of social interrelationship'.[66] His reason for taking this position is that exchange is prior

---

63 See the discussions of the music of the Darmstadt serialists, Boulez, Messiaen and others in previous chapters.
64 Sohn-Rethel 1978.
65 Sohn-Rethel 1978, p. 20.
66 Sohn-Rethel 1978, p. 6.

to abstract labour in two senses: logically prior because abstract labour depends on a system of generalised commodity production, which by definition 'depends on exchange' – in other words it is 'the exchange process which accomplishes the abstraction'; and historically prior because systems of abstract cognition predate the existence of capitalism, emerging, according to Sohn-Rethel, in those pre-capitalist societies in which commodity exchange took place and money played a significant role.[67] Thus Sohn-Rethel's emphasis on exchange rather than wage labour enables his theory to account for the forms of abstract thought in mathematics and philosophy which arose in ancient Greece. These developments are, if anything, related negatively to labour for Sohn-Rethel, in that they are intimately bound up with the historical separation of intellectual labour from manual labour.

Sohn-Rethel emphasises the abstract character of the act of exchange. The exchange value of a commodity is marked by a complete absence of quality, by the total disregard of the material characteristics of the object and the use to which it may be put. In addition, use and exchange are mutually exclusive in time: in order for exchange to take place, its separation from use must be strictly observed. The object whose social status is to change through a transfer of ownership must be abstracted from the temporal world, and its material status must remain unchanged, or, rather, must be assumed to remain unchanged, for the period of the act of exchange. Not only is it highly undesirable for goods, even second-hand goods, to be in use while the contract of exchange is under negotiation, but while brand new goods stand in shop windows with price tags attached, their condition is held to be absolutely immutable, unaffected by the natural processes of decay and corrosion that are in reality at work on every material object, however slowly. Time stands still in the act of exchange.

Not surprisingly, these conditions are found in their most extreme form in the universal medium of exchange – money. Money is abstraction in material form, which, strictly speaking, is a contradiction in terms. Its existence is only possible because those who use it tacitly accept that its value is not determined by its material characteristics. This was not true of the early use of metal as medium of exchange, which needed to be weighed out to the appropriate quantity and tested for purity. But with the advent of coinage, money's value became guaranteed by the issuing authority rather than residing in its physical

---

67   R. Bellofiore cited in Bonefeld 2010, p. 257. Eldret and Hanlon cited in Bonefeld 2010, p. 258. Support for the position that abstract labour plays a determining role only later comes from Marx: 'The proportions in which [commodities] are exchangeable are at first quite a matter of chance' (Marx 1977, p. 91).

properties. A coin's or a banknote's materiality is merely the carrier of its social function. As Sohn-Rethel says:

> A coin, therefore, is a thing which conforms to the postulates of the exchange abstraction and is supposed, among other things, to consist of an immutable substance, a substance over which time has no power, and which stands in antithetic contrast to any matter found in nature.[68]

Sohn-Rethel stresses that though a separation of value from use is an absolute condition of exchange, it does not arise in the minds of the exchanging agents: for the purchaser especially, use value remains, of course, the prime motivation.

> It is the action of exchange, and the action alone, that is abstract. The consciousness and the action of the people part company in exchange and go different ways.... The abstractness of their action will... escape the minds of the people performing it. In exchange, *the action is social, the minds are private*.[69]

Participants in the act of exchange do not require a conscious understanding of the abstraction that underpins it: they misrecognise it as a simple act between individual property owners. However, it is Sohn-Rethel's argument that the abstraction involved is nevertheless not lost to thought, but finds expression in 'the abstract intellect, or the so-called "pure understanding" – the cognitive source of scientific knowledge'.[70] Slavoj Žižek comments on the significance of the unconscious aspect of the process:

> This misrecognition brings about the fissure of the consciousness into 'practical' and 'theoretical': the proprietor partaking in the act of exchange proceeds as a 'practical solipsist': he overlooks the universal, socio-synthetic dimension of his act, reducing it to a casual encounter of atomized individuals in the market. This 'repressed' *social* dimension of his act emerges thereupon in the form of its contrary – as universal Reason turned towards the observation of nature (the network of categories of 'pure reason' as the conceptual frame of natural sciences).[71]

---

68   Sohn-Rethel 1978, p. 59.
69   Sohn-Rethel 1978, pp. 28–9.
70   Sohn-Rethel 1978, p. 34.
71   Žižek 1989, p. 20.

The paradigm of such thought is mathematics, of the kind initiated by figures such as Pythagoras in the first society based on commodity production:

> The interrelational equation posited by an act of exchange leaves all dimensional measurements behind and establishes a sphere of non-dimensional quantity. This is the pure or abstract quality of cardinal numbers, with nothing to define it but the relation of greater than (>) or smaller than (<) or equal to (=) some other quantity as such. In other words, the postulate of the exchange equation abstracts quantity in a manner which constitutes the founding of free mathematical reasoning.[72]

The exchange abstraction also finds its reflection in conceptions of time and space. For the purposes of exchange, time must be emptied of all its concrete components – births and deaths, human interaction with nature, the seasons, and so on – all of which pertain to the sphere of use. Concrete times and their effects are suspended and time is conceived only in terms of the instants at which exchange takes place. Similarly, all qualitative aspects of space are disregarded leaving only the abstract distance which needs to be traversed in order to complete the exchange with the delivery of goods. The quantitative equation of exchange does not depend on any particular place or time, or, alternatively, is held to apply equally at all places and all times. So from the point of view of exchange, time becomes unhistorical and space ungeographical, while both are absolutely homogeneous and limitless:

> Time and space rendered abstract under the impact of commodity exchange are marked by homogeneity, continuity and emptiness of all natural and material content, visible or invisible (e.g. air). The exchange abstraction excludes everything that makes up history, human and even natural history. The entire empirical reality of facts, events and description by which one moment and locality of time and space is distinguishable from another is wiped out. Time and space assume thereby that character of absolute historical timelessness and universality which must mark the exchange abstraction as a whole and each of its features.[73]

---

72   Sohn-Rethel 1978, p. 47.
73   Sohn-Rethel 1978, pp. 48–9.

Sohn-Rethel argues that it is precisely these categories which form the basis of mathematical and scientific knowledge from its beginnings with the ancient Greeks to the bourgeois era. With the Greeks:

> the geometry of the measurement became something quite different from the measurement itself. The manual operation became subordinated to an art of pure thought which was directed solely towards grasping quantitative laws of number or of abstract space. Their conceptual content was independent not only from this or that particular purpose but from any practical task.[74]

For Sohn-Rethel, it is no accident that it is with the Greeks too, that the systematic separation of intellectual from manual labour takes place for the first time. The possibility of intellectual activity is often understood as having its roots in the emergence of a social class who have been freed from the obligation to labour. But the force of Marx's and Engels's historical materialist maxim, 'mankind must first of all eat, drink, have shelter and clothing, before it can pursue politics, science, art, religion, etc'.[75] goes much deeper than simply stating that work must be taken care of before the philosophising can begin. Sohn-Rethel posits a direct connection between the emergence of a class of intellectuals who assume responsibility for the thought of a society and the form that their thought takes. The knowledge deployed by an artisan or manual worker has the character of 'practical know-how', which would be meaningless if severed from the tasks to which it relates, and takes a form which is more amenable to being passed on by demonstration than by explanation alone. Where it is conveyed by the written word – Sohn-Rethel uses cookery books as an example – common language usage is sufficient because such knowledge is part of the fabric of empirical life. By contrast, the foundational precepts of modern physics, for example, are marked by their dependence on the suspension of the conditions pertaining to real existence in the world. Galileo's concept of inertial motion, which formed the basis for the Newtonian mechanics that has underpinned science for the last three hundred years, is entirely abstract. As Koyré points out, it rests on presuppositions which could not possibly apply in the empirical world: the isolation of a physical body from its environment; a Euclidian concept of empty, homogeneous, infinite space; and a conception of

---

74   Sohn-Rethel 1978, p. 102.
75   Engels 1989, p. 467.

movement as the translation of a body from one geometrical point to another which is held to have no other effect on the body in question.[76]

Therefore, Sohn-Rethel argues, the knowledge produced by societies in which exchange provides the social synthesis and in which the intellectual sphere has separated itself from the sphere of work, displays particular characteristics. It is a form of thought that is non-empirical which requires abstract, 'pure' concepts for its representation. Because the social synthesis upon which it is based is an abstraction that excludes the material interaction of humans with nature, it is also thought in which nature appears as an object world, to which pertain abstract laws of cause and effect. It is thought whose concepts:

> being non-empirical, ... bear no trace of the locality, the date or any other circumstances of their origin. They stand outside the realm of sense-perception without, however, forfeiting their own prime claim to reality.[77]

Having cut itself off from its social origin through its abstractness and its exclusion of empirical content, such thought 'develops a normative sense of its own – its "logic"'. In its purest forms, such as mathematics, physics and philosophy, its claim to validity rests upon the internal consistency of its procedures in a way which amounts to self-justification. Sohn-Rethel comments:

> It is the science of intellectual labour springing from the second nature which is founded upon non-empirical abstraction and on concepts of an *a priori* nature. The form elements of the exchange abstraction are of such fundamental calibre – abstract time and space, abstract matter, quantity as a mathematical abstraction, abstract motion, etc. – that there cannot be a natural event in the world which could elude these basic features of nature. They make up between them a kind of abstract framework into which all observable phenomena are bound to fit. Anything descriptive of this framework such as, for example, the geometry of homogeneous space, would be applicable to such phenomena with *a priori* assured certainty.[78]

---

76 Sohn-Rethel 1978, pp. 126–7. Interestingly, Herbert Marcuse posits precisely the opposite cause of developments in science, arguing that capitalist society has rendered intellectual thought 'one-dimensional' by excluding all concepts which cannot be represented by operational procedures: e.g. the concept of length measurement has become synonymous with the empirical practice of length measurement (see Marcuse 1964, pp. 12–13).
77 Sohn-Rethel 1978, p. 67.
78 Sohn-Rethel 1978, p. 73.

The highest philosophical expression of an epistemology resting on an *a priori* framework of abstractions is, of course, that of Kant. Sohn-Rethel believes, however, that there is nothing *a priori* about such categories: 'The basic categories of intellectual labour... are replicas of the elements of the real abstraction, and the real abstraction is itself that specific characteristic which endows commodity exchange with its socially synthetic function. Therefore, intellectual labour, in employing these categories, moves in the mould of the formal elements of the social synthesis'. Žižek sums up the core of Sohn-Rethel's argument:

> Before thought could arrive at pure *abstraction*, the abstraction was already at work in the social effectivity of the market.... Before thought could arrive at the idea of a purely *quantitative* determination, a *sine qua non* of the modern science of nature, pure quantity was already at work in money, that commodity which renders possible the commensurability of the value of all other commodities notwithstanding their particular qualitative determination.[79]

By identifying the empirical and historically specific practice which gives rise to abstract categories of cognition, Sohn-Rethel's analysis serves to undermine their claim to neutrality and timelessness. On this reading, the principles of geometry and the theories of physics are not so much *discoveries* about the world as *ideological representations* of it.[80]

But to what extent is this a critique of abstract thought? Does Sohn-Rethel's analysis amount to a judgment that these abstractions are false or wrong? To draw this conclusion would be to misunderstand the nature of the argument. Sohn-Rethel's materialist procedure recognises that a critique undertaken at the level of theory alone would collapse into the very idealism with which it seeks to accuse bourgeois epistemology. 'Consciousness is not the function of a "mind" capable of absolute self-criticism on lines of pure logic. Pure logic does not control, but is controlled by, its timeless idea of the truth; of this idea itself there is no immanent criticism or confirmation'.

Nevertheless, Sohn-Rethel's is a critique, not merely an exposé, of abstract cognition, but not one that simply argues that such thought is an error. Its materialism provides an antidote to critiques, like Bergson's, of the spatialisation

---

79 Žižek 1989, p. 17.
80 A more sociological account of the effect of a money economy on consciousness is given by Simmel, who comments on its tendency to 'transform the world into an arithmetic problem' (Simmel 2010, p. 105).

of time discussed in Chapter 3, which fail to understand the material and social roots of forms of consciousness. Sohn-Rethel believes that the epistemology that he has analysed is deficient, but represents what he terms 'necessary false consciousness'. However, he writes:

> Necessary false consciousness ... is not faulty consciousness. It is, on the contrary, logically correct, inherently incorrigible consciousness.... Necessary false consciousness is false, not as a fault of consciousness, but by fault of the historical order of social existence causing it to be false.[81]

Thus, the concept of abstract time is not a simple misrecognition of the 'reality' of time, but the necessary form taken by thought when the social synthesis is accomplished by exchange. Its falsehood lies in its misrepresentation of itself as based on a 'pure reason', but more importantly because the form of society of which it is a product is itself false.[82]

Though, as we have seen, Sohn-Rethel links epistemological abstraction to the practice of commodity exchange and the division of labour, rather than capitalism, it is nevertheless with capitalism as a society of generalised commodity production that such thinking reaches its apogee. It was between the seventeenth and nineteenth centuries that abstract concepts such as those of space and time spread beyond intellectual circles and came to influence the thinking of entire societies. In this sense, Sohn-Rethel's philosophical analysis conforms to the timescale of the sociological developments discussed at the start of this chapter.

Monopoly Capitalism and the Discipline of Abstract Time

These findings may help to explain how meter established itself as the norm for the temporal organisation of music at the dawn of the bourgeois era in Europe, but do little to illuminate the transformation of meter into groove around the turn of the twentieth century. However, Sohn-Rethel goes on to identify developments at precisely this historical moment that can form the basis for such an analysis. These developments are the outcome of the

---

[81] Sohn-Rethel 1978, pp. 197–8.
[82] Arguments to support this latter claim are not part of a study of bourgeois epistemology. The standard against which a social formation may be regarded as 'false' can be derived on the basis of ethics (justice), economics (crisis), ecological sustainability, immanent critique (inability to deliver its avowed aims), or in other ways.

inception of monopoly capitalism in the last two decades of the nineteenth century, specifically, the new forms of management introduced to meet the demands of the new production processes required by capitalism on this scale. As John Bellamy Foster explains:

> While these tendencies of the capitalist division of labor were already evident in the nineteenth century, it was not until the maturation of monopoly capitalism in the twentieth century that they came to be applied systematically. The development of the division of labor, as Adam Smith observed, was dependent on the extent of the market and the scale of production. Its full development was therefore impracticable for the small family firm that still predominated in the nineteenth century. With the rise of the giant corporation in the late nineteenth century, however, all of this changed. It is in this context that one has to understand the rise to prominence of Frederick Winslow Taylor and scientific management, or Taylorism, in the early twentieth century.[83]

So-called scientific management emerges in the late nineteenth century with 'the beginnings of monopolistic organisation of industry, and the purposive and systematic application of science to production'. It marked the beginning of a fully-fledged capitalist organisation of production which had finally established itself in place of the range of putting-out and subcontracting arrangements that had characterised the early period of industrialisation. Centralised production became the norm surprisingly late in the nineteenth century. Maurice Dobb testifies that a system in which workers were employed by a subcontractor, who was both an employee and a small employer of labour, was still in operation in many American industries in 1870.[84] Under these arrangements, management set the tasks only in general terms, leaving the workers themselves to devise the ways to perform them.[85] Braverman regards these systems as evidence that early capitalists sought 'to disregard the difference between labor power and the labor that can be gotten out of it', treating the purchasing of labour in the same way as that of raw materials.[86] Monopoly capitalism, therefore, marks the end of these 'transitional forms' of labour management, and the point at which capital finally assumes the function of full control over the labour process and seeks to maximise the quantity of

---

83 Foster 1998, p. xvi.
84 Braverman 1998, pp. 42–3.
85 Braverman 1998, p. 62.
86 Braverman 1998, p. 8.

value that can be produced from every unit of labour power by dictating the precise manner in which tasks are to be carried out.[87]

Despite its scientific pretensions, Braverman argues, the focus of the new management techniques was the organisation of labour, not the development of technology: 'It enters the workplace not as the representative of science, but as the representative of management masquerading in the trappings of science'.[88] The crucial parameter focused upon by Taylor as he developed the foundational techniques of scientific management was time. The heart of the system was 'time study', 'defined as the measurement of elapsed time for each component operation of a work process; its prime instrument is the stopwatch, calibrated in fractions of an hour, minute, or second'.[89] But this was a concept of time shorn of all empirical elements. As Taylor himself said: 'time study is a success only if it enables you to know exactly how long the studied job *should* take', rather than how long it *does* take. So the timings which were imposed on workers to set the pace of their work, and which purported to be accurate to a fraction of a second, were not derived observationally from the performance of the concrete tasks in question, but were entirely abstract. Sohn-Rethel describes this procedure as 'coercive timing', in which 'time is abstractified to a quantifiable dimension into which the scientific intellect can refit carefully selected items of content', in order to create norms which carry the validating stamp of scientific and mathematical neutrality.[90]

For Sohn-Rethel, this represents not only an expression of the increasing domination of living labour by the dead labour of machinery as it imposes its own tempo on those who operate it, but also a new extreme in the division of mental and manual labour. Under Taylorism, all the mental aspects of work, all the elements of knowledge involved in skilled labour, are removed from the workers and are undertaken by management in the office. Taylor argued:

> The most prominent single element in modern scientific management is the task idea. The work of every workman is fully planned out by the management... in advance,... describing in detail the task which he is to accomplish, as well as the means to be used in doing the work.... This task specifies not only what is to be done, but how it is to be done and the exact time allowed for doing it.[91]

---

87   Braverman 1998, pp. 43, 62.
88   Braverman 1998, p. 59.
89   Braverman 1998, p. 119.
90   Sohn-Rethel 1978, p. 155.
91   Braverman 1998, p. 82.

Taylor's first successes were achieved simply by setting more challenging targets for the completion of specific tasks.[92] But scientific management later developed its techniques to an extraordinary degree of refinement. Time study became time and motion study as each task was broken down into the individual body movement required to perform it and allocated a timing value in TMUs, or one hundred thousandths of an hour. For example, to pick up a pencil was deemed by one system to involve three movements – *Transport Empty*, *Pinch Grasp*, and *Transport Loaded* – each of which was to be performed in a specified time period. For other tasks, there was even a formula to allow for 'Eye Travel Time'![93] A journal article on the subject exposed the extent of the abstract thinking behind such practices:

> ... as an element in a control system, a man may be regarded as a chain consisting of the following items: (1) sensory devices ... (2) a computing system which responds on the basis of previous experience ... (3) an amplifying system – the motor-nerve endings and muscles ... (4) mechanical linkages ... whereby the muscular work produces externally observable effects.[94]

Here, labour, along with the body of the labourer, has become abstract not only at the level of the system as a whole, but for each individual unit of capital. Henry Ford's oft-quoted question, 'Why is it that each time I ask for a pair of hands, they come with a brain attached'?, expresses the view of the monopoly capitalists. The two aspects of human labour – knowledge and action – have been completely separated from each other; the former understood as abstract, autonomous intellectual activity, the latter subjected to the discipline of abstract, measured time.

Sohn-Rethel argues that the coercive use of abstract time in the labour process marks the onset of a new period in capitalism.[95] This period of monopoly

---

92   He claims to have increased the quantity of pig iron shifted per man per day at the Bethlehem Steel Works from 12½ tons to 47½ tons (Braverman 1998, pp. 71–3).
93   Braverman 1998, pp. 121–2.
94   Braverman 1998, p. 124.
95   Sohn-Rethel comes to different conclusions from Postone in this respect. He suggests that the Taylorism of monopoly capitalism represents the beginnings of an emergence of an alternative mechanism for the commensuration of labour based on the conscious apportioning of living labour to specific tasks, rather than occurring blindly through the exchange mechanism. Of course, the influence of the market has not been superseded; ultimately it remains the competitive dynamic of the market which enforces the norm of socially necessary labour time. However, Sohn-Rethel believes, in line with Engels's

capitalism marks the point when abstract time, already at work in society through the mechanism of socially useful labour time, becomes imposed consciously and coercively on workers by the agents of capital. This way of understanding the problem allows a class dimension to appear in the analysis, one that is entirely absent from Postone's account.[96] For there is no doubt that the spread of clock time impinged on different sections of society to varying extents and varying degrees. Whether the material source of conceptual abstraction is commodity exchange or abstract labour, it is clear that the idea of abstract time is first taken up and used by the intellectuals of society – the philosophers and the scientists. Clock time gradually makes itself felt on the mass of the population through the regulation of work time, but for several generations it directly affects the proletariat only at the start and end points of the working day, influencing what happens in between only via their employers through the value mechanism. With the imposition of Taylorism, abstract clock time now manifests itself acutely and continuously for the entire duration of every working day, not simply as idea, but as material reality. It is, therefore, only with monopoly capitalism that the mass of the population comes to feel the full effect of a reified, homogenous empty time, a time without beginning or end, immanent to itself, 'whose passing ticks and tocks human activity'.[97]

The abstract time of capitalism also made itself felt on working people in another new way at this point in history. Thrift regards the expansion of

---

formulation cited in fn. 58, that monopoly capitalism is a manifestation of the increasing socialization of production within a system of the private appropriation of the social product (Sohn-Rethel 1978, pp. 171, 178). In this sense, for Sohn-Rethel the practices of scientific management contain within themselves the seeds of a rational allocation of labour suitable for use by a 'society of production' as opposed to the current 'society of appropriation'. For this, he earns the criticism of Postone for whom abstract labour is the hallmark of the exploitative rationality of capitalism, and who consequently rejects as trivial any change in the organisation of production which retains industrial practices. In this respect, Postone's position is similar to that taken by John Holloway in his *Crack Capitalism*, where he writes: 'The abstraction of doing into [abstract] labour is the homogenization of time' (Holloway 2010, pp. 135–40). For him, abstract labour and abstract time must be overcome or refused and replaced by 'doing', or unalienated labour, in order to achieve a free society. As we shall see, this approach has implications for the musical arguments, and on the question of time situates Holloway's autonomism closer to Bergson's idealism than to Sohn-Rethel's historical materialism, with Postone occupying ground somewhere in between.

96 Bonefeld 2010, p. 272, fn. 3.
97 Bonefeld 2010, p. 267.

consumerism in the late nineteenth century and the extension of credit to wider layers of the population upon which it depended as the key factors which spread an abstract orientation on the future to the mass of working people. As we have seen, the logic of investment had long since had an effect on the time consciousness of industrialists, but as domestic loans became more common a version of those same influences were felt by those they employed: 'The new economic calculation put a financial value on future time so that a putative future became part of the habitus of the worker'.[98] However, as discussed in relation to Postone's analysis, the conception of the future generated by abstract time and by the expectation that debts will be paid is of a rather limited kind. It is the projection of a static present into the future rather than an idea of the future as genuinely novel; this futurity is merely the abstract continuation of being, rather than true becoming.

World Time

There are other historical developments that can be cited to endorse the thesis that the final years of the nineteenth century mark the final victory of abstract time over the lives of the population of the advanced capitalist world. This is also the period in which clock time achieved the standardisation which is logically implied by its concept. For a long period, the diffusion of clock time was uneven within national territories. Even where the clock had achieved a dominance in civic life, different localities tended to adhere to their own time zones; for instance, the official times of London and Plymouth diverged by sixteen minutes. The process of standardisation was driven by the mechanism and the needs first of a national postal service and then by the railways. In Britain, most railway companies switched to Greenwich Mean Time on December 1st 1847 and most towns had brought their public clocks into line by 1852.[99]

What was distinctive about monopoly capitalism, apart from the unprecedented size of the units of capital, was its global character. What is often described as the 'first era of globalisation'[100] brought about the international standardisation of clock time. World time was inaugurated in Washington at the International Meridian Conference of 1883 and the process was completed in 1913 with the transmitting of a wireless signal from the Eiffel Tower to set the

---

98   Thrift 1996, p. 559.
99   Thrift 1996, pp. 560–4.
100 Bordo and Meissner 2007.

standard.[101] World time is intimately implicated with space through the marking out of time zones on the basis of their longitudinal distance from London. Thus there is a sense in which world time is the temporal expression of space: longitude and clock time can be expressed in each other's measurements, the culmination of a development initiated by Harrison's solution of the 'longitude problem' with his H.4 chronometer in 1759.[102] But these developments not only took the spatialisation of time to a new level, they also generated a degree of instantaneity which was inconceivable earlier in history. Marconi's first news services were established in Cornwall and Cape Cod in 1904, linking both sides of the Atlantic with events on the other on the basis of a simultaneous timescale. The BBC began broadcasting the Greenwich Time Signal in 1924, two years after its creation. Adam comments that these developments effectively produced a tangible 'global present' in which 'instantaneity and simultaneity ... replaced sequence and duration'. In a global capitalist economy, abstract, quantifiable time applies equally everywhere, just as money does. Within the world time of the global economy, resetting one's watch on arrival in a distant time zone is analogous to changing one's money into the local currency.

We are now in a position to pick up and expand the historico-geographical analysis begun in Chapter 2 in relation to African music. If the materialist assumption behind this book – that the temporal organisation of music is an expression of the temporal forms of the society that produces it – is correct, then meter proper (as opposed to a regular pulse) emerges as a result of a reorganisation of temporal relations by the onset of European modernity. The invention and spread of the mechanical equal-hours clock is both evidence of a new abstract concept of time and the mechanism which reinforces this concept in the daily lives of increasing numbers of people. Underlying the expansion of clock time, however, are the new needs of industrial capitalism for time regulation, time discipline, time thrift and time measurement.

Marx's value theory takes us deeper still into the analysis, revealing that at the heart of an economic system of generalised commodity production and exchange lies a system of value determined by abstract labour measured by abstract time. Marx understands these as 'real abstractions' – abstractions in the material conditions of social reproduction – rather than abstractions arising solely at the level of thought. Postone's development of this analysis adds weight to the view that metrical music is the music of capitalism by exposing the temporal processes which govern the dynamic of capitalism itself, in particular 'socially necessary labour time'. As a result of the interaction of abstract

---

101 Adam 2004, pp. 117–18.
102 Landes 1983, p. 150.

time-as-measure of labour and a historical time associated with the development of productive forces, time is experienced in capitalism as a particular combination of presentness and futurity: a constant present projected into an abstract future. Importantly, this is not simply the mental conception of time that capitalism tends to produce; it is the temporality of the system itself.

Abstract time, however, is found also at the level of thought, as part of a general system of abstract intellectual thinking which Sohn-Rethel traces to the act of commodity exchange and the separation of mental from manual labour. Sohn-Rethel's contribution allows us to historicise further, both to explain the occurrences of abstract thought in mathematics and philosophy before the rise of capitalism, and to trace more recent developments. Chief among these, for the purposes of our argument, are changes brought about by the monopolisation of capital around the turn of the twentieth century. Abstract time, already present as a disciplining force through the market, now divided into ever finer and more accurate gradations, becomes deployed consciously as a coercive force by capital in the techniques of Taylorism. Combined with the completion of a standardisation process which renders clock time an all-encompassing system, for the first time the mass of the population comes under the direct regulation of abstract time, experienced as an objective force beyond human control. This quantitative intensification of the experience of accurately measured time at this historical moment threatens to become a qualitative transformation of social temporality as capital moves to incorporate those spheres of human activity which hitherto had remained outside of its logic and thereby retained elements of substantive and concrete temporalities. This is the period of the rise of the 'culture industry', which increasingly subsumed the leisure time of workers to the dynamic of capital by commodifying its activities.

This moment is a turning point in time consciousness. It produces a cultural crisis in which a section of society – intellectuals, artists and those influenced by them – mount a sustained critique of abstract, spatialised conceptions of time and attempt to promote a less rigid, humanised temporality as a model for society. Broadly speaking, this critique falls under the category of modernism, and includes, in their different ways, two of the key thinkers discussed in earlier chapters, Bergson and Adorno. In the main, because of the acute division of labour wrought by mature capitalism, the sections of society that adopt this position are those who feel the effects of abstract time in thought, but are not directly affected by the 'real abstraction' of capitalism. For the mass of the population, the working class, rejecting abstract time is not a possibility, because for them, that is the reality of time. From this point onwards, a marked divergence opens up between the temporality of the cultural products of intellectuals and those of the working class, between 'high' art and mass art, between 'serious' and 'popular' culture. In the field of music, from roughly the beginning of the twentieth century, 'serious' or 'classical' music tends to try to break free from metricality and eschew even a discernible regular pulse, while popular music adopts the groove.

The question to be tackled in the next chapter is how groove should be characterised in aesthetic terms. Does it represent, as both Adorno and Deleuze believed, a capitulation to unfreedom, to a sterile and formulaic abstraction which degrades music's artistic value? Or can the temporality of the era of monopoly capitalism be the foundation for valid – that is, critical – artistic expression?

CHAPTER 7

History, Modernism, and the Time of Music

By the dawn of the twentieth century, Western societies had reached a point where the abstract, measured time of the clock had come to dominate a large part, if not the entirety, of the lives of the vast majority. In many ways, it was this temporality which was the target of the revolt against established cultural norms waged by the artistic modernisms of the early twentieth century. These revolts, despite taking place in the sphere of aesthetics, and comprising critiques of modes of artistic representation, were fundamentally political. They necessarily involved a critique of the society which had generated such a one-dimensional and repressive temporality, and sought to posit transformative or utopian alternatives.

We have already encountered some examples of these critiques, in particular Adorno's charge against certain kinds of modern music, both popular and 'serious', that fail to capture the dialectically emergent structure of historical time. But Bergson's critique of spatialised time, which finds an echo in Adorno's formulation, might also be considered an example of this modernist impulse, albeit one operating in the philosophical, rather than the aesthetic, realm.

As we have seen, Adorno champions modernist temporal procedures in music which avoid the regularity of pulse, meter and repetition. But similar experiments in the treatment of time were central to modernist currents in many artforms. Lunn describes the weakening or even disappearance of temporal structure in modernist literature and theatre, and its replacement by other ways of ordering events:

> Instead of narrating outer sequential or additive time, modern novelists explore the simultaneity of experience in psychological time, in which are concentrated past, present and future.

Such work is no longer sustained by a framework consisting of a succession of events unfolding in historical time, but 'is often without apparent causal progression and completion'.[1] This temporal ambiguity is closely connected to the abandonment of a unitary perspective on events, what Lunn describes as 'the demise of the integrated individual subject or personality'.[2] Instead, modernist

---

1 Lunn 1984, p. 35.
2 Lunn 1984, p. 37.

writers often occupy multiple, contradictory and fallible vantage points in their portrayal of events, techniques which were paralleled in painting by the simultaneous, multiple perspectives of cubism and constructivism, and the distortions of expressionism. In general, the techniques inaugurated by the various schools of artistic modernism sought to fragment, distort, or subvert any sense of time or history as a unitary, coherent, continuous, comprehensible process.

What is interesting from the point of view of a study of groove music, is that groove emerges at precisely the same historical moment as artistic modernism, but represents an aesthetic of time which appears to be radically different from both modernism and the dominant norms of the nineteenth century. For Adorno, this bifurcation in musical style, which maps directly onto the popular/serious split, is an aspect of commodification, the colonisation of artistic products by the capitalist market and its prioritisation of exchange value over use value. Hence his oft-quoted, 'both are torn halves of an integral freedom, to which however they do not add up'.[3] Because groove has its origins in this tumultuous historical moment, it may be profitable to investigate whether there are other aspects of the aesthetic debates of the period which can illuminate it.

Time and Narrative

George Lukács is known for his particularly thorough elaboration of Marx's theory of commodity fetishism and yet is to be found on the other side of the aesthetic debate from Adorno, as a trenchant critic of modernism. The question of time is central to Lukács's defence of realism against modernism in these debates. In his pre-Marxist *Theory of the Novel*, Lukács appears to believe that there can be a realist artistic representation of time; that is, that there is such a thing as 'real' time and that it can be portrayed realistically in literature. He explicitly identifies real time as Bergson's *durée*, and goes on to argue that the novel is the temporal form of literature in the fullest sense: unlike older literary forms such as epic, it is time itself that gives form to the novel.[4] He argues, 'only in the novel, whose very matter is seeking and failing to find the essence, is time posited together with the form'; 'real duration, real time [is]

---

3 Adorno 1997b, p. 123.
4 Lukács 1971a, p. 121.

the life-element of the novel'.[5] Explaining the way in which time provides the unifying force for a novel's events and characters, he writes:

> This victory [of unifying] is rendered possible by time. The unrestricted, uninterrupted flow of time is the unifying principle of the homogeneity that rubs the sharp edges off each heterogeneous fragment and establishes a relationship... between them. Time brings order into the chaos of men's lives and gives it the semblance of a spontaneously flowering, organic entity; characters having no apparent meaning appear, establish relations with one another, break them off, disappear again without any meaning having been revealed. But the characters are not simply dropped into that meaningless becoming and dissolving which preceded man and will outlast him. Beyond events, beyond psychology, time gives them the essential quality of their existence: however accidental the appearance of a character may be in pragmatic and psychological terms, it emerges from an existent, experienced continuity, and the atmosphere of thus being borne upon the unique and unrepeatable stream of life cancels out the accidental nature of their experiences and the isolated nature of the events recounted.[6]

Lukács can be read here as making the trivial point that the novel achieves unity by means of time simply in virtue of its chronology. However, it is clear that Lukács does not believe that the mere existence of a chronological thread is the basis of the novel's temporality. What distinguishes the novel from the epic is a certain distancing of meaning from the immediate chronology of events and characters:

> In the epic the life-immanence of meaning is so strong that it abolishes time: life enters eternity as life, the organic retains nothing of time except the phase of blossoming; fading and dying are forgotten and left entirely behind. In the novel, meaning is separated from life, and hence the essential from the temporal; we might almost say that the entire inner action of the novel is nothing but a struggle against the power of time.[7]

Time is pictured here as the source of destruction and passing away; the meaning of life is not to be gleaned from immersion in its immediacy because life is

---

5 Lukács 1971a, pp. 122, 151.
6 Lukács 1971a, p. 125.
7 Lukács 1971a, p. 122.

a struggle against time. Therefore death – the non-temporal, or the limit of temporality – is necessary for any realistic and meaningful representation of time.

In Lukács's later Marxist masterwork, *History and Class Consciousness*, the necessity of distancing is addressed more thoroughly but this time in the context of commodity fetishism and the 'reification' of social structures that it produces. Lukács regards the issue of the commodity 'as the central, structural problem of capitalist society in all its aspects'.[8] The commodity structure 'penetrate[s] society in all its aspects and... remould[s] it in its own image', generating a 'phantom objectivity' whose apparent rationality and autonomy conceal the social relations which underpin it.[9] 'This rationalisation of the world appears to be complete, it seems to penetrate the very depths of man's physical and psychic nature', condemning people to a servitude to a 'second nature' based upon reification.[10]

One aspect of this reification is an abstract time, the idea of which Lukács ostensibly draws from Marx, but in fact, by identifying it with space, has more in common with Bergson's formulation.[11] Lukács states that the rationalisation of the work process in commodity production 'reduces space and time to a common denominator and degrades time to the dimension of space'.[12] He goes on:

> Thus time sheds its qualitative, variable, flowing nature; it freezes into an exactly delimited, quantifiable continuum filled with quantifiable 'things' (the reified, mechanically objectified 'performance' of the worker, wholly separated from his total human personality): in short, it becomes space.[13]

The overall result of reification is that:

> Man in capitalist society confronts a reality 'made' by himself (as a class) which appears to him to be a natural phenomenon alien to himself; he is wholly at the mercy of its 'laws', his activity is confined to the exploitation of the inexorable fulfilment of certain individual laws for his own (egoistic)

---

8   Lukács 1971b, p. 82.
9   Lukács 1971b, pp. 82–3.
10   Lukács 1971b, pp. 86, 101.
11   Osborne 2008, p. 18.
12   Lukács 1971b, p. 89.
13   Lukács 1971b, p. 90.

interests. But even while 'acting' he remains, in the nature of the case, the object and not the subject of events.[14]

Lukács argues that in the context of a situation in which there seems to be an unbridgeable gulf between human action and objective reality as a totality, such that human subjectivity is overwhelmed by the power of a reified objectivity, the principle of art acquires an importance denied to it in other historical periods. 'This principle is the creation of a concrete totality that springs from a conception of form orientated towards the concrete content of its material substratum. In this view form is therefore able to demolish the 'contingent' relation of the parts to the whole and to resolve the merely apparent opposition between chance and necessity'.[15]

Art is the arena in which an unreified relation between subject and object, content and form, can be modelled. This notion that artistic form should not be preconceived and arbitrarily imposed upon its content, but should result only from the elaboration of the material of which it is composed, echoes, as we have seen, a prime aesthetic concern of Adorno's and is paralleled by the critique of commodification by both writers.

But despite the shared features of their analyses of both the underlying historical condition and the significance to it of the unity of form and content in the artwork, the two thinkers drew opposite conclusions about modernist art. While for Adorno, the adoption of avant-garde techniques offered the only hope of resisting the commodification of art and thereby keeping alive the promise of another kind of society, for Lukács the disjointed, fractured, and multiple perspectives of modernism represented a capitulation to the reification of modern capitalism. The seeds of modernism's failings were already present in 'naturalism', Lukács's term for the literature of authors such as Flaubert and Zola in the second half of the nineteenth century which represented for him a decline from the high point of realism. Naturalism, for Lukács, treated the circumstances in which events took place and characters found themselves as objectively given, reducing them to the background for the plot. By implicitly denying the possibility that characters could change those circumstances, could shape history, naturalism reinforces rather than challenges reification by confirming that the world is essentially unchangeable.[16] In this kind of literature, therefore, the split between subject and object is maintained through a strict aesthetic separation between the immediate phenomena of

---

14 Lukács 1971b, p. 135.
15 Lukács 1971b, p. 137.
16 Lunn 1984, p. 80.

events and their underlying historical essence. It is this that explains the drift in modernism towards extreme forms of subjectivism on the one hand and a vulgar materialism on the other.[17]

Here Lukács develops the idea, encountered earlier, of the problem of immediacy. He argues that a key weakness of bourgeois thought is that it is mired in immediacy, that it fails to grasp the mediations involved in our attempts to come to terms with reality. In an epistemological register this is a critique of positivism, but it also has ramifications for aesthetics. We have already seen the sense in which, for Lukács, the novel succeeds in being a temporal artistic form by positioning the reader outside of its own temporality. Similarly, Lukács argues that the representation of nature in a landscape painting necessarily involves the observer standing outside the landscape, 'for if this were not the case it would not be possible for nature to become a landscape at all... landscape only *starts* to become landscape at a definite distance from the observer'.[18] Without that spatial distance, there is no aesthetic meaning, only the immediacy of living in a natural environment.

Where the realist novel was able to achieve this distance through the use of an omniscient authorial voice, modernism's subjectivism and its rejection of a unitary perspective reduces it to reliance on immediacy. Indeed, a form such as montage fetishises immediacy, rejecting any attempt to make sense of elements by arranging them within a coherent whole in favour of presenting them as disconnected 'facts' shorn of causality. For Lukács, modernism's predilection for drawing attention to its own artistic procedures was evidence of an aesthetic attitude which had become more interested in expressing isolated subjectivities than in attempting to make the world comprehensible as a totality.[19]

If Lukács is right in insisting that art and knowledge, and art as a form of knowledge, must go beyond immediacy, beyond bare empirical reality, then any defense of artistic techniques which rests on mimesis, on reflecting the world as it appears, is ruled out. We have encountered the notion, apparently validated by Adorno's analysis of the role of primitive art, that all art contains a mimetic element. A claim that can be made for the modernisms of the early twentieth century is that the world which witnessed a seemingly unstoppable drive towards the industrialised mass destruction of the First World War, in which the bold hopes for progress of the early Victorian era had turned into pessimism and nihilism in the face of the soullessness of 'mass society', a world

---

17   Lunn 1984, p. 81.
18   Lukács 1971b, p. 158.
19   Lunn 1984, pp. 80–1.

whose complexities had made it resistant to being grasped as a comprehensible totality, this world could no longer be adequately represented using the transparent procedures of nineteenth century realism. Art required the fractured and distorting techniques of modernism in order to be adequate to a fractured and distorting world, or, we might say, to continue to be realistic.[20] In other words, as Brecht argued against Lukács, the techniques of realism should not be viewed ahistorically as fixed for all time. Both Adorno and Lukács express versions of this historicising thesis: Adorno in recognising the 'impossibility' of tonality and the sonata form beyond the end of the nineteenth century, and Lukács in theorising the decline of literature from the high point of realism as the result of the passing of the 'heroic' phase of the bourgeoisie, as marked definitively by the revolutions of 1848.[21] In other words, as Jameson puts it, realism, in the form that Lukács understands it, 'depend[s] on those privileged historical moments ... which [allow] access to society as a totality'.[22]

Yet Lukács resists drawing from this historical argument the pessimistic conclusion arrived at by Adorno, one which questioned the very possibility of art in a thoroughly commodified world. For Lukács, modernism was not the necessary form that art must take in a world in crisis; rather, by uncritically reflecting the dehumanisation and alienation of modern society such art failed in its duty to go beyond the 'facts', and effectively submitted itself to that society.[23] And despite his antipathy to the non-linear temporal techniques of modernist literature, it is difficult to infer any support for a musical aesthetic of measured time in his work. Although he appears to believe that there is a 'real' time which needs to be represented in artworks, it is not the abstract, quantifiable time of capitalism, which is merely a surface phenomenon obscuring the deeper reality of society. Real time is Bergsonian flux or *durée*, or, more politically, it is history. In this respect, despite their differences over the political and aesthetic role of modernism, Lukács is in agreement with Adorno: the abstract time of bourgeois positivism functions to annul and arrest the real time of history. Nevertheless, we are left with the general problem of how to balance the competing claims within art of reality and utopia, of addressing the world the way it is while avoiding suggesting that it could not be otherwise. This problem is made particularly acute if we are to take seriously the argument made in the previous chapter that abstract time is not mere appearance masking essence, but is the reality of time in capitalism: that abstract time is a

20   See Jameson 1988, p. 131; Wayne 2007, pp. 165–83.
21   Lukács 1936, p. 10.
22   Jameson 1971, p. 205.
23   Lunn 1984, p. 83.

'real abstraction'. The materialism entailed by this position precludes the possibility, or at least the effectiveness, of simply adopting the correct theoretical or artistic stance, or a simple desire to alter the situation, which as Lukács correctly points out would be no more than a subjective wish.[24] After all, the whole point of Lukács's essay is to explore the historical conditions under which the hold of reification on the proletariat can be broken in the only sphere it can be – in practice.

The Structure of History

Though the concept of history appears as a term in this debate, and both Adorno and Lukács consider themselves to be thoroughly historical thinkers, its precise contours remain unclarified. History appears as the periodisation of the past and its concept provides the basis for a politics of change, mobilised in order to disprove the claim that capitalist society is the terminus of humanity's development. History is change, conceived at the level of human societies; it is the fact that things have been different in the past, thereby providing the logical basis for an argument that things will be different in the future. This is history as story, history as told. What is left uninterrogated, especially in the case of Lukács, is the *quality* of the historical consciousness that underlies such a concept of history; or rather, Lukács's treatment of the question of time in the novel assumes that historicity takes this narrative form. This is where the question of time consciousness and the nature of temporality intersects with the wider question of history.

There are good reasons for regarding narrativity to be the basis of historicity. Paul Ricoeur uses a combination of insights from both Husserl and Heidegger to ground such a claim. Ricoeur argues that historicity is that form of temporal consciousness which is capable of uniting subjective and objective times, 'lived' time and 'universal' time, or the 'time of the soul' and the 'time of the world'. These two apparently irreconcilable poles are represented by the two main traditions in the philosophy of time: respectively, the Augustinian 'present', capable of producing a differentiated past and future on the basis of self-referentiality; and the Aristotelian 'instant', from which is generated a serial succession capable of measuring time and identifying a 'before' and 'after', but incapable of ascribing pastness and futurity.[25] Ricoeur seeks a way of reconciling these two consciousnesses of time in a way avoids the pitfall of

---

24   Lukács 1971b, p. 160.
25   Osborne 1995, p. 48.

reducing the first to the second such that 'now' is conceived abstractly as the instant of utterance by a subject, and past and future are reduced to the series of instants 'before' and 'after' this point. This conception effectively takes the presence out of the present, reducing the 'now' to one instant among others in a reversible, spatialised continuum. As Osborne comments, it 'fails to grasp the dynamism of the now as a permanent relation of differentiation and unification, upon which the before and after depends for its sense of temporal direction'.[26]

Ricoeur is committed to a phenomenological conception of consciousness in which the present is not instantaneous, but which, as discussed in Chapter 4, incorporates past and future into its structure through the Husserlian mechanisms of retention and protention. The problem, as Ricoeur sees it, is how to connect this essentially subjective conception of time to 'objective', cosmic or universal time. Against Heidegger, for whom conceptions of time based on Aristotle's endless succession of instants are the basis of 'within-time-ness', the inauthentic temporality of time reckoning, of dateability, measurement and clocks, Ricoeur asserts that this ordinary, everyday conception of time is 'an authentic apprehension of the independent infinity of cosmological time'. Heidegger was wrong to say, 'There is no nature-time, since all time belongs essentially to Dasein', as that would represent a reversion to the neo-Kantian idealism which phenomenology sought to escape.[27] Ricoeur insists that there is an exterior, cosmological time which 'surrounds us, envelops us, and overpowers us with its awesome strength': it is ultimately the time because of which we die.[28]

Ricoeur's contribution to an understanding of historicity is his positing of the existence of a distinct 'historical time' which mediates between phenomenological time and cosmological time and establishes a unity of time, visible at the level of a poetics of narrative.[29] This historical time arises from the '(re)inscription of lived time onto cosmic time', resulting in a 'network of interweaving perspectives' between the time of human action and its everyday interpretation and the chronological framework of cosmological time. Because the mediation it effects is imperfect, the structure of historical time is inherently open-ended, futural, denying the possibility of historical totalisation, and leaving the historical present open to initiative and action.[30] But the form that

---

26   Osborne 1995, p. 49.
27   Heidegger 1988, p. 262.
28   Ricoeur 1984, p. 17; Osborne 1995, pp. 64–5.
29   Osborne 1995, p. 52.
30   Osborne 1995, p. 53.

this historical time takes is that of narrative, and there is a sense in which it is only through this narrative mediation that the other two forms of time – phenomenological and cosmological – can be grasped at all. As Ricoeur says, 'No thought about time without narrated time'.[31]

What is it about narrative that allows it to mediate in this way? Ricoeur argues that narratives comprise two dimensions of temporality: one chronological, or episodic; the other non-chronological, or configurational. The episodic dimension is that aspect of storytelling which 'tends towards the linear representation of time' because of the 'and then' and 'what next?' aspects of its open-ended structure as a series of events following the irreversible order of ordinary time. The configurational dimension displays temporal features which are opposed to this episodic time because it groups events together under single categories or 'thoughts' (for example, the Renaissance, the Industrial Revolution, etc.). This dimension should not be misunderstood as atemporal: it is actually more deeply temporal than the episodic aspect. It also imposes 'the sense of an ending' upon the open-endedness of episodic succession. The retelling of a story reinforces this configurational aspect: events are grasped together under the heading, for instance, 'the ending'. The combination of these two dimensions means that narrative (plot) does more than establish humanity (actions and passions) 'in' time; it also takes us from 'within-time-ness' to historicality, from 'reckoning with' to 'recollecting' time, to use Heidegger's terminology.[32] We can see that both of the dimensions of time that Ricoeur identifies contribute to the distancing of narrative from the temporality of the events it describes, but the configurational more so because of the non-linear form that it takes.

The idea that historical consciousness depends on narrative is one that, as we have seen, is present in Lukács's valorisation of the realist novel. The self-evident political value of art's ability to portray the inner movement of history can also be detected in Adorno's discussion of Beethoven's dialectical and emergent temporal techniques (see Chapter 5). Adorno himself does not describe this as narrative, but others, such as Small, Newcomb and Maus, do regard the Western art-music tradition as essentially narrativistic or dramatic.[33] History as narrative is also central to Fredric Jameson's approach to the

---

31   Ricoeur 1984, p. 241.
32   Ricoeur 1980, pp. 178–9.
33   Though Adorno does refer to Mahler's music as 'a narrative which relates nothing' (Adorno 1996, p. 75). Small 1977, p. 176; Maus 1997; see also Newcomb 1987 for an analysis of the narrative techniques of a particular composer within this tradition, and Pasler 1989 for a discussion in relation to music of Ricoeur's ideas. Nattiez's distinction that music

hermeneutics of aesthetic representation, summed up by his injunction, 'always historicize!'.[34] Such an approach includes both a commitment to critical distance from the 'booming, buzzing confusion' of immediacy, and the belief that the key to understanding the meaning of works of art is to situate them within a unified human history:[35]

> [Their themes] can recover their original urgency for us only if they are retold within the unity of a great single collective story; only if, in however disguised and symbolic a form, they are seen as sharing a single fundamental theme – ... the collective struggle to wrest a realm of Freedom from a realm of Necessity; only if they are grasped as vital episodes in a single vast unfinished plot.[36]

More recently, Jameson has sought to develop his theorisation of the ways by which narrative texts function to express, or figure, time. The result is a much more sophisticated elaboration of the claim that time and history are narrative forms.

It is in the nature of time, Jameson asserts, that it is not directly representable; to the extent that it is conceivable at all, time must always be represented in terms of something else. This explains why Aristotle, for instance, was forced to define it in terms of movement. As Ricoeur says, 'there can be no pure phenomenology of time'. Because, during our everyday lived experience, time as such is not visible to us, we depend on narrative texts to make time and history appear.

Moreover, it is only the narrative literary form that can do this. Time comes into view as a result of a process of narrative emplotment. Literary texts can thus succeed in presenting time where philosophy has consistently failed. According to Jameson, then, time is 'accessible only to narrative interpretation and not philosophical systemisation – to narrative intelligence rather than abstract reason'.[37]

We might interpret this as a defence of the role and importance of art, a claim relating to the specific contribution that artistic forms can make to cognition. The idea that art is capable of cognitive effects which are distinct from

---

       itself cannot be a narrative but can invite a narrative listening strategy does not contradict an argument for the narrative character of some music (Nattiez, 1990, p. 249).
34   Jameson 1983, p. ix.
35   Jameson 1991, p. 400.
36   Jameson 1991, p. 35.
37   Jameson 2010, p. 529.

those of scientific and philosophical knowledge is an attractive one. If time might plausibly be considered as a suitable object of such 'aesthetic knowledge', then it surely makes sense to include temporal arts such as music among those capable of contributing to it.

Jameson does not do so. Instead he develops a theory about how narrative texts work to make time visible which rests on the fact that all narrative acts combine at least two temporalities, the time of the narrated events and the time of the narrative act. On this basis, Jameson argues that the appearance of time in a literary text depends on its holding together multiple temporalities in a single dialectical configuration: 'Time can only appear at the intersection of various times'.[38]

For Ricoeur, as we have seen, narrative serves to mediate between the various times, specifically the objective time of the universe and the subjective time of the individual, producing history in the process. Jameson rejects the possibility of such a concordant unification. For him, the temporalities at work are much more manifold and diverse than a simple opposition between objective and subjective times; and their 'random and multiple intersections', though regulated by the 'emplotment' of narrative, defy assimilation to a single overarching temporal structure.[39]

The emphasis Jameson places here on multiple, intersecting temporalities is certainly a step forward compared to the earlier formulation of a 'single, collective story'. As Bernstein points out, to understand historical materialism as simply asserting a collective history on a trajectory towards 'freedom' or socialism, is to reduce it to an abstract, agentless teleology. 'Marxism thus becomes a collective narrative which is no one's narrative, a narrative searching for an agent, a hero to complete it'.[40] However, Jameson seems to think that the only way to avoid this kind of historicism is to eschew all 'modernist' ambitions to reconcile disparate temporalities and endorse a postmodern celebration of difference. The literary text's ability to make time appear through its presentation of incommensurable intersecting temporalities:

> constitutes the superiority of the postmodern aesthetic over its modernist predecessor in this respect. For while the latter pursued that mirage of unification which it still shared with philosophy, the former chose to embrace dispersal and multiplicity; and the slogan 'Difference relates' ... turns out to be the best working program for this deployment of temporal

---

38 Jameson 2010, p. 498.
39 Jameson 2010, p. 529.
40 Bernstein 1984, p. 261.

levels, in the absence of the thing itself.... Reading is the momentary and ephemeral act of unification in which we hold multiple dimensions of time together for a glimpse that cannot prolong itself into the philosophical concept.[41]

Just as with Deleuze's invocation of multiplicity in relation to music, it is unclear how a 'pell-mell jumble' of incommensurable difference is capable of making time appear with any clarity, let alone history.[42] Moreover, by making the individual reader the focus of the process whereby time is made to appear, Jameson seems to give up on any concept of history which subsists in a collective or social consciousness. Time and history can appear only 'fitfully' and 'ephemerally' in the mind of the solitary reader of narrative.

This retreat to individual subjectivity is strange given that Jameson rebukes Ricoeur for a 'rigorous limitation to individual human consciousness and the individual subject, and the refusal to theorize agency on the level of the collective'.[43] In fact, it was precisely Ricoeur's aim to overcome the individuality of phenomenological conceptions of time and to emphasise the social, and indeed universal, aspects of time consciousness. Jameson himself discusses those elements of Ricoeur's theory – calendars, generations – which are socially and collectively derived, but despite this, persists with his claim that time is individual, History is collective, and Ricoeur theorises only the former.

Jameson's own attempt to collectivise the issue rests on the suggestion that History has only become possible as a result of globalisation: History is itself the product of history. Prior to the existence of a single world system there were at best multiple histories, the partial and limited temporalities of isolated peoples:

> A single history begins to come into view only with the destruction of these multiple collective temporalities, with their unification into a single world system, and it is not yet complete in current globalization, but will only be completed by universal commodification, by the world market as such. Making history 'appear' is then dependent on this process of unification, whose vicissitudes alone can generate the discontinuous situations in which such a glimpse is possible: which is to say that the 'appearance' of History is dependent on the objective historical

---

41 Jameson 2010, p. 532.
42 Jameson 2010, p. 529.
43 Jameson 2010, p. 501.

situations themselves. There is here a unity of theory and practice according to which the cognitive (or representational) possibility of grasping the unity of history is at one with situations of praxis as well.[44]

Even if it makes sense to argue that a fully universal history is only now just becoming possible, it is a mistake to imply that *any* history has as yet been impossible. To do so would be to ignore the demonstrable development of historical consciousness over at least the last couple of centuries, itself the product of the *de facto* existence of a world system (albeit incomplete) for well over a century. It would also logically imply that 'modernist' narrative strategies which attempt to unify or commensurate multiple temporalities are ahead of their time (so to speak) while postmodern ones are becoming increasingly anachronistic. The fact that Jameson seeks to endorse the latter at the expense of the former seems inconsistent with this thesis.

Where Jameson does offer a valuable insight is when he grasps that the possibility of historical consciousness is not the product of a disinterested engagement with the world, but is dependent on taking sides, on politics, or praxis. He writes, '[t]here is here a unity of theory and practice according to which the cognitive (or representational) possibility of grasping the unity of history is at one with situations of praxis as well'.[45]

Of course, for Marx, all knowledge was the product of a critical synthesis of theory and practice, and history was no exception. But the recognition of an essential praxial aspect to history immediately takes us away from narrative, which indeed recedes in importance at this point in Jameson's argument. There is an explanation for this: narrative, because of its temporal distancing of told events from lived present, remains essentially contemplative in nature, and is thus a structurally unsuitable vehicle for the kind of praxial historical consciousness Jameson seeks. For Jameson it is always about 'making History *appear*', whereas what counts is *making* History.

Postmodern theory is hostile to any attempt to conceive time, or times, as history; and although its tenets find expression in branches of the musical avant garde, they will be of no help in understanding groove, which can in no way be described as a postmodern development. Groove is a modern phenomenon, so in order to explore its temporal ramifications, we will need to address the question of modernity, not simply as the preconditional site for the emergence of historical consciousness, but as a particular, itself historically

---

44   Jameson 2010, p. 588.
45   Ibid.

determined, form of historicisation or temporalisation. As Adorno puts it, 'Modernity is a qualitative, not a chronological, category'.[46]

The Historical Consciousness of Modernity

What is the principal defining quality of modernity? According to Osborne, drawing upon Koselleck and Blumenburg, it is its self-reflexiveness or self-consciousness. Modernity as a form of temporal consciousness combines two aspects: it designates its own contemporaneity according to the time of its classification, i.e., 'now'; and it understands this contemporaneity as always qualitatively new in relation to even the most recent past. In this way, as Koselleck argues, history becomes temporalised by a process which valorises the present over the past.

But the concept of the present holds a paradoxical position within modernity. On the one hand, it is central to modernity's system of historical designation. As Blumenburg says, 'Modernity ... was the first and only age that understood itself as an epoch and, in so doing, simultaneously created the other epochs'. On the other hand, modernity's tendency to generate an abstract chronological structure threatens 'to eliminate the present by conceiving it as simply the vanishing point between a changing past and an indeterminate future – "now" as a "gap in time"'. Osborne suggests that modernity, therefore, 'is a form of historical consciousness, an abstract temporal structure which ... totaliz[es] history from the standpoint of an ever-vanishing, ever-present present'.[47]

The single concept which best encapsulates the time consciousness of modernity and the problematic role of the present within it is that of 'progress'. Absent from pre-modern conceptions of temporality, progress is 'the continuous self-justification of the present, by means of the future that it gives itself, before the past, with which it compares itself'.[48] Departing from a classical conception of history which continued to dominate through the Middle Ages and the Renaissance in which 'nothing qualitatively new can occur', 'the idea of progress extrapolates from a structure present in every moment to a future that is immanent in history'.[49] In the concept of progress, the present's privileged position, which it holds by virtue of its being the newest element of

---

46   Adorno 1978, p. 218.
47   Osborne 1995, pp. 11–14.
48   Quoted in Callinicos 1997, p. 148.
49   Koselleck 1987, p. 148; quoted in Callinicos 1997, p. 148.

history, is continuously undermined by its inevitable usurpation by a future which is immanent to it. The abstract temporal structure which valorises the present as the most important and unique moment in history is simultaneously the cause of the present's perpetual devaluing to one of a series of identical instants in a chain of temporal succession.

It was this constant eclipsing of the present and its potential for newness or difference which Walter Benjamin attacked in his critique of 'historicism'. As another key participant in the Marxist aesthetic debates of the early twentieth century, Benjamin goes beyond the dichotomy of abstract time versus historical time to problematise historical time itself. For Benjamin, historicism was bound up with the world of the commodity, whose temporal logic is expressed in the concept of fashion. This continuous displacement of existing mass-produced articles by new ones which are 'ever-always-the-same' is the source of the 'homogeneous empty time' of historicism. Modernism, for Benjamin, is the 'affirmative cultural self-consciousness of the abstract temporality of modernity' in which novelty becomes reinscribed as eternity, in which 'the new appear[s] within the ever-always-the-same and the ever-always-the-same within the new'.[50] This 'blank chronologism' is the 'hell' of commodity fetishism, and its political counterpart, historicism, is an ideology which naturalises history as a form of pre-ordained progress, ruling out the possibility of genuine historical change. 'Historicism contents itself with establishing a causal connection between various moments in history', effectively conferring historical status on events 'posthumously' in a way which suggests that the course of history could not have been other than it was. Benjamin detected this 'rosary bead' concept of history not only in the pronouncements of the apologists for Western capitalism and their Social Democratic counterparts, for whom any negative aspects of society's development were to be instantly forgotten and any victims of its inexorable march were to be regarded simply as so much collateral damage.[51] But it was also present in the 'orthodox Marxism' of Benjamin's own lifetime, which tended to regard revolution as the inevitable consequence of the working out of the dialectical contradictions of capitalism, as the result of movement along the 'iron rails of history'.

Benjamin argues that any political project for social transformation, for the inauguration of the genuinely new, must be based on a critique of the notion of historical progress and of the concept of homogeneous, empty time on which it is based. Rather than a notion of the present which is a transition, a historical materialist needs one 'in which time stands still and comes to a stop'.

---

50 Osborne 2000, pp. 79–81; Benjamin 1985, p. 43.
51 Benjamin 1999, p. 255.

Only in such a present can history be made, rather than simply passed through. Making history involves 'mak[ing] the continuum of history explode', the seizing of moments of the present which are not part of an incessant succession of instants but which are 'blasted out of the continuum of history'. Benjamin's term for such moments is *Jetztzeit* – 'now-time'. He insists: 'History is the subject of a structure whose site is not homogeneous, empty time, but time filled by the presence of the now [*Jetztzeit*]', and he praises the revolutionary Parisian workers of 1830 who fired on the city's clocktowers in an attempt to stop time.[52]

The paradigm of historical representation in the era of modernism is not, therefore, narrative, whose linear structure can only succeed in perpetuating the ideology of time's essential continuity and indifference, but a 'dialectical image' capable of figuring the qualitative experience of the 'now'. The dialectical image is a monad whose structure captures, from the point of view of the oppressed, the entirety of history in a single snapshot, thereby opening historical time to the possibility of revolutionary rupture. As Leslie puts it,

> History breaks down into images not stories – it is the flash, not the continuum that is important. Precisely it is the continuum that is to be arrested. Its method counters historicism at each move. It refuses continuity, linearity, in favour of a synoptic glare, in which each element of the whole is unfolded from each other element.[53]

For Benjamin, revolution does not emerge from historical continuity, does not 'swell inevitably from the process of social evolution', but is a messianic irruption into history, the seizing of a present filled to bursting with the entirety of past oppressions in order to shatter the homogeneous course of history.[54]

While appreciating Benjamin's contribution to a critique of vulgar Marxist historicism, Callinicos regards such a conception of revolution as ultimately unhelpful. Against historical fatalism or objectivism, Callinicos wants to

---

52 Benjamin 1999, pp. 252–4.
53 Leslie 2000, p. 197.
54 Callinicos 1987, p. 180. Post-Marxist thinkers have also posited the necessity of temporal rupture in the transition from the 'ordinary' continuity of events to a new form of society. To the measured continuity of *Chronos* Negri counterposes *Kairòs*, the modality of time excluded from flux, the creative restlessness of temporality expressed by 'being on the brink', being 'on a razor's edge', the moment when the 'archer looses the arrow' (Negri 2003, p. 152). For Badiou, the crucial temporal-ontological form is the 'event', the emergence of a radically unpredictable moment of 'not-being' which exceeds the historical situation which produces it (Badiou 2007, p. 190). The relationship between this idea and Benjamin's critique of historicism is addressed in Callinicos 2006, p. 103.

emphasise the subjective component of history, the fact that history does not simply unfold but is made, but he believes that Benjamin's position 'makes revolution so discontinuous with the ordinary sequence of events as to be unthinkable':

> Revolution belongs to *Jetztzeit*, the time of redemption, qualitatively distinct from the historical world in which men and women live and work and struggle. It is so starkly counterposed with the 'continuum of history', the Hell of commodity fetishism, ... that the emergence of the one from the other appears unthinkable. Conceiving revolution as a Messianic irruption into history is a decisive break with the evolutionism of vulgar Marxism. But in the absence of any analysis of the processes by virtue of which the working class is likely 'to brush history against the grain', then the obvious terminus of Benjamin's critique of the concept of historical progress is the pessimism of Adorno.[55]

But although Callinicos puts the phrase in inverted commas, he seems to accept the 'continuum of history' as an adequate way of conceiving the temporality of non-revolutionary periods. Against this 'normal' time, Benjamin's *Jetztzeit* can only appear as a radical alternative which comes from outside. However, if the analysis presented above is correct, modernist temporalisation involves a presencing, or a privileging of the 'now', alongside its tendency towards an abstract historicism which undermines the uniqueness of the present. On this view, Benjamin's *Jetztzeit* does not emerge from 'outside of history' but is present, at least in embryonic form, in the temporality of modernity. Rather, now-time, or what we might call the heightened present of decision making and action, is that aspect of modernist temporality which must be grasped in any project to 'make history', against modernity's historicist tendency to depict the future as a mere continuation of the past. For Daniel Bensaïd, Benjamin's focus on an active present represents the primacy in his thought of politics over history, the determination not to accept the future as determined or closed, but to grasp the possibility of struggle whose outcome can shape events but cannot be predicted. 'Messianic anticipation is never the passive certainty of an advent foretold, but is akin to the concentration of a hunter in the lookout for the sudden emergence of what is possible'. Every instant contains a plurality of possibilities, with struggle deciding between

---

55   Callinicos 1987, pp. 181–2.

them. 'The Benjaminian critique of historical reason thus leads "from a time of necessity to a time of possibilities" '.[56]

The importance of Benjamin's critique of abstract, linear time is that, unlike Adorno's, which is conceived as a desperate rearguard action mounted from the few remaining spheres of life yet to be subjected to the reifying effects of commodification, the condition of possibility for Benjamin's critique is precisely modernity's incessant circulation of commodity forms. As Osborne explains, 'the very *indifference* of the new as ever-always-the-same that is the basis for the quantification of time in historicism becomes, for Benjamin, the ground for a quite different, *qualitative* experience of the "now" as a historical present'. He continues:

> The instantaneity of the 'now', experienced for the first time within modernity as a form of *historical* (rather than merely natural) temporality, is seen to contain within its monadic structure the possibility of an experience of eternity, a Messianic 'cessation of happening', combined with a 'recurrence', a 'yet once again', which can only be understood as a new form of remembrance. In the time of this 'now', nature and history are one, as eternal. The past will be gathered up within the present, in the perspective of redemption, as an explosive historical 'experience'. In opposition to the regressive, psychologically defensive, historicist experience of the temporal order of modernity, whereby an incident is assigned a precise point in time 'at the cost of the integrity of its contents' in order to transform it into 'a moment that has been lived' – intellectually appropriating it as a merely quantitative relation, in compensation for the failure to establish any living relationship to it, we are offered a historico-metaphysical experience of the same temporal order: 'nowbeing' (*Jetztsein*).[57]

In other words, this critique of abstract, homogeneous time emerges from within the structure of modernist temporal experience by focusing on the intense presencing quality of its experience. It is this presencing by the ever-new that, according to Habermas's reading of Benjamin on Baudelaire, rescues modernity from triviality and grounds 'actuality':

> On this account, the authentic world is radically bound to the moment of its emergence; precisely because it consumes itself in actuality, it can

---

56 Bensaïd 2002, pp. 84, 88–9.
57 Osborne 2000, p. 82.

bring the steady flow of trivialities to a standstill, [and] break through normality....[58]

The ideological effect of the dominance of a culture of measured time which mimics cosmic time is a naturalisation of history as an autonomous process which is beyond human control. This is the problem of historicism. And yet, the same process, viewed from the opposite side, results in a historicisation of nature, the realisation that each instant in the abstract continuum of time has been and remains a lived, human moment. As a way of grasping historical time, Benjamin's represents a completely different approach from the narrativism of Lukács, Adorno, Ricoeur and Jameson, which is predicated upon the subject's distancing from, or standing outside of, historical experience. We might say, following Bernstein, that artistic forms which adopt this non-teleological temporal structure are praxial rather than simply representational, engaged rather than contemplative, and are capable of 'realis[ing] the temporal synthesis of human action at the level of historicality'.[59] *Jetztzeit's* critical potential lies in its ability to crack historicism *from within*: its present is not the blank cosmological instant of the kind which historicism regards as its ontological ground, nor is it the extended, phenomenological present of Bergson or Husserl; rather it makes present all of history as once-having-been-present, acting as a synecdoche for history as a whole.

We are now in a position to explore the significance of this for music's temporality. Benjamin's *Jetztzeit* provides us with an alternative to a straightforward rejection of the presence within music of abstract, measured time in the form of meter and, in particular, groove. It allows us to grasp the groove concept, not as at odds with the modernist sensibility which emerged in the late nineteenth century and took hold in the early twentieth, as it had previously appeared, but, in its immediate and non-narrative representation of time, as an exemplary manifestation of modernist culture.

We have already noted, in Chapter 5, the assertions by Shepherd and Small that music of the Western art tradition appears to situate the listener outside of its own temporality. This conforms to the position articulated by Lukács and others discussed in this chapter that the representation of temporality, now conceived as history, is best achieved by a narrative structure. We can argue that eighteenth- and nineteenth-century art music's use of meter was the prime device that served to generate a narrative-type musical temporality, one which Adorno felt was capable, at least in the hands of Beethoven, of representing

---

58 Habermas 1987, p. 9.
59 Bernstein 1984, pp. 264–5.

the movement of history, in a way which was broadly analogous to the realist novel. The incorporation of abstract, measured time in music was necessary in order to produce a genuinely temporal music, rather than a static or cyclic one, but a key condition of its use for this narrativistic purpose is that it should remain subservient to the musical material – the development of themes (referred to, significantly, in musicological language as 'subjects'). Its role was to erect a temporal framework within which the material could be articulated, rather than to measure time for its own sake.

The threat represented by the qualitative intensification of meter that we have identified as groove is precisely the overwhelming of the musical material by abstract temporal measure. Adorno identifies this domination of form over content as intimately bound up with the triumph of the commodity form over all aspects of life, the result of the marginalisation of use value by exchange value in a system of generalised commodity production. Benjamin's conception of modernist time, however, allows us to formulate another view of this process. The broad character of groove music is one in which temporality – figured as the abstract continuum of historicism – has displaced thematic material as the subject matter of the music. Of course, thematic material is not done away with completely, but there has been a reversal of roles: whereas, in non-groove music, meter is at the service of the material, in groove music, the material – especially the rhythm section material – functions to articulate and elaborate the groove. That explains the relative increase in the latter of the importance of pithy, repeatable elements of material such as riffs, stabs and fills, to a point where it makes more sense to talk about musical 'events' than musical 'themes'.

Groove deploys a reproduction of an abstract temporal continuum, a web of instants, organised hierarchically in relation to a system of time measurement. The effect of such temporal organisation, contrary to the accusation of predictability, is to impart a heightened significance to the present, or in practice, to the articulation of each beat of the groove. In non-groove pulsed music, meter plays a role analogous to chronology in narrative: the ordering of events in relation to each other into a whole, which, like all wholes, needs to be appreciated from the outside. Groove, by adopting the quasi-natural structure of historicism, draws the participant/listener into its temporal structure as a web of lived 'nows'. The web is fabricated from a particular weave of musical events, occurring in relation to an abstract metrical system. It is less the case that each musical event is positioned in relation to the groove, than that each musical event, through its temporality, makes a contribution to the articulation of the groove. It is not as though each event is marked by an auxiliary time stamp which gives its temporal position (on or off a certain beat, etc.); rather each event is the actualisation of its temporal position. In accordance with Zuckerkandl's analysis of meter, discussed in Chapter 1, each event's musical significance is defined by a temporal character derived from its relationship to the metrical scheme.[60] What counts here, consistent with a conception of meter which is fully hierarchical to the extent that it encompasses an entire piece of music, is the temporal character derived from the *whole* metrical scheme, rather than that of a single bar. This means that there is a sense in which all of the past of the groove is gathered into each new event, analogously to Benjamin's concept. In contrast to non-groove pulsed music, where many notes occur between the beats, every musical event in groove music is also a beat at some level of the metric hierarchy. This gives each event/beat the character of intense, pregnant presentness – a nowtime – which is lacking in the narrative-style art music tradition. And the inherently collective nature of groove, produced as a result of its practical instantiation by human bodies in space (as discussed in Chapter 4), guarantees that the experience of successive 'nows' is verified intersubjectively, in a way which does not depend on a purely internal, subjective time-consciousness of the Husserlian type.

Groove as a Musical Modernism

In its preoccupation with the present, groove music reveals itself to be consistent with other artistic modernisms. In this respect, it confirms Moore's assertion that both modernism and mass culture should be viewed as 'sibling expressions of modernity'.[61] Hauser claims that 'the time experience of our age consists above all in an awareness of the moment in which we find ourselves – an awareness of the present', and as we have seen, this awareness is expressed in modernist literature's general rejection of the Aristotelian prescription of beginning, middle and ending for aesthetic forms.[62] But groove's presencing takes a different form from that of other modernisms. Kramer

---

60 One excellent example of this is the use in some popular music styles of metric displacement techniques on a phrase to explore the alteration in temporal character produced, e.g. Dizzy Gillespie's 'Salt Peanuts' or this backing riff on Louis Jordan's 'Saturday Night Fish Fry' of 1949:

61 Moore 2003, p. 172.
62 Quoted in Kramer 1988, p. 17.

identifies two types among the temporal techniques of twentieth-century avant garde composers. The first, 'moment time' or 'moment form', derived from techniques pioneered by Debussy and Stravinsky, was conceptualised by Karl-Heinz Stockhausen as a musical stasis which produced 'a concentration on the present moment – on every present moment – [capable of] mak[ing] a vertical cut… across horizontal time perception, extending out to a timelessness I call eternity… an eternity that is present in every moment'.[63] More extreme than moment time is what Kramer calls vertical time, found in some avant garde music and also in minimalism:

> Vertical music denies the past and the future in favor of an extended present.… Such music tries to thwart memory in order to focus on the present, the now.… The future, to the extent that it is anticipated at all, is expected to be the same as the present. This kind of music tries to create an eternal now by blurring the distinction between past, present, and future, and by avoiding gestures that invoke memory or activate expectation.[64]

These types of modernist presencing aim to produce timelessness or eternity through an infinitely extended present. Their goal is akin to meditation: an intense focus on the minutiae of the present to achieve a state of atemporal relaxation or ecstasy.[65] Groove's presencing is quite different. Its focus on the present does not involve a withdrawal or escape from 'ordinary' time, from temporal succession, or an occluding of memory and expectation, but rather highlights the unique significance and potential of each of the series of presents which comprise temporal continuity. Kramer concedes that because all music requires temporal succession for its performance, moment time's attempt to escape worldly time cannot ultimately succeed, resulting in the paradox that 'moment time uses the linearity of listening to destroy the linearity of time'.[66] Groove, by contrast, avoids any such paradox by using the linearity of abstract time to produce its presencing effect. To use Edward T. Hall's distinction, whereas other modernist musics seek a non-worldly 'sacred time', groove music is an aesthetic of 'profane time', which 'marks minutes and hours, the days of the week, months of the year, years, decades, centuries – the entire

---

63   Stockhausen quoted in Kramer 1988, p. 201.
64   Kramer 1988, pp. 375–6.
65   Kramer 1988, p. 377.
66   Kramer 1988, p. 219.

explicit, taken-for-granted system which our civilization has elaborated".[67] We might say that groove music conforms thoroughly to that sense of the word 'temporal' which means profane, worldly.

Despite this important difference, the temporality generated by groove is, like much modernist music, immediate and non-teleological. Because of that, groove musics often share the tendency of moment and vertical music to seek to avoid openings and particularly closings, the effect of which is inevitably to situate the listener outside the music's temporality and reduce its sense of presencing. Stockhausen recognised that for practical purposes music must start and stop, but he wanted his moment forms not to begin or end.[68] Pieces of groove music similarly often blur the sense of beginning by establishing the groove layer by layer within a repetitive vamp, and avoid endings by facilitating a seamless transition to the next groove through the use of fade-out or medley.

What Benjamin helps us to understand is why a temporal structure which appears to replicate the abstract temporal continuum of historicism is capable, like Baudelaire's poetry, of 'winning the new with heroic effort from the "ever-always-the-same" '.[69] It provides an antidote to Adorno's, and indeed Jameson's, pessimistic position that resistance to reification can only emerge from spheres of humanity which have not yet fallen fully under the sway of commodification, of which there remain precious few, by directing our attention to the possibilities of fracture from within. On this basis, music which adopts the abstract temporal measure of groove has not capitulated to the reification of time, as Adorno argues, but instead points to the character of presentness – now-time – which has the potential to cause its disintegration.

Temporal Quality, Quantity and Measure

This discussion of the temporality of modernism, with its fixation on the new within the accelerating circulation of commodities, returns us to the question of the time of capitalism which was addressed in the previous chapter. Bensaïd points out that for Marx, although it functions as the measure of value in capitalism, time was not a given, not an unproblematic or straightforward yardstick lying outside of the system which it measured. On the contrary, 'time is constituted by the rhythms and periodicities of capitalism itself – "an economy

---

67   Hall quoted in Kramer 1988, p. 17.
68   Kramer 1988, p. 203.
69   Benjamin 1985, p. 43.

of time"'.[70] In *Capital* Marx identifies several 'times of capitalism': not only the time which measures exchange value which we have already encountered, but also a 'negative time' of circulation, whose devaluing tendency must be overcome by accelerating turnover; and a time of reproduction which, because it is the product of the system as a whole, retrospectively determines the other two. 'The mechanical time of production, the chemical time of circulation, and the organic time of reproduction are thus coiled and slotted inside one another, like circles within circles, determining the enigmatic patterns of historical time, which is the time of politics'. Time is thus cast as a measure of social relations but one which is itself determined by social relations, contradicting any formal definition of time. For example, in line with Postone's analysis, the movement of capitalism means that 'the value of a machine is determined not by the time that *was* required for its production in practice, but by the time *currently necessary* for its reproduction'. Bensaïd comments:

> The time and motion of capital are therefore determined reciprocally. Social time measures the accumulation of capital, whose turnovers determine the social substance of time. So time appears simultaneously as a measure of value and as its substance. This substance is continually modified according to the changing conditions of social production.... Combining measure and substance, [time] represents a *social relation in motion*.[71]

In line with the concept of measured time as 'real abstraction' outlined in the previous chapter, it becomes clear from this that a simple opposition between concrete, unmeasurable time on the one hand and abstract, measured time on the other does not adequately capture the situation within capitalism. The binary of qualitative versus quantitative time is complicated by the emergence at the heart of social relations of a substantive time which is also a measured time. The abstract, measured time of capitalism is clearly not a 'lived' time in any sense that implies freedom, since it confronts us as a reified, objectified structure, beyond subjective control, to which we must comply. But neither is it just an external, neutral scale of measurement. Abstract time is not simply the measure of value in capitalism; rather, it *is* value, it has a quality of denseness which fluctuates with the productivity of labour, and therefore manifests a 'realness' which is experienced by all whose activities come under its sway.

---

70   Bensaïd 2009, p. 74.
71   Bensaïd 2009, pp. 77–81.

If we accept that time has the character of substance within capitalism in this way, then Hegel's discussion of the relationship between quality, quantity and measure may be illuminating for an understanding of how it manifests itself. Hegel defines quality relatively straightforwardly as 'the character identical with being: so identical that a thing ceases to be what it is, if it loses its quality'.[72] Quantity is initially defined in contrast to quality, having a character which is external to being, or as pure being, 'where the mode or character is no longer taken as one with the being itself, but explicitly put as superseded or indifferent'. However, there is a mode of quantity which possesses determinate being: it is quantum (how much), that is, a specific quantity or a particular value. A quantum's character has both quantitative and qualitative components: quantitative, in that it is external to itself; and qualitative because of its independence, its Being-for-self.[73] This is made visible when two quanta are brought into relationship with each other in a ratio. In a ratio it is not the quantitative values of the quanta that are important – the ratio 2:4 can be replaced by 3:6 – the purely quantitative elements of each quantum cancel each other out. The quantitative and qualitative aspects of quantum, respectively its externality to Being and its Being-for-self, which were formerly external to each other, are now mediated, producing Measure. 'Thus quantity by means of [this] dialectical movement..., turns out to be a return to quality... [but] not a mere return to quality, as if that were the true and quantity the false notion, but an advance to the unity and truth of both, to *qualitative quantity*, or Measure'.[74]

Measure is the terminus of the dialectic of quality and quantity which demonstrates that 'quality is implicitly quantity, and conversely quantity is implicitly quality'.[75] It is this dialectic which allows us to grasp examples of the transformation of quantity into quality such as the incremental increase in the temperature of water which eventually turns it into steam, or the final straw that breaks the camel's back.[76] But the crucial insight for our purposes is Hegel's clarification of the distinction between Quantity and Measure. He writes:

> Measure is the qualitative quantum, in the first place as immediate – a quantum, to which a determinate being of a quality is attached. Measure,

---

72   Hegel 1972, p. 157.
73   Hegel 1972, p. 190.
74   Hegel 1972, pp. 199–200 (emphasis added).
75   Hegel 1972, p. 205.
76   Hegel 1972, pp. 202–3.

where quality and quantity are in one, is thus the completion of Being. Being, as we first apprehend it, is something utterly abstract and characterless: but it is the very essence of Being to characterise itself, and its complete characterisation is reached in Measure.[77]

The idea of distance remains abstract until the measurement of length makes it concrete. The concept of heaviness is abstract without the existence of weighing scales and a system of weight measurement. If we apply the same thought to time, it follows that abstract time and measured time are not synonymous, as has been assumed so far. On the contrary, the measuring of time is required to achieve its characterisation, to transform it, in Hegel's terminology, from abstract Being to determinate Being.

The conclusion to be drawn from this is that if it is justifiable to think of time as simultaneously abstract and substantive – and our analysis suggests that for capitalism it is – then it is through measure that it is made determinate, that it achieves its complete characterisation. Nor does measure necessarily reduce time to space, as Bergson and those who follow him insist. In one sense, the act of music-making is indeed a spatialisation of time, but in an entirely different sense to Bergson's spatialisation, one in which time retains its essentially temporal character.[78] The terms abstract, measured and spatialised when applied to time do not automatically imply each other.

This has tremendous importance for arguments about measured time in music. The burden of the various arguments made by those who criticise meter and temporal regularity has, as we have seen, been borne by the idea that to measure time is to degrade it from concrete, lived experience to empty abstraction. Hegel provides the basis not only for the opposite argument – that the quality of time, as time, not as the events which comprise it, is only made determinate through measurement – but also for an explanation of why those musics which eschew temporal measure which were discussed in earlier chapters seem unable to represent time as such.

The determining effect of measure provides an explanation for the way groove functions. The analysis presented in Chapter 1 demonstrated that the various elements of groove combine to form a powerful system for the measurement of time which far surpasses the forms of musical time measurement that predate it. A simple pulse is capable of marking off regular intervals in time, but does not go beyond the count of 1 – 1 – 1 – 1 – 1 ..., less powerful as a means of measurement even than a stick with notches on it for measuring

---

77   Hegel 1972, p. 201.
78   As McNally points out, concrete time is always also spatial (McNally 2004, p. 200).

length, since the latter can rely on the addition of counting (i.e. more numbers) to produce a result. Meter, as found in the Western art music tradition of the post-Renaissance period, represents an increase in measuring power by superimposing upon the music's pulse a slower periodicity, giving its structure the form 1 – 2 – 3 – 1 – 2 – 3 ... or 1 – 2 – 3 – 4 – 1 – 2 – 3 – 4.... Groove's addition of many more related periodicities, both slower and faster, to produce a deeply hierarchical metrical scheme, plus its emphasis on those points of the scheme which have the most measuring power – the off-beats – complete the transformation of pulse and meter into a fully developed time measuring system. And such a system is necessary because this is music which *seeks to express time*, music *for whom time is its subject matter*. Measure is the only mechanism by which the pure Being of time can be concretely characterised.

Why should music be about time? Because, simply put, under the conditions of advanced, or monopoly capitalism, our whole existence is shaped and structured by time. As we saw in the previous chapter, industrialisation brought with it an increasingly rigid temporal organisation of daily lives through the spread of clock time to entire populations. More deeply, we have also traced the ways in which capitalism can be regarded as fundamentally an economy of time, a system of productive relations in which time is the determining category. Capitalism enforces a regime in which value is measured by time, in which value and time are effectively synonymous. But it is also a regime in which time is not simply a standard measure, a universal yardstick, but is itself determined by the system of value which it measures. Some critics of capitalism have deduced from this that, under conditions of 'real subsumption', time has become purely tautological and has ceased to have meaning as a measure. Negri writes that:

> ... since time has become entirely hegemonic over the process, in so far as it is its only measure, it also reveals itself as its only substance. But this complete superimposition of measure and substance denies any dialectical significance to the relationship, reducing it therefore to pure and simple tautology.[79]

---

79 Negri 2003, p. 27. Jameson makes a structurally similar argument in a cultural register when he suggests that modernism's acute sensitivity to temporal matters was predicated on the continued existence of a non-capitalist world – the countryside and the colonies – against which a comparison could be made with life in the industrialised urban centres. Late twentieth-century globalisation has collapsed that distinction, resulting in the 'end of temporality' and postmodern culture's obsession with space instead (Jameson 2003, pp. 699–701).

Negri's mistake is to assume the existence of time-as-measure existing independently of capitalism before the emergence of real subsumption, that is, before capitalism came to dominate the entirety of social relations. Such a thought involves the illegitimate abstraction of time from its social determinants. It is of course the case that time is not entirely a social phenomenon; it has ontological roots in the movements of the planets and the stars and the effects of those movements on the nature of the earth – diurnal, tidal and seasonal rhythms. Pre-capitalist time-as-measure is little more than the social acknowledgement of the rhythms of universal or 'natural' time. Under the development of capitalism, this time is not simply adopted and deployed as a measure of value, but undergoes a radical transformation. On the one hand, time is further abstracted from its universal roots as economic activity becomes less determined by diurnal and seasonal rhythms. The notion of homogeneous, empty time emerges alongside other forms of abstract thought. On the other hand, as we have seen, capitalism, through its revolutionising of the means of production and the resulting increases in the productivity of labour, constantly undermines the universality of temporal measure upon which its value system rests. Negri believes that this means that time can no longer be understood as measure, 'but rather must be presented as the global phenomenological fabric, as base, substance and flow of production in its entirety'.[80] He is wrong in the first aspect but right in the second. Time is still measure, but, as Bensaïd argues, 'no longer a sort of supposedly uniform standard of reference, but a social relation that is determined in production, exchange and conflict'.[81] He continues:

> ... values initially require a common measure that is itself invariant, an invariant general commodity equivalent. Yet as commodities, all values are social magnitudes that vary with the class struggle. The measure determined by its object constantly changes with it. This is why qualities seem to manifest themselves in time, whereas, in reality, it is time that is the nascent new quality.[82]

Under capitalism, time becomes substance. Time-as-measure is no longer abstract, empty and homogeneous but concrete and full of the various rhythms of capitalist production and exchange. Because he identifies that capital uses time to measure labour-power, rather than labour, Marx is able to say that:

---

80 Negri 2003, p. 29.
81 Bensaïd 2009, p. 250.
82 Bensaïd 2009, p. 252.

one man during an hour is worth just as much as another man during an hour. Time is everything, man is nothing; he is, at the most, time's carcase. Quality no longer matters. Quantity alone decides everything; hour for hour, day for day....[83]

But at the same time he describes labour-time as more or less 'condensed', more or less 'porous', more or less 'intense', depending on the level of productivity involved.[84] For capitalism, time is determined by both its quality and its quantity.

It is, therefore, no wonder that the music of the era of 'real subsumption', of a capitalism which has subordinated to its logic, to its temporality, all aspects of human activity, including culture, should take time as its subject matter. 'Time-as-measure become time-as-substance' is not an inappropriate way to describe the dialectical transformation of both temporality in general wrought by capitalism, and musical time by the emergence of groove music. But this returns us again to the question of the aesthetic value of such music. Is groove music simply the music *of* capitalism, in the sense that it is merely the uncritical cultural expression of the dynamics of the system?

The Politics of an Aesthetic of Measured Time

We have already discussed the problems associated with a simple rejection of measured time in the creation of music. That option was adopted by the social stratum traditionally associated with cultural and artistic production in Western societies, as a protest against the encroachment of capitalist social relations on their area of activity. We might characterise it, perhaps overharshly, as a reactionary response to monopoly capitalism in its implicit hankering for a return to a cultural sphere free of market pressures, or, at least, a utopian response which simply tries to evade reality. In any case, it was hardly a position which it was possible for anything other than a minority of society to adopt, certainly not those whose lives were already thoroughly imbued, chiefly by work, with the measured and measuring time of capitalism. It is, of course, from these strata, from working people, broadly speaking, that groove music originated and from which it continues to be sustained. In his study of popular music's relationship with history, George Lipsitz refutes the suggestion that popular musicians are classless:

---

83   Marx 1976, p. 127.
84   Marx 1988, p. 345.

> ... having specific class roots means that rock and roll contains specific class imagery, with biases towards specific class ideologies. Artists themselves may no longer be part of the working class when they achieve success as musicians, but the dialogue from which they emerge, and the one they maintain with their fans, prevents them from becoming completely detached from their class backgrounds.[85]

He goes on to make an argument suggesting that the rhythm of popular music represents a reaction to the time discipline imposed upon workers in industrial capitalism:

> Instead of the regular beat that measured time by the clock, working-class musics embraced polyrhythms and irregular time signatures as a way of realizing in culture the mastery over time denied workers in the workplace.... [Rock-and-roll wins an audience] by inverting the icon of the clock and using it to measure out doses of pleasure instead of units of labor.[86]

In fact, as we have seen, irregular time signatures have been marginal to the history of popular music and tend to undermine the groove concept, so their inclusion in this argument is misplaced; and though Lipsitz's reliance on the concept of 'pleasure' is insufficiently rigorous, it echoes jazz clarinetist Don Byron's view that groove is 'about feeling like time itself is pleasurable'.[87] The idea that working-class culture involves the aesthetic transformation and mastery of the alienated measured time to which workers are subjected is a powerful one. Groove music appears here as simultaneously utopian and non-utopian: it is non-utopian in that it does not follow the course of most 'high' modernist music in simply turning its back on, or wishing away, the domination of measured time in industrial society; but by detaching it from its utilitarian purpose and using it as a raw material for creative expression, groove humanises measured time and presents a utopian picture of an unalienated existence. In this sense, then, groove might be said to belong within the tradition of working-class resistance to time discipline whose early examples were studied by E.P. Thompson and cited in the previous chapter. On this analysis, such resistance would be present, implicitly, in any music to the extent that its groove was successful, irrespective of its other content, lyrical or otherwise.

---

85   Lipsitz 1990, p. 109.
86   Lipsitz 1990, p. 113.
87   Monson 1996, p. 68.

The consciously political jazz drummer, Max Roach, is among those cited as having detected this resistive quality in the rhythm of otherwise apolitical rap music: 'the politics was in the drums'.[88]

But there may be a deeper sense in which groove's expropriation of the alienated time of modern capitalism expresses a liberatory project. In his classic text, *The Society of the Spectacle*, Guy Debord traces the development in history of historical consciousness, the full achievement of which would represent true liberation. Taking as his starting point Marx's view that 'History itself is a real part of natural history – of nature developing into man',[89] Debord argues that,

> History has always existed, but not always in its historical form. The temporalization of man, as effected through the mediation of a society, is equivalent to a humanization of time. The unconscious movement of time becomes manifest and *true* in historical consciousness.[90]

Debord argues that the ruling classes of early class societies were able to monopolise historical time through their mastery of knowledge and because their populations were immersed in the cyclical time of agricultural existence. 'Separated off from the collective organization of time that predominated as a function of the repetitive form of production which was the basis of social life, historical time flowed independently above its own, static, community'. In these old societies 'irreversible time was the prerogative of whoever ruled... Those who *possessed history* gave it an orientation – a direction, and also a meaning', but their history remained separate from the reality of the majority of people.

For these dry chronologies to become conscious history, large groups of people had to experience real participation in historical events. Consciousness of history is the manifestation in thought of the actual making of history, and 'to reflect upon history is also, inextricably to reflect upon power'. The first representations of an irreversible time open to all, according to Debord, were those of the monotheistic religions. But these representations were only semi-historical and only partially democratised because they remained entirely orientated to a single final event: the Last Judgment. Their goal was an eternity lying *beyond* irreversible time.[91]

---

88   Quoted in Lipsitz 1994, p. 38.
89   Marx 1975b, pp. 303–4.
90   Debord 1995, p. 92.
91   Debord 1995, pp. 94–9.

Historical consciousness takes another leap forward with the rise to power of the bourgeoisie:

> The victory of the bourgeoisie was the victory of a *profoundly historical time* – the time corresponding to the economic form of production, which transformed society permanently, and from top to bottom.... History, which had hitherto appeared to express nothing more than the activity of individual members of the ruling class, and had thus been conceived of as a chronology of events, was now perceived in its *general movement* – an inexorable movement that crushed individuals before it.[92]

But, says Debord, because the time of capitalism is inscribed in the mass production of commodities, the historical time of bourgeois society is a time of *things*, an alienated time rather than a lived time. 'The bourgeoisie unveiled irreversible historical time and imposed it on society only to deprive society of its *use*'. Capitalism inaugurates a truly historical time, eradicating all vestiges of cyclical time and imposing a generalised time across the whole globe. But instead of being a lived time, this global irreversible time is simply the time of production, rooted in labour time, and consequently ends up being a denial of history. It is a fragmented, abstract, reified time. Like its development of the productive forces, capitalism creates the preconditions for an unalienated society in which individuals can live history, but fails to deliver such a society. Nevertheless, those at the base of society – workers – are no longer estranged from history, 'for now the irreversible is generated from below'. The struggle for a liberated society, therefore, is the demand to *live* the historical time that the proletariat creates.[93] Debord sums up:

> Time's natural basis, the sensory data of its passage, becomes human and social inasmuch as it exists *for human beings*.... The revolutionary project of a classless society, of a generalized historical life, is also the project of a withering away of the social measurement of time in favor of an individual and collective measurement of time which is playful in character and which encompasses, simultaneously present within it, a variety of autonomous yet effectively federated times....[94]

---

[92] Debord 1995, pp. 104–5.
[93] Debord 1995, pp. 105–7.
[94] Debord 1995, p. 116.

The notion of 'federated times' is interestingly at odds with the vision of temporal freedom which emerged earlier from Bergsonian thinkers like Deleuze as well as Jameson's celebration of temporal incommensurability.[95] It maintains the sense of diversity inherent in a multiplicity of times while at the same time endorsing the possibility, even the necessity, for a collective integration of those times. Debord's invocation of 'playfulness' also allows us to grasp the aesthetic component of such a political project and apply it directly to the musical questions we have been exploring up to this point. It is easy to see the parallels in groove. In addition to the idea, expressed above, that groove's metricality de-instrumentalises measured time, thereby effecting an aesthetic critique of it, the elements of polyrhythm and syncopation, often in practice generated through improvisation rather than compositional decree, suggest alternative pulses and tempos which nonetheless remain integrated within the metrical framework. In contrast to Adorno, who condemns these rhythmic deviations as mere gestures towards subjective freedom which ultimately betray their autonomy by conforming to the all-powerful beat, it is better to understand the relationship dialectically and to see in the objectified collectivity of meter the precondition for rhythmic individuation. As we saw in Chapter 5, both Zuckerkandl's formulation of the relationship between rhythm and meter, and Marx's notion of society as necessary for individuation, express this thought in their respective ways.

That is not to say that in all groove music the relationship between collective and individual, between objective and subjective, is satisfactorily achieved. There are plenty of instances – both of individual pieces and of styles or genres – where the objective component overwhelms and stifles the subjective, where the groove is reduced to little more than the basic pulse articulated by, say, the bass drum. Such music has proliferated especially in the field of 'dance music' composed on computers, a method which, by definition, is blind to the concept of individual parts and tends towards total centralisation. We might describe music with such an overbearing metronomic pulse as having a poor groove, or we might conclude from its paucity of syncopation and its shallow metrical structure that it does not deserve classification as groove music at all. But the existence of such music should not detract from the fact that over the last century the groove principle has been employed to great effect in a huge range of genres to produce what are, truly, musics for our times. Groove, in its best manifestations, bears within itself an aesthetic critique of the alienated temporality of contemporary capitalism, and figures a demand for the collective

---

95   See Chapter 3.

control of time and history in which the time of the universe and the time of humanity would finally be reconciled.

Groove is the praxial, concrete, aesthetic figuration of an emancipated, collective temporality. Praxial because it avoids the contemplative and individualistic representation of time through narrative in favour of a collective making of time. Concrete because it uses as its raw material the abstract, alienated time of capitalism rather than an ideal liberated time. Groove is an aesthetic practice which, through the mimetic grasping of the measured time of capitalism, achieves a praxial figuration of a liberated temporality.

References

Adam, Barbara 2004, *Time*, Cambridge: Polity.
Adorno, Theodor 1973a, *Philosophy of Modern Music*, translated by Anne G. Mitchell and Wesley V. Blomster, New York: Seabury Press.
——— 1973b, *Negative Dialectics*, translated by E.B. Ashton, London: Routledge and Keegan Paul.
——— 1976, *Introduction to the Sociology of Music*, translated by E.B. Ashton, New York: Seabury Press.
——— 1978, *Minima Moralia: Reflections from Damaged Life*, translated by Edmund Jephcott, London: Verso.
——— 1983 [1953], 'Perennial Fashion – Jazz', in *Prisms*, translated by Samuel Weber and Shierry Weber Nicholsen, Cambridge, MA: MIT Press.
——— 1996 [1960], *Mahler: A Musical Physiognomy*, translated by Edmund Jephcott, Chicago: Chicago University Press.
——— 1997a, *Aesthetic Theory*, translated by Robert Hullot-Kentor, London: Continuum.
——— 1997b [1936], 'Letter to Benjamin', in *Aesthetics and Politics*, New York: Verso.
——— 2002a [1932], 'On the Social Situation of Music' in *Adorno: Essays on Music*, edited by Richard Leppert, Berkeley, CA: University of California Press.
——— 2002b [1933], 'Farewell to Jazz', in *Adorno: Essays on Music*, edited by Richard Leppert, Berkeley, CA: University of California Press.
——— 2002c [1936], 'On Jazz', in *Adorno: Essays on Music*, edited by Richard Leppert, Berkeley, CA: University of California Press.
——— 2002d [1938], 'On the Fetish-Character of Music and the Regression of Listening', in *Adorno: Essays on Music*, edited by Richard Leppert, Berkeley, CA: University of California Press.
——— 2002e [1941], 'On Popular Music' [With the assistance of George Simpson], in *Adorno: Essays on Music*, edited by Richard Leppert, Berkeley, CA: University of California Press.
——— 2002f [1953], 'On the Contemporary Relationship of Philosophy and Music', in *Adorno: Essays on Music*, edited by Richard Leppert, Berkeley, CA: University of California Press.
——— 2005, *In Search of Wagner*, translated by Rodney Livingstone, London: Verso.
——— 2006, *Towards a Theory of Musical Reproduction*, translated by Henri Lonitz, Cambridge: Polity.
Agawu, Kofi 2003, *Representing African Music: Postcolonial Notes, Queries, Positions*, London: Routledge.
Alén, Olavo 1995, 'Rhythm as Duration of Sounds in Tumba Francesa', *Ethnomusicology*, 39, 1: 55–72.

Alperson, Philip 1980, '"Musical Time" and Music as an "Art of Time"', *Journal of Aesthetics and Art Criticism*, 38:4: 407–417.
Anderson, Perry 1998, *The Origins of Postmodernity*, London: Verso.
Ansell Pearson, Keith and John Mullarkey (eds.) 2002, *Henri Bergson: Key Writings*, London.
Arbeau, Thoinot 1966 [1588], *Orchésographie*, translated by Mary Evans, London: Dover.
Arom, Simha 1991, *African Polyphony and Polyrhythm: Musical Structure and Methodology*, translated by Martin Thom, Barbara Tuckett and Raymond Boyd, Cambridge: Cambridge University Press.
Attali, Jacques 1985, *Noise: The Political Economy of Music*, translated by Brian Massumi, Manchester: Manchester University Press.
Badiou, Alain 2007, *Being and Event*, translated by Oliver Feltham, London: Continuum.
Bailey, Derek 1992, *Improvisation, its Nature and Practice in Music*, London: The British Library National Sound Archive.
Bartholomew, Douglas 1985, 'Preamble to a Phenomenology of Music', *Journal of Musicological Research*, 5: 319–60.
The Beatles 1969, 'Here Comes the Sun' (George Harrison), *Abbey Road*, London: Apple Records.
Beethoven, Ludwig van 1986 [1805], *Leonore Overture No.3 Op. 72a*, Leipzig: Eulenburg.
Belgrad, Daniel 1998, *The Culture of Spontaneity: Improvisation and the Arts in Postwar America*, Chicago: University of Chicago Press.
Benjamin, Andrew and Peter Osborne (eds.) 2000, *Walter Benjamin's Philosophy: Destruction and Experience*, Manchester: Clinamen Press.
Benjamin, Walter 1985 [1939], 'Central Park', *New German Critique*, 34: 32–58.
——— 1999, *Illuminations*, London: Pimlico.
Bensaïd, Daniel 2009, *Marx For Our Times: Adventures and Misadventures of a Critique*, translated by Gregory Elliot, London: Verso.
Berger, John 1972, *Ways of Seeing*, London: BBC.
Bergson, Henri 1996, 'Essai sur les données immédiates de la conscience', in Moore, F.C.T., *Bergson: Thinking Backwards*, Cambridge: Cambridge University Press.
——— 2002a, 'Creative Evolution' in *Henri Bergson: Key Writings*, edited by Keith Ansell Pearson and John Mullarkey, London: Continuum.
——— 2002b, 'Time and Free Will' in *Henri Bergson: Key Writings*, edited by Keith Ansell Pearson and John Mullarkey, London: Continuum.
——— 2002c, 'Concerning the Nature of Time' in *Henri Bergson: Key Writings*, edited by Keith Ansell Pearson and John Mullarkey, London: Continuum.
——— 2002d, 'The Perception of Change' in *Henri Bergson: Key Writings*, edited by Keith Ansell Pearson and John Mullarkey, London: Continuum.
Berlin, Ira 1992, *Slaves Without Masters*, New York: New Press.

Berman, Marshall 1983, *All That Is Solid Melts Into Air: The Experience of Modernity*, London: Verso.

Bernstein, J.M. 1984, *The Philosophy of the Novel: Lukács, Marxism and the Dialectics of Form*, Brighton: Harvester Press.

Bloch, Ernst 1985 [1925], 'On the mathematical and dialectical character in music' in *Essays on the Philosophy of Music*, translated by Peter Palmer, Cambridge: Cambridge University Press.

Bogue, Ronald 2003, *Deleuze on Music, Painting and the Arts*, London: Routledge.

Bonefeld, Werner 2010, 'Abstract labour: Against its nature and on its time', *Capital and Class*, 34, 2: 257–76.

Bordo, Michael D. and Christopher M. Meissner 2007, 'Foreign Capital and Economic Growth in the First Era of Globalization', NBER, www.nber.org/papers/w13577.

Brackett, David 2000, *Interpreting Popular Music*, Berkeley: University of California Press.

Braverman, Harry 1998, *Labor and Monopoly Capitalism: The Degradation of Work in the Twentieth Century*, New York: Monthly Review Press.

Brubeck, Dave (The Dave Brubeck Quartet) 1959, 'Take Five', *Time Out*, Columbia Records.

Buchanan, Ian and Marcel Swiboda (eds.) 2004, *Deleuze and Music*, Edinburgh: Edinburgh University Press.

Burning Spear 1975, 'Marcus Garvey', *Marcus Garvey*, Island Records. Audio CD.

Caffentzis, George 2005, 'Immeasurable Value? An Essay on Marx's Legacy', *The Commoner* 10, 3: <thecommoner.org.uk/10caffentzis.pdf>.

Callinicos, Alex 1987, *Making History*, Cambridge: Polity.

―――― 1997, *Theories and Narratives*, Cambridge: Polity.

―――― 2006, *The Resources of Critique*, Cambridge: Polity.

Campbell, Edward 2010, *Boulez, Music and Philosophy*, Cambridge: Cambridge University Press.

Capek, Milic 1968, 'Time in Relativity Theory: Arguments for a Philosophy of Becoming', in *Voices of Time*, edited by J.T. Fraser, Harmondsworth: Penguin.

Chernoff, John Miller 1979, *African Rhythm and African Sensibility: Aesthetics and Social Action in African Musical Idioms*, Chicago: University of Chicago Press.

Chester, Andrew 1970, 'Second Thoughts on a Rock Aesthetic: The Band', *New Left Review* 62: 75–82.

Clarke, Eric 1987, 'Levels of Structure in the Organization of Musical Time', in *Contemporary Music Review* 2: 211–38.

―――― 1999, 'Rhythm and Timing in Music', in *The Psychology of Music*, edited by Diana Deutsch, London: Academic Press.

Clemence, G.M. 1968, 'Time Measurement for Scientific Use', in *Voices of Time*, edited by J.T. Fraser, Harmondsworth: Penguin.

Clifton, Thomas 1983, *Music As Heard: A Study in Applied Phenomenology*, London: Yale University Press.
Colebrook, Claire 2006, *Deleuze: A Guide for the Perplexed*, London: Continuum.
Cone, Edward, 1968, *Musical Form and Musical Performance*, New York: Norton.
Cook, Nicholas 2004, 'Making Music Together, or Improvisation and its Others', *The Source: Challenging Jazz Criticism* 1: 5–25.
Cooper, Grosvenor and Leonard Meyer 1960, *The Rhythmic Structure of Music*, Chicago: University of Chicago Press.
Danielsen, Anne 2006, *Presence and Pleasure: The Funk Grooves of James Brown and Parliament*, Middletown, CT: Wesleyan University Press.
Davis, Mike 2005, 'Urban Renaissance and the Spirit of Postmodernism', in *New Left Review* 151: 106–113.
Day, Gail 2011, *Dialectical Passions: Negation in Postwar Art Theory*, New York: Columbia University Press.
Debord, Guy 1995, *Society of the Spectacle*, New York: Zone Books.
Deleuze, Gilles and Félix Guattari 1988, *A Thousand Plateaus*, London: Continuum.
Derrida, Jacques 1991, 'Speech and Phenomena' (extract), in *The Derrida Reader*, edited by Peggy Kamuf, Hemel Hempstead: Harvester Wheatsheaf.
Deutsch, Diana 1999, *The Psychology of Music*, London: Academic Press.
Dexy's Midnight Runners 1982, 'Come On Eileen', *Too-Rye-Ay*, Mercury Records.
The Eagles 1976, 'Hotel California', *Hell Freezes Over*, Asylum Records.
Eagleton, Terry 1990, *The Ideology of the Aesthetic*, Oxford: Blackwell.
—— 2007, *The Meaning of Life: A Very Short Introduction*, Oxford: Oxford University Press.
Engels, Frederick, 1960, 'Socialism: Utopian and Scientific' in *Marx, Engels, Lenin, The Essential Left*, London: Unwin Books.
—— 1989 [1883] 'Speech at the grave of Karl Marx', *Karl Marx and Frederick Engels Collected Works*, Volume 24, London: Lawrence & Wishart.
Epstein, David, 1987, *Beyond Orpheus: Studies in Musical Structure*, Oxford: Oxford University Press.
Fanon, Frantz 1967, *Black Skin, White Masks*, translated by Charles Markmann, New York: Grove Press.
Farmelo, Allen, 1997, 'The Unifying Consequences of Grooving: An Introductory Ethnographic Approach to Unity Through Music', <http://www.musekids.org/UCS.html>.
Floyd, Samuel A. 1991, 'Ring Shout! Literary Studies, Historical Studies, and Black Musical Inquiry', *Black Music Research Journal*, 11, 2: 265–87.
Foster, John Bellamy 1998, 'Introduction', in *Labor and Monopoly Capitalism: The Degradation of Work in the Twentieth Century*, by Harry Braverman, New York: Monthly Review Press.

REFERENCES

——— 2000, *Marx's Ecology: Materialism and Nature*, New York: Monthly Review Press.
Foucault, Michel 1977, *Discipline and Punish: The Birth of the Prison*, translated by Alan Sheridan, London: Allen Lane.
Franklin, Benjamin 1748, 'Advice to a Young Tradesman, Written by an Old One', *The Writings of Benjamin Franklin: Philadelphia, 1726–1757*, available at <http://www.historycarper.com/resources/twobf2/advice.htm>.
Fraser, J.T. (ed.) 1968, *Voices of Time: A Co-operative Survey of Man's Views on Time, as Expressed by the Sciences and the Humanities*, Harmondsworth: Penguin.
Frith, Simon 1998, *Performing Rites: Evaluating Popular Music*, Oxford: Oxford University Press.
Gates, Henry Louis Jr. 1984, 'The Blackness of Blackness: a Critique of the Sign and the Signifying Monkey', in *Black Literature and Literary Theory*, edited by Henry Louis Gates, London: Methuen.
Gershwin, George, 1934, *'I Got Rhythm' Variations for Piano and Orchestra*, New York: New World Corp.
Getz, Stan and Charlie Byrd 1962, *Jazz Samba*, Verve Records.
Giddens, Anthony 1981, *A Contemporary Critique of Historical Materialism: Volume 1: Power, Property and the State*, London: Macmillan.
Gilroy, Paul 1993, *The Black Atlantic: Modernity and Double Consciousness*, London: Verso.
Goodman, Nelson 1976, *Languages of Art: An Approach to a Theory of Symbols*, Indianapolis: Hackett.
Gordon, Peter 2009, 'The Artwork Beyond Itself: Adorno, Beethoven and Late Style', in *The Modernist Imagination*, edited by Warren Breckman et al., New York: Berghahn Books.
Gracyk, Theodore 1996, *Rhythm and Noise: An Aesthetic of Rock*, London: Tauris.
Griffiths, Paul 1985, *Olivier Messiaen and the Music of Time*, London: Faber and Faber.
Habermas, Jürgen 1987, *The Philosophical Discourse of Modernity: Twelve Lectures*, translated by Frederick Lawrence, Cambridge: Polity.
Hainge, Greg 2004, 'Is Pop Music?' in *Deleuze and Music*, edited by Ian Buchanan and Marcel Swiboda, Edinburgh: Edinburgh University Press.
Hegel, Georg William 1972, *The Logic of Hegel, The Encyclopaedia of the Philosophical Sciences*, translated by William Wallace, Oxford: Oxford University Press.
——— 1977, *Phenomenology of Spirit*, translated by Arnold Vincent Miller, Oxford: Oxford University Press.
Heidegger, Martin 1978, *Being and Time*, translated by John Macquarrie and Edward Robinson, Oxford: Wiley-Blackwell.
——— 1988, *The Basic Problems of Phenomenology*, translated by Albert Hofstadter, Bloomington IN: Indiana University Press.
Holloway, John 2010, *Crack Capitalism*, London: Pluto Press.

Horner, Bruce and Thomas Swiss (eds.) 1999, *Key Terms in Popular Music and Culture*, London: Blackwell.

Hudson, Richard, 'Rubato', *Grove Music Online. Oxford Music Online*, available at <http://www.oxfordmusiconline.com/subscriber/article/grove/music/24039>.

Hughes, Timothy 2003, *Groove and Flow: Six Analytical Essays on the Music of Stevie Wonder*, PhD dissertation, University of Washington, available at <http://www.surrey.ac.uk/Music/NewsGenInfo/AcademicStaff/Hughes/GrooveAndFlow.pdf>.

Husserl, Edmund 1964, *The Phenomenology of Internal Time-Consciousness*, translated by James H. Churchill, Bloomington, IN: Indiana University Press.

Iyer, Vijay 2002, 'Embodied Mind, Situated Cognition, and Expressive Microtiming in African-American Music', *Music Perception*, 19, 3: 387–414.

Jameson, Fredric 1971, *Marxism and Form*, Princeton, NJ: Princeton University Press.

―――― 1983, *The Political Unconscious*, London: Routledge.

―――― 1988, *The Ideologies of Theory, Essays 1971–1986*, Volume 2, London: Routledge.

―――― 1991, *Postmodernism, or, The Cultural Logic of Late Capitalism*, London: Verso.

―――― 1997, 'Culture and Finance Capital', *Critical Inquiry*, 24, 1: 246–65.

―――― 1998, 'The Brick and the Balloon: Architecture, Idealism and Land Speculation', *New Left Review*, 228: 25–46.

―――― 2003, 'The End of Temporality', *Critical Inquiry*, 29, 4: 695–718.

―――― 2010, *Valences of the Dialectic*, London: Verso.

Jones, Arthur Morris 1959, *Studies in African Music*, Volume 1, London: Oxford University Press.

Jones, Norah 2002, 'Don't Know Why', *Come Away With Me*, New York: Blue Note Records.

Jordan, Louis and Ellis Lawrence Walsh 2000, 'Saturday Night Fish Fry', *Louis Jordan and his Tympany Five, Saturday Night Fish Fry: The Original and Greatest Hits*, Jasmine Records.

Joplin, Scott 1998, *Complete Rags For Piano*, New York: Schirmer.

Jung, C.G. 1968, *The Archetypes and the Collective Unconscious*, London: Routledge.

Katz, Mark 2012, *Groove Music: The Art and Culture of the Hip-Hop DJ*, New York: Oxford University Press.

Keil, Charles 1966, *Urban Blues*, Chicago: University of Chicago Press.

―――― 1995, 'The Theory of Participatory Discrepancies: a Progress Report', in *Ethnomusicology*, 39, 1: 1–19.

―――― n.d., 'Groovology and the Magic of Other People's Music', available at <http://musicgrooves.org/articles/GroovologyAndMagic.pdf>.

Keil, Charles and Steven Feld 1994, *Music Grooves*, Chicago: University of Chicago Press.

Kennedy Michael 1984, *The Oxford Dictionary of Music*, Oxford: Oxford University Press.

Kernfeld, Barry n.d., 'Groove (i)', *The New Grove Dictionary of Jazz*, in *Grove Music Online*, *Oxford Music Online*, second edition, edited by Barry Kernfeld, available at <http://www.oxfordmusiconline.com/subscriber/article/grove/music/J582400>.
Kingman, Daniel 1979, *American Music: A Panorama*, New York: Schirmer.
Kivy, Peter 1984, *Sound and Semblance: Reflections on Musical Representation*, Princeton, NJ: Princeton University Press.
Klumpenhouwer, Henry 2001, 'Late Capitalism, Late Marxism, and the Study of Music', *Music Analysis* 2, 3: 367–405
Koselleck, Reinhart 1985, *Futures Past: On the Semantics of Historical Time*, Cambridge, MA: MIT Press.
Kramer, Jonathan 1988, *The Time of Music: New Meanings, New Temporalities, New Listening Strategies*, London: Collier Macmillan.
Krims, Adam 2003, 'Marxist Music Analysis without Adorno: Popular Music and Urban Geography', in *Analyzing Popular Music*, edited by Allen Moore, Cambridge: Cambridge University Press.
——— 2007, *Music and Urban Geography*, Cambridge: Cambridge University Press.
Kubik, Gerhard, 'Africa' n.d., *Grove Music Online*. *Oxford Music Online*, available at <http://www.oxfordmusiconline.com/subscriber/article/grove/music/00268>.
Landes, David 1983, *Revolution in Time: Clocks and the Making of the Modern World*, London: Harvard University Press.
Langer, Susanne 1953, *Feeling and Form*, London: Routledge Keegan and Paul.
——— 1957, *Philosophy in a New Key*, Cambridge, MA: Harvard University Press.
Larkin, Colin (ed.) 2006, *Encyclopedia of Popular Music*, fourth edition, *Oxford Music Online*, available at <http://www.oxfordmusiconline.com/subscriber/article/epm/63171>.
Latham, Alison 2002, 'Metre', *The Oxford Companion to Music*, *Oxford Music Online*, edited by Alison Latham, available at <http://www.oxfordmusiconline.com/subscriber/article/opr/t114/e4387>.
——— 2002 'Rubato', *The Oxford Companion to Music*, *Oxford Music Online*, edited by Alison Latham, available at <http://www.oxfordmusiconline.com/subscriber/article/opr/t114/e5796>.
Lecourt, Dominique 1977, *Proletarian Science?*, translated by Ben Brewster, London: New Left Books.
Leppert, Richard (ed.) 2002, *Adorno: Essays on Music*, Berkeley, CA: University of California Press.
Lerdahl, Fred and Ray Jackendoff 1981, 'On the Theory of Grouping and Meter', *Musical Quarterly*, 67, 4: 479–506.
——— 1983, *A Generative Theory of Tonal Music*, Cambridge, MA: MIT Press.
Leslie, Esther 2000, *Walter Benjamin: Overpowering Conformism*, London: Pluto Press.

Lipsitz, George 1990, *Time Passages: Collective Memory and American Popular Culture*, Minneapolis: University of Minnesota Press.

—— 1994, *Dangerous Crossroads: Popular Music, Postmodernism and the Poetics of Place*, London: Verso.

London, Justin, 'Metre', *Grove Music Online*, *Oxford Music Online*, available at <http://www.oxfordmusiconline.com/subscriber/article/grove/music/18519>.

Lukács, György 1936, 'Eulogy for Maxim Gorky: A Great Proletarian Humanist', *International Literature* 8, reproduced in *Red Flag*, Journal of the CP (MLM), March 2007, available at <http://neworleans.media.indypgh.org/uploads/2007/02/red_flag_no._1.pdf>.

—— 1971a, *The Theory of the Novel*, London: Merlin.

—— 1971b, 'Reification and the Consciousness of the Proletariat' in *History and Class Consciousness*, translated by Rodney Livingstone, London: Merlin.

Lunn, Eugene 1984, *Marxism and Modernism; An Historical Study of Lukács, Brecht, Benjamin and Adorno*, Berkeley, CA: University of California Press.

Marcuse, Herbert 1964, *One-Dimensional Man: Studies in the Ideology of Advanced Industrial Society*, Boston: Beacon Press.

Marley, Bob 1974, 'No Woman, No Cry', *Natty Dread*, Island Records.

Marothy, János 1974, *Music and the Bourgeois, Music and the Proletarian*, Budapest: Akadémiai Kiado.

Marx, Karl 1973, *Grundrisse: Foundations of the Critique of Political Economy*, translated by Martin Nicolaus, London: Pelican with New Left Review.

—— 1975a [1841], 'The Difference Between the Democritean and Epicurean Philosophy of Nature', *Karl Marx & Frederick Engels, Collected Works*, Volume 1, London: Lawrence & Wishart.

—— 1975b, *The Economic and Philosophic Manuscripts of 1844, Karl Marx & Frederick Engels, Collected Works*, Volume 3, London: Lawrence & Wishart.

—— 1976 [1847], 'The Poverty of Philosophy', *Karl Marx & Frederick Engels, Collected Works*, Volume 6, London: Lawrence & Wishart.

—— 1977 [1867], *Capital: A Critique of Political Economy*, Volume 1, London: Lawrence and Wishart.

—— 1981 [1859], *A Contribution to the Critique of Political Economy*, translated by Salomea Volfovna Ryazanskaya, London: Lawrence and Wishart.

—— 1988, 'Economic Manuscripts of 1861–63', *Karl Marx & Frederick Engels, Collected Works*, Volume 30, London: Lawrence & Wishart.

—— 1989 [1881], 'Marginal Notes on Adolph Wagner's *Lehrbuch der politische Oekonomie*', *Karl Marx & Frederick Engels, Collected Works*, Volume 24, London: Lawrence and Wishart.

—— 1994 [1864], 'Economic Manuscripts', *Karl Marx & Frederick Engels, Collected Works*, Volume 34, London: Lawrence and Wishart.

Marx, Karl and Frederick Engels 1960 [1848], 'The Manifesto of the Communist Party', in *Marx, Engels, Lenin, The Essential Left*, London: Unwin Books.

Maus, Fred Everett 1997, 'Narrative, Drama, and Emotion in Instrumental Music', *Journal of Aesthetics and Art Criticism*, 55, 3: 293–303.

McClary, Susan 2000, *Conventional Wisdom: The Content of Musical Form*, Berkeley: University of California Press.

McNally, David 2004, 'The Dual Form of Labour in Capitalist Society and the Struggle over Meaning: Comments on Postone', *Historical Materialism*, 12, 3: 189–208.

McNeill, William 1995, *Keeping Together in Time: Dance and Drill in Human History*, Cambridge, MA: Harvard University Press.

Merriam, Alan 1982, 'African Musical Rhythm and Concepts of Time-Reckoning', in *African Music in Perspective*, London: Garland.

Middleton, Richard 1990, *Studying Popular Music*, Buckingham: Open University Press.

Moore, Allen (ed.) 2003, *Analyzing Popular Music*, Cambridge: Cambridge University Press.

Moore, Francis Charles Timothy 1996, *Bergson: Thinking Backwards*, Cambridge: Cambridge University Press.

Miller, Izchak 1984, *Husserl, Perception, and Temporal Awareness*, Cambridge, MA: MIT Press.

Miller, Karen 2004, 'The Question of Time in Postone's *Time, Labor and Social Domination*', *Historical Materialism*, 12, 3: 209–37.

Monson, Ingrid 1996, *Saying Something: Jazz Improvisation and Interaction*, Chicago: Chicago University Press.

Mumford, Lewis 1963 [1934], *Technics and Civilization*, Orlando: Harvest/Harcourt Brace.

——— 2000, 'The Monastery and the Clock' (The Human Prospect), in *The City Cultures Reader*, edited by Malcolm Miles et al., London: Routledge.

Murphy, Timothy and Daniel Smith 2001, 'What I Hear Is Thinking Too: Deleuze and Guattari Go Pop', in *Echo*, 3, 1, available at <http://www.echo.ucla.edu/Volume3-Issue1/smithmurphy/index.html>.

Mursell, James 1964, *The Psychology of Music*, Westport, CT: Greenwood Press.

Muzzetto, Luigi 2006, 'Time and Meaning in Alfred Schütz', *Time and Society*, 15, 1: 5–31.

Myers, D.G. 1990, 'Signifying Nothing', *New Criterion* 8: 61–4.

Nattiez, Jean-Jacques 1990, 'Can One Speak of Narrativity in Music?', *Journal of the Royal Musical Association*, 115, 2: 240–57.

Negri, Antonio 2003, *The Constitution of Time*, translated by Matteo Mandarini, London: Continuum.

Nesbitt, Nick 2004, 'Deleuze, Adorno, and the Composition of Musical Multiplicity', in *Deleuze and Music*, edited by Ian Buchanan and Marcel Swiboda, Edinburgh: Edinburgh University Press.

Neubauer, Eckhard and Veronica Doubleday n.d., 'Islamic Religious Music', *Grove Music Online*. *Oxford Music Online*, available at <http://www.oxfordmusiconline.com/subscriber/article/grove/music/52787>.

Newcomb, Anthony 1987, 'Schumann and Late Eighteenth-Century Narrative Strategies', *19th-Century Music*, Volume 11, 2: 164–74.

Newton, Francis (Eric Hobsbawm) 1959, *The Jazz Scene*, London: MacGibbon and Kee.

Newton, Isaac 1934 [1729], *Philosophiae Naturalis Principia Mathematica*, Book 1, translated by A. Motte, Berkeley: University of California Press.

Oliver, Paul 1970, *Savannah Syncopators: African Retentions in the Blues*, West Sussex: Littlehampton Book Services.

Osborne, Peter 1992, 'Modernity is a Qualitative, Not a Chronological Category', *New Left Review*, 192: 65–84.

——— 1995, *The Politics of Time*, London: Verso.

——— 2000, 'Small-scale Victories, Large-scale Defeats: Walter Benjamin's Politics of Time', in *Walter Benjamin's Philosophy: Destruction and Experience*, edited by Andrew Benjamin and Peter Osborne, Manchester: Clinamen Press, 2000.

——— 2008, 'Marx and the Philosophy of Time', *Radical Philosophy*, 147: 15–22.

Paddison, Max 1982, 'The Critic Criticised: Adorno and Popular Music' in *Popular Music 2: Theory and Method*, edited by Richard Middleton and David Horn, Cambridge: Cambridge University Press.

——— 1991, 'The Language-Character of Music: Some Motifs in Adorno', *Journal of the Royal Musical Association*, 16, 2: 262–79.

——— 1997, *Adorno's Aesthetics of Music*, Cambridge: Cambridge University Press.

——— 2004, *Adorno, Modernism and Mass Culture: Essays on Critical Theory and Music*, London: Kahn and Averill.

Pasler, Jann 1989, 'Narrative and Narrativity in Music', in *Time and Mind: Interdisciplinary Issues*, edited by Julius Thomas Fraser, Maddison, CT: International University Press.

The Police 1983, 'Every Breath You Take', *Synchronicity*, A&M Records.

Postone, Moishe 1993, *Time, Labor, and Social Domination: A Reinterpretation of Marx's Critical Theory*, Cambridge: Cambridge University Press.

Prögler, Josef 1995, 'Searching for Swing: Participatory Discrepancies in the Jazz Rhythm Section', *Ethnomusicology*, 39, 1: 21–54.

Pryer, Anthony 2002, 'Mensural music', *The Oxford Companion to Music*, *Oxford Music Online*, edited by Alison Latham, available at <http://www.oxfordmusiconline.com/subscriber/article/opr/t114/e4353>.

Queen 1978, 'Don't Stop Me Now', *Jazz*, London: EMI.

Rainbow 1979, 'Since You've Been Gone', *Down to Earth*, London: Polydor.

Rampley, Matthew 2000, *Nietzsche, Aesthetics and Modernity: Retrieving the Repressed*, Cambridge: Cambridge University Press.

Reinhardt, Django 2001 [1937], 'Sweet Georgia Brown', *All Star Sessions*, Parlophone France.
Ricardo, David 2004, *On the Principles of Political Economy and Taxation*, London: Dover.
Ricoeur, Paul 1980, 'Narrative Time', *Critical Inquiry*, 7, 1: 169–90.
—— 1984, *Time and Narrative*, Volume 3, translated by Kathleen McLaughlin and David Pellauer, Chicago: Chicago University Press.
Robinson, Bradford. 'Stride', *Grove Music Online. Oxford Music Online*, available at <http://www.oxfordmusiconline.com/subscriber/article/grove/music/ 26955>.
Rose Royce 1976, 'Car Wash', *Car Wash Soundtrack*, MCA Records.
Russell, Matheson 2006, *Husserl: A Guide for the Perplexed*, London: Continuum.
Scaff, Lawrence 2005, 'The Mind of a Modernist: Simmel on Time', *Time and Society*, 14: 5–23.
Schleifer, Ronald 2000, *Modernism and Time: The Logic of Abundance in Literature, Science, and Culture 1880–1930*, Cambridge: Cambridge University Press.
Scholes, Percy and Judith Nagley 2002, 'Syncopation', *The Oxford Companion to Music, Oxford Music Online*, edited by Alison Latham, available at <http://www.oxfordmusiconline.com/subscriber/article/opr/t114/e6605>.
Schuller, Gunther 1968, *Early Jazz: Its Roots and Musical Development*, New York: Oxford University Press.
Schutz, Alfred 1951, 'Making Music Together: A Study in Social Relationship', *Social Research*, 18,1/4: 76–97.
—— 1962, 'Scheler's Theory of Intersubjectivity and the General Thesis of the Alter Ego', in *Collected Papers I*, The Hague: Martinus Nijhoff.
—— 1966, *Collected Papers III*, The Hague: Martinus Nijhoff.
—— 1976, *The Phenomenology of the Social World*, London: Heinemann.
Schutz, Alfred and Fred Kersten 1976, 'Fragments on the Phenomenology of Music', *Journal of Musicological Research*, 2, 1: 5–71.
Scruton, Roger 1999, *The Aesthetics of Music*, Oxford: Clarendon Press.
Shepherd, John 1977, 'The Musical Coding of Ideologies' in *Whose Music? A Sociology of Musical Languages*, edited by John Shepherd, Phil Virden, Graham Vulliamy and Trevor Wishart, London: Latimer.
—— 1982, 'A Theoretical Model for the Sociomusicological Analysis of Popular Musics', *Popular Music*, Volume 2: 145–77.
Sherlaw Johnson, Robert 1975, *Messiaen*, Berkeley: University of California Press.
Simmel, Georg 2010 [1903], 'The Metropolis and Mental Life', in *The Blackwell City Reader*, edited by Gary Bridge and Sophie Watson, Oxford: Blackwell.
Skarda, Christine 1979, 'Alfred Schutz's Phenomenology of Music', *Journal of Musicological Research*, 3, 1: 75–132.
Small, Christopher 1977, *Music, Society, Education*, London: Calder.

—— 1987, *Music of the Common Tongue*, London: Calder.
—— 1997, *Musicking: The Meanings of Performing and Listening*, Middletown, CT: Wesleyan University Press.
Smith, F. Joseph 1979, *The Experiencing of Musical Sound: Prelude to a Phenomenology of Music*, London: Gordon and Breach.
Snead, James 1984, 'Repetition as a Figure of Black Culture', in *Black Literature and Literary Theory*, edited by Henry Louis Gates Jr., London: Methuen.
Snyder, Bob 2000, *Music and Memory*, Cambridge, MA: MIT Press.
Sohn-Rethel, Alfred 1978, *Intellectual and Manual Labour: A Critique of Epistemology*, London: Macmillan.
Southern, Eileen 1984, *The Music of Black Americans*, New York: W.W. Norton.
Stambaugh, Joan 1964, 'Music as a Temporal Form', *Journal of Philosophy*, 62, 9: 265–80.
Stevens, John et al. 'Troubadours, trouvères', *Grove Music Online, Oxford Music Online*, available at <http://www.oxfordmusiconline.com/subscriber/article/grove/music/28468>.
The Stranglers, 1981, 'Golden Brown', *La Folie*, Liberty Records.
Survivor 1982, 'Eye of the Tiger', or 'Theme from Rocky IV', *Eye of the Tiger*, Scotti Brothers Records.
Tagg, Philip 1984, 'Understanding Time Sense', available at <http://tagg.org/articles/timesens.html>.
—— 1989, 'Open Letter about "Black Music", "Afro-American Music", and "European Music"', in *Popular Music*, 8, 3: 285–298.
—— 1996, 'Popular Music Studies versus the "Other"', available at <http://www.tagg.org/articles/cascais.html>.
—— 1999, 'Introductory Notes to the Semiotics of Music', available at <www.tagg.org/xpdfs/semiotug.pdf>.
Tagg, Philip and Bob Clarida 2003, *Ten Little Title Tunes: Towards a Musicology of the Mass Media*, New York: Mass Media Music Scholars' Press.
Tamlyn, Garry 1998, *The Big Beat: Origins and Development of Snare Drum Backbeat and Other Accompanimental Rhythms in Rock 'n' Roll*, unpublished Ph.D. thesis, University of Liverpool.
—— 2003, 'Groove', in *Continuum Encyclopedia of Popular Music of the World. Volume II: Performance and Production*, edited by John Shepherd et al., London: Continuum.
Thompson, Edward Palmer 1967, 'Time, Work Discipline, and Industrial Capitalism', *Past and Present*, 38, 1: 56–97.
Thrift, Nigel. 1996, 'Owners' Time and Own Time: The Making of a Capitalist Time-Consciousness 1300–1800', in *Human Geography: An Essential Anthology*, edited by John Agnew et al., London: Wiley-Blackwell.

Toscano, Alberto 2008a, 'The Open Secret of Real Abstraction', *Rethinking Marxism*, 20, 2: 273–87.
——— 2008b, 'The Culture of Abstraction', *Theory, Culture and Society*, 25, 4: 57–75.
Van Der Merwe, Peter 1989, *The Origins of the Popular Style: The Antecedents of Twentieth-Century Popular Music*, Oxford: Clarendon.
Van Halen 1984, 'Jump', *1984*, Warner Brothers.
Vannoy Adams, Michael 1996, *The Multicultural Imagination: Race, Color, and the Unconscious*, New York: Routledge.
Waterman, Richard 1948, '"Hot" Rhythm in Negro Music', *Journal of the American Musicological Society*, 1, 1: 24–37.
——— 1951, 'African Influence on the Music of the Americas', in *Acculturation in the Americas*, edited by Sol Tax, Chicago: University of Chicago Press.
Wayne, Michael 2007, 'Theses on Realism and Film', *International Socialism*, 116: 165–83.
Weber, Max 1958, *The Rational and Social Foundations of Music*, translated by Don Martindale, Johannes Riedel and Gertrude Neuwirth, Carbondale, IL: Southern Illinois University Press.
——— 2003 [1930], *The Protestant Ethic and the Spirit of Capitalism*, translated by Talcott Parsons, Mineola, NY: Dover.
Whittall, Arnold 2002, 'Rhythm', *The Oxford Companion to Music*, *Oxford Music Online*, edited by Alison Latham, available at <http://www.oxfordmusiconline.com/subscriber/article/opr/t114/e5635>.
Whitrow, Gerald James 1968, 'Time and the Universe' in *Voices of Time: A Co-operative Survey of Man's Views on Time, as Expressed by the Sciences and the Humanities*, edited by J.T. Fraser, Harmondsworth: Penguin.
Wilson, Olly 1974, 'The Significance of the Relationship Between Afro-American and West African Music', *The Black Perspective in Music*, 2, 1: 3–22.
Withers, Bill 1977, 'Lovely Day', *Menagerie*, Columbia Records.
Witkin, Robert 1998, *Adorno on Music*, London: Routledge.
Zahavi, Dan 2007, 'Perception of Duration Presupposes Duration of Perception – or Does It? Husserl and Dainton on Time', *International Journal of Philosophical Studies*, 15, 3: 453–71.
Zaner, Richard 2002, 'Making Music Together While Growing Older: Further Reflections on Intersubjectivity', *Human Studies*, 25: 1–18.
Žižek, Slavoj 1989, *The Sublime Object of Ideology*, London: Verso.
Zuckerkandl, Victor 1973, *Sound and Symbol: Music and the External World*, Princeton, NJ: Princeton University Press.
——— 1976, *Man the Musician (Sound and Symbol: Volume 2)*, Princeton, NJ: Princeton University Press.

Index

abstraction   112, 122, 197, 199, 200, 206–213, 217, 219–21, 229, 246, 248, 250
Adam, Barbara   193, 194, 195, 218fn, 218, 219
Adorno, Theodor,   5, 6, 9, 13, 14, 15, 86, 103, 147–186, 203, 205, 206, 220, 221, 222, 223, 226–9, 231, 236, 239–42, 245, 255
Africa   12, 19, 22, 30, 40, 59, 61–91, 138, 184, 219
African(Afro)-American music   19, 24, 30, 64–6, 70–72, 75, 90
Agawu, Kofi   78, 81, 82fn, 83, 89–90
Alén, Octavo   28fn
alienation   8, 10, 174, 203, 228
Alperson, Philip   92, 114
America   6, 56, 58, 61–78, 80, 90, 91, 214
Anderson, Perry   6fn
Ansell Pearson, Keith   95fn
anticipation   35–7, 40–2, 113, 121–3, 134, 152, 153, 195, 239
Arbeau, Thoinot   26
Aristotle   2, 119, 229, 230, 232, 243
Arom, Simha   78–81, 83–6
atonality   162, 164, 174
Attali, Jacques   6–7
Augustine   229
Average White Band   72

Bach, Johann Sebastian   6, 42, 85, 167
back-beat   49–59
Badiou, Alain   238fn
Bailey, Derek   23fn, 106fn
Baroque music   42, 59, 178
Bartholomew, Douglas   117, 118, 120fn
Bartok, Bela   60, 75
Baudelaire   240, 245
Beatles, The   40
Beckett, Samuel   174
Beethoven, Ludwig van   34, 38, 103, 124, 152, 155–9, 162–3, 167, 182, 183, 206, 231, 241
Belgrad, Daniel   179fn
Bellofiore, R.   207fn
Benjamin, Walter   6, 205, 237–43, 245
Bensaïd, Daniel   183, 239–40, 245–6, 250
Berg, Alban   158, 162
Berger, John   2

Bergson, Henri   2, 14, 92–8, 100, 101, 103–5, 107–115, 119, 123, 124, 125, 130, 138, 139, 145, 148, 156–8, 161, 170, 185, 186, 212, 217fn, 220, 222, 223, 225, 228, 241, 248, 255
Berio, Luciano   101
Berlin, Ira   74fn
Berliner, Paul F.   21
Berman, Marshall   187
Bernstein, J.M.   233, 241
Bernstein, Leonard   38
black music   12, 18, 56, 64–77, 184
black nationalism   63, 71, 72
blackness   66, 68–70
Bloch, Ernst   169
blues   21, 45–6, 61, 73, 75–6
Blumenburg, Hans   236
Bogue, Ronald   102fn
Bonefeld, Werner   207fn, 217fn
Bordo, Michael D.   218fn
Boulez, Pierre   98, 101, 206fn
Brackett, David   22–3, 56, 69
Brahms, Johannes   163–4, 172–3
Brandel, Rose   82–3
Braverman, Harry   214–6
Brecht, Berthold   6, 228
Britain   32, 218
Brown, James   12, 45, 60, 69, 70, 72
Brubeck, Dave   46
Bukharin, Nicolai   145fn
Burning Spear   56–7
Byron, Don   20fn, 252

Cage, John   6, 101
cakewalk   34, 35
Callinicos, Alex   236fn, 238–9
Campbell, Edward   101fn, 102fn
capitalism   6, 7fn, 8, 10, 14–17, 89, 115, 157, 168, 175, 187–221, 226, 228, 237, 245–56
Carter, Elliot   83
Chailley, Jacques   85
Chase, Gilbert   73
Chernoff, John Miller   22, 78–9, 83, 88
Chic   12
China   189, 191

INDEX 271

Chopin, Frédéric   54
Christianity   25, 90, 188
cinema   96, 98
Clarida, Bob   10fn
Clarke, Eric   43, 45fn, 48fn, 51fn
classical music   1, 10, 24, 26, 27, 30–1, 33–4, 37, 42, 46, 47, 49, 59, 67, 71, 85, 90, 140, 142, 149, 163, 181–2, 185, 221
Clemence, G.M.   12
Clifton, Thomas   126
Clinton, George   18, 45, 60
clocks and clock time   93, 104, 110, 115, 123, 144, 157, 166, 175, 187–95, 217–20, 222, 230, 238, 249, 252
Colebrook, Claire   97fn, 98fn
commodification   15–16, 181, 184, 220, 223, 226, 228, 234, 240, 245
common practice era   11, 33, 48, 59, 140, 141
Cone, Edward   44fn
convention   4–5, 7, 11, 12, 13, 19, 26, 56, 59, 103, 163, 164, 170
Cook, Nicholas   140–2, 181
Cooper, Grovesnor   43fn

Danielsen, Anne   40, 45, 60, 70, 79fn
Darmstadt   206fn
Davis, Mike   6fn
Day, Gail   200fn
Debord, Guy   253–5
Debussy, Claude   244
Deleuze, Gilles   97–104, 114, 221, 234, 255
density referent   34, 46, 53, 79
Dexy's Midnight Runners   27
Dobb, Maurice   214
Doubleday, Veronica   25fn
drums   21, 26, 29, 31, 49, 54, 56, 57, 61, 77, 81, 106fn, 149–50, 159, 170, 171, 253, 255
Dylan, Bob   18fn

Eagles, The   36
Eagleton, Terry   16fn, 180
Earth, Wind and Fire   12, 18fn
Einstein, Albert   2
Engels, Frederick   199fn, 204fn, 210, 216fn
Epicurus   145
Epstein, David   136
Europe   4, 6, 7, 19, 25, 26, 54, 59, 61–3, 65fn, 66–75, 77, 79, 80, 85–7, 89, 90, 184, 187–9, 191, 213, 219

Europe, James Reese   71
Evans-Pritchard, E.E.   87

Fanon, Franz   65
Farmelo, Allen   23, 137
Feld, Steven   20fn, 21, 23–4
figurative painting   2, 3
Floyd, Samuel A. Jr.   65–6, 68–9, 71–2, 75, 76, 77
folk music   26, 33, 54, 59, 62, 71, 73–5, 86, 89, 185
Foster, John Bellamy   145fn, 214
Foucault, Michel   193
Fraisse, Paul   45
Franklin, Benjamin   194
Frith, Simon   69–71
Fukuyama, Francis   166
funk   18, 21, 45, 46, 70, 72, 77, 90

Galileo   210
Gates, Henry Louis   19, 65, 68–9, 77
Gershwin, George   41, 46, 69
Gesualdo   6
Getz, Stan   58
Giddens, Anthony   192fn
Gillespie, Dizzy   243fn
Gilroy, Paul   77fn
Glass, Philip   103
globalisation   1, 218, 234, 249
Goodman, Benny   62
gospel music   19, 56, 90
Gracyk, Theodore   49
Gramsci, Antonio   15
Greece   189, 207
Gregorian plainchant   25, 85, 124
Griffiths, Paul   102, 103fn
Groove Armada   18fn
groovology   20–1, 22fn
Guattari, Félix   98–104

Habermas, Jürgen   240–1
Hainge, Greg   104fn
Hall, Edward T.   244
Harrison, George   40
Harrison, John   219
Hauser, Arnold   243
Haydn, Joseph   59fn, 155, 170
Hegel, G.W.F.   247–8
Heidegger, Martin   116fn, 119, 229–31

hemiola 37–8
Hindemith, Paul 150
Hobsbawm, Eric 16fn, 60fn
Holloway, John 217fn
Horner, Bruce 19
'hot rhythm' 62–3
Hudson, Richard 27
Husserl, Edmund 116–25, 128, 138–9, 143, 145, 147, 205fn, 229–30, 241, 243
Huygens, Christaan 190

ideology 8, 10, 16, 69, 72, 237–8
improvisation 23–4, 66, 69, 73, 75, 106fn, 129, 135, 140–2, 150, 178–9, 182, 255
India 189
Industrial Revolution 191, 231
iPod 1, 12
Islam 25, 74–5, 189
isochrony 25–6, 29–32, 42, 53, 59, 78–81, 84–6, 88–9
Ives, Charles 83
Iyer, Vijay 26, 28, 29, 30, 54, 66fn

Jackendoff, Ray 43fn, 48fn, 51fn
Jackson, Milt 18fn
Jamerson, James 70, 72
James, William 105fn, 112, 119, 122
Jameson, Fredric 5–6, 11, 15, 195fn, 200fn, 228, 231–5, 241, 245, 249fn, 255
Japan 191
jazz 18, 20–2, 27–31, 34, 38, 43, 45, 46, 48, 49, 53, 60, 61–3, 64, 66, 69, 70, 73, 80, 86, 90, 135, 140–2, 147, 149–52, 154, 159, 160, 162, 165, 172, 179–80, 184, 252, 253
Jobim, Carlos Antonio 58
Jones, A.M. 74, 77–83
Jones, Norah 37
Joplin, Scott 41
Jordan, Louis 243
Judaism 25, 69, 188
Jung, Carl 65

Kaluli (Papua New Guinea) 24
Kant, Immanuel 92, 114, 163, 212, 230
Katz, Mark 18
Keil, Charles 12fn, 20–4, 29, 56, 76
Kennedy, Michael 25
Kern, Jerome 46

Kernfeld, Barry 19fn
Kersten, Fred 122–9fns, 138
Kingman, Daniel 72fn, 73, 75fn, 76, 77fn
Kivy, Peter 3fn
Klumpenhouwer, Henry 15
Koselleck, Reinhart 236
Koyré, Alexandre 210
Kramer, Jonathan D. 103, 243–5
Krims, Adam 15, 147
Kubik, Gerhard 79–83, 88fn
Kuhn, Thomas 4

Landes, David 187–91, 194, 219fn
Langer, Susanne 13, 92–4
Latham, Alison 25fn, 27
Latin American music 38, 58, 82, 89
Le Goff, Jacques 188, 195
Lerdahl, Fred 48fn, 51fn
Leslie, Esther 238
Limp Bizkit 18
Lipsitz, George 251–3
Liszt, Franz 28
London, Justin 32fn
Lukács, George 6, 147, 203, 223–9, 231, 241
Lunn, Eugene 222, 226, 227fn, 228fn

Madonna 18
Marconi, Guglielmo 219
Marcuse, Herbert 211fn
Marley, Bob 35
Marothy, János 11
Marxism 5, 6, 11, 13, 14, 15, 16, 147, 156, 183, 185, 200, 223, 225, 233, 237, 238, 239
Marx, Karl 7fn, 8, 15, 16, 144–5, 151fn, 179, 180fn, 183, 196–207, 210, 219, 223, 225, 235, 245, 246, 250–1, 253, 255
Maus, Fred Everett 231
McClary, Susan 4–5, 7–8, 10–11, 13, 19
McNally, David 197fn, 248fn
McNeill, William 151fn
medieval music 26, 84–5, 89, 189
melisma 25, 75
mensural music 25, 84–5, 89
mensural notation 168, 176
Merriam, Alan 86–9
Messiaen, Olivier 101–2, 206fn
meter 1, 4, 11, 20, 27, 29, 32, 37–48, 50–3, 59–60, 64, 75, 78, 80–6, 89, 91, 94, 97,

INDEX

100–7, 109–11, 115, 117, 136–7, 141–2, 144, 146, 149–52, 160, 169–74, 176, 177, 179, 180, 185, 187, 206, 213, 219, 222, 241–3, 248–9, 255
metronome   29, 30, 46, 62, 78–80, 93, 104, 110, 135–6, 166
Meyer, Leonard B.   3, 8, 43fn
Middleton, Richard   19–20, 47
Miller, Izchak   116fn, 120fn, 121, 122
Miller, Karen   204
Milton, John   16
modernism   5–6, 60, 148, 157, 162, 166, 174–5, 184, 220, 222–3, 226–8, 237–8, 243, 245, 249fn
Monson, Ingrid   19–20, 22, 26, 140–2, 252fn
Monteverdi   42
Moore, Allan   243
Moore, F.C.T.   95fn, 112fn
Mozart, Wolfgang Amadeus   27–8, 47, 48fn, 59fn, 155, 170
Mullarkey, John   95fn
Mumford, Lewis   187–8, 190, 193
Murphy, Timothy   103fn
musical form   4–7, 9–11, 14, 17, 19, 21, 24fn, 43, 47, 65, 66, 67, 80, 92, 100
Muzzetto, , Luigi   119fn, 121fn, 128
Myers, D.G.   68–9

Nagley, Judith   32fn
narrative   17, 19, 47, 98, 223, 229–35, 238, 241–3, 256
Nattiez, Jean-Jacques   231–2fn
Needham, Joseph   189
Negri, Antonio   238fn, 249–50
Nesbitt Nick   103fn
Neubauer, Eckhard   25fn
New Musicology   5, 7–8
New Orleans   74
Newcomb, Anthony   231
Newton, Francis   16fn, 60fn
Newton, Isaac   2, 189, 201, 210
Nietzsche, Frederick   159
notation   12, 24fn, 25, 44, 81, 82–3, 85, 86, 99, 117, 126, 168–73, 176, 179

Oliver, Paul   76fn
orchestra   26, 28, 30–3, 135, 160
orthodox Marxism   11, 183, 237
Osborne, Peter   225fn, 229fn, 230, 236, 237fn, 240

Oxley, Tony   106fn

Paddison, Max   147–8, 159fn, 164fn, 165fn, 167fn, 168, 170fn, 177fn, 178fn, 181
Palestrina   124
Parliament   70
Pasler, Jann   231fn
performance   8–9, 12, 19, 23–5, 26, 27, 28, 29, 30, 46, 56, 59, 60, 64, 66, 75, 77, 79, 82, 83, 84, 86, 110, 125–7, 134–42, 143, 144, 146, 168, 178–9, 180, 244
periodisation   5–7, 229
phenomenology   14, 31, 116–46, 181, 205fn, 230–1, 232, 234, 241, 250
Picasso, Pablo   3, 5
poetry   25, 106, 245
Police, The   55–6
political economy   7, 204fn, 206
polka   24
polymeter   37, 40, 83–4
polyrhythm   32, 35, 37–42, 58, 59, 64, 65, 78, 83, 150, 153, 252, 255
postmodernism   6, 15, 67–8, 195fn, 200fn, 233, 235, 249fn
Postone, Moishe   188–91, 196–206, 216fn, 217, 218, 219, 246
praxis   235, 241, 256
Prog Rock   27, 46
Prögler, Josef   21, 29
proletariat   16, 192, 217, 229, 254
Pryer, Anthony   25fn
pulse   11, 19, 20, 22–3, 24–32, 34, 42, 44, 45, 53, 59, 60, 63, 66, 78–86, 88–9, 98, 99, 101–3, 106, 107, 110, 115, 136, 142, 144, 149, 158, 161, 169–70, 173, 219, 221, 222, 242–3, 248–9, 255
Pythagoras   127, 209

Queen   40

ragtime   34, 41, 54, 60, 61
Rainbow   37
Rameau, Jean-Philippe   167
Rampley, Matthew   159fn
rationalisation   167–71, 173, 185–6, 225
realism   6, 223, 225, 226, 227, 228, 231, 242
Reich, Steve   103
Renaissance   26, 55, 84, 115, 231, 236, 249
rhythm and blues   61
Ricardo, David   199fn

Ricoeur, Paul   143–4, 229–34, 241
riff   47–8, 65, 242, 243fn
Ring Shout   65, 66fn, 75
Roach, Max   253
Robinson, Bradford   54fn
rock music   13, 23fn, 27, 37, 38, 40, 42, 46, 49, 54–5, 90, 103, 252
Romantic music   26, 29, 42, 59
Rose Royce   57
Rousseau, Jean-Jacques   84
rubato   20, 27–30, 34, 60, 79, 158, 173
rumba   38–41, 58, 90, 150
Russell, Matheson   121–2

Scaff, Lawrence   2fn
Schoenberg, Arnold   5, 42, 149, 158, 162–5, 172–4
Scholes, Percy   32fn
Schubert, Franz   33, 53fn
Schuller, Gunther   49, 53
Schutz, Alfred   13, 14, 31, 116, 119, 122–46, 147
Scruton, Roger   20
semiotics   10, 22, 23
Sessions, Roger   93
Shaw, George Bernard   34fn, 38fn
Shepherd, John   9fn, 10, 181, 241
Shuker, Roy   18
Signifyin(g)   19, 65–68
Simmel, Georges   212fn
slavery   61, 64, 65, 66, 72, 76
Small, Christopher   8–10, 12, 13, 17, 22, 70–1, 89, 138, 143, 181–2, 231fn, 241
Smith, Adam   214
Smith, Daniel   103fn
Smith, F. Joseph   117, 118, 126
Snead, James A.   67–9, 71
Snyder, Bob   34
Sohn-Rethel, Alfred   206–17, 220
Southern, Eileen   73fn
space   2, 92, 94–5, 100, 107–9, 114, 122, 125, 134–5, 138, 153–4, 156, 161, 166, 187, 193, 209–11, 213, 218–9, 225, 243, 248, 249fn
spatialisation of time   86, 94–7, 102, 107–8, 114–5, 117, 119, 124–5, 138, 149, 156, 158–9, 161, 170–1, 212–3, 219–20, 222, 230, 248
Stambaugh, Joan   4, 92
Stevens, John   25fn
Stockhausen, Karl-Heinz   42, 101, 244–5
Stranglers, The   45

Stravinsky, Igor   60, 149, 150, 158, 159–60, 162, 165, 172, 177, 244
stride piano   54
Stuckey, Sterling   65–6
style-system   3, 4, 5
Survivor   39
Swan Silvertones   19
swing   19, 20, 21–2, 23fn, 46, 66, 70, 90
Swiss, Thomas   19
symbolism in music   7–13, 22, 93, 232
syncopation   29, 31–42, 48, 50, 53, 54–5, 58, 59, 61, 63, 81–2, 91, 149–53, 171, 172–3, 175, 255
Szwed, John   179

Tagg, Philip   10, 30, 64
Talking Heads   148
Tamlyn, Garry   23, 24fn
Tangerine Dream   6
Taylor, Frederick Winslow (Taylorism)   214–7, 220
tempo   22, 26, 27–8, 30, 31, 37, 79, 83, 98, 135–6, 255
Thompson, Edward Palmer   188, 191, 192, 193fn, 252
Thrift, Nigel   192, 193fn, 217–8
time consciousness   3, 13, 14, 115, 118–24, 129, 133, 138–9, 143–6, 173, 175, 188, 189, 191, 199, 205fn, 218, 220, 229, 234, 236, 243
Tin Pan Alley   16fn, 43
tonality   4, 7–8, 10–11, 13, 48, 60, 100, 105, 162, 164, 167, 169, 174, 181, 228
Toscano, Alberto   199–200
Tower of Power   12
troubadours, trouvères   25

USSR   204fn

vamp   48, 65, 245
Van der Merwe, Peter   34fn, 43, 44, 46, 73fn, 74–7
Van Halen   42
Vannoy Adams, Michael   65fn
Velasquez   3
Von Uexküll   98

Wagner, Richard   149, 158–9, 160, 161
Waterman, Richard A.   62–3, 78–9, 83
Wayne, Michael   228fn

INDEX

Weber, Max   119, 167, 168–70, 173, 176, 194
Webern, Anton   158
Wertheimer, Max   105fn
Whittall, Arnold   42
Wilson, Olly   64–5, 69, 71, 72, 76, 77
Winner, Langdon   49
Withers, Bill   39
Witkin, Robert   158
Wonder, Stevie   12

Zahavi, Dan   120fn
Zaner, Richard   133
Zappa, Frank   148
Žižek, Slavoj   208, 212
Zuckerkandl, Victor   45, 50–1, 58, 81, 104–15, 171–2, 176, 243, 255